Rez
Ramblings

Living on the Pine Ridge as a
21st Century "Injun"

Leon Blunt Horn Matthews
Forward by Russell Means

Rez Ramblings
Living on the Pine Ridge as a 21st Century "Injun"

First Edition 2012

Copyright @ Blunt Horn Production
blunthorn@gmail.com

ISBN: 978-0-9885114-0-8
Printed In USA For World Wide Distribution

For more copies write to :
Blunt Horn Production
Pine Ridge, SD USA
blunthorn@gmail.com
Website: www.rezramblings.com

Table of Contents

Foreward

Leon Matthews is a man who fights for our rights and wellbeing through his writing. He understands the needs of American Indians. He is respected, successful and has the mind to carry on the fight for the American Indian. He is well regarded among the Oglala of the Pine Ridge Indian Reservation and he is a writer for the Lakota Country Times. His family owns a successful coffee house on the Pine Ridge Indian Reservation. His life experiences are varied and many. He left the Reservation and came back in 1995 to live and help the people. Leon is unique because of his life experiences. He grew up in the struggles of the Relocation program in a family that held tight to their Lakota roots. This meant he spent time on and off of the Reservation in his formative years. His faith as a Christian is strong and nothing will change his faith. He has experienced firsthand the oppression, prejudice, and attempts by the United States of America to exterminate American Indians and his faith.

In my youth, my generation was able to take a lot of our direction from the old people who were born in the 1800s. The elders never went to boarding school, and they still had a clear vision of who they were. They were not yet mixed up by the oppressive policies of assimilation, relocation, and reservation life. It is their vision that I have spent my life fighting and seeking to restore for our people. Today I am joined in this fight by the next generation of American Indians who also seek to restore freedom and an authentic Indian life for the next generation of American Indians. Leon Matthews understands the history and lives the life of a modern day Lakota. His words tell of life on the Pine Ridge Indian Reservation, and he challenges readers to look towards the possibilities that lie ahead for the Lakota Nation. Most of all, he has the vision our ancestors wanted......for our people to live free.

Russell Means

5

Preface

Rez Ramblings began as an effort to bring light to daily life on the Pine Ridge Reservation. It is not exhaustive, and it does not inspire to show all aspects of life on the Indian Reservation. It is not meant to be politically correct, but uses language common to the people of the Pine Ridge. Reservation life is a hybrid culture; it has developed because of the situation Indian people were thrust into in the latter part of the 19th Century. Indian Reservations were meant to confine and concentrate a people, and this has caused great damage to the people of the Plains, known as the Lakota or Sioux. When I was approached to write for the Lakota Country Times, I did so with the intent of eventually completing a book with my columns. This book contains columns, noted by date, and blogs I have written during the past four years.

My parents were born and raised on the Pine Ridge Reservation. I came home to Pine Ridge to live when I was fourteen. This book shares my many stories, experiences, and ideas; but, you must remember it comes from me.

I dedicate my book to my grandchildren because I want them to know their grandfather. Before my mother passed away she told me I should take my great, great grandfather's name. His name was John Blunt Horn. He fought at the Little Big Horn and came home to Wounded Knee to live out his life. During the Massacre at Wounded Knee in 1890 he served as a lay minister. He rang the church bells as the mass grave was being filled. When asked why he was doing this, he said that some of the people killed were Christian, and it was the right thing to do. I have taken John Blunt Horn's name because my mother wanted to give it to me, and I hope I can serve without fear as he did in 1890. Just as I have read and learned about my great, great grandfather, I want my grandchildren to be able to know about their grandfather as I live my life as an American Indian in the 20th and 21st Century.

7

Western thought is linear, and I have been educated in this context. Indian thought is circular. I am Indian and have lived among my people. In my writing I believe or in the very least attempt to capture the way our people think. It is circular, and it may seem like I am rambling in the book. It should be noted I have sat among the elders and leaders of my people. I have listened and experienced their way of thinking. So as you read, it is imperative to keep in mind this is the work of an Oglala Lakota Man.

The book spans four years of writing, but its reflections and stories span my life. Lakota storytelling is the way our people have kept our lives intact for future generations. Many people are part of the stories and were influential as I was writing and developing each entry.

I seek to be inspired by my relatives but also through every day American life. I chose to watch ABC's The View and develop hot topics in the daily life on the Pine Ridge Reservation. What you will find are the stories that have impacted life on the Reservation at any given time. This comes at an important time in our history, as we see so many of the Civil Rights leaders of 1960s and 70s finding their final resting place. I was privileged to spend time with some amazing leaders both from AIM, the American Indian Movement, and people on the other side known as the GOONS, or Guardians of the Oglala Nation.

Amanda Takes War Bonnet was the person who approached me to write, and she was instrumental in the completion of this book. She saw something in me. I was on the Voice of the Lakota Nation, or KILI Radio, for about ten years. Amanda listened to my weekly show. I appreciate the support, and I hope I was able to capture the radio experience in my writing.

My desire is to give the reader an opportunity to walk alongside this Lakota Man as I travel through life. You will be able to sit, read, and see what an Oglala Lakota man deals with on a daily basis. Each word is my own, and it is an opportunity for you to experience a little of the daily life on the Pine Ridge Indian Reservation. Thank you for allowing me to be a part of your life.

Introduction

....from 10-02-08

Rez Ramblings started with a need to write my thoughts out. It has helped me as I began the journey one of my mentors asked me to start three years ago, which is writing.

I started writing for the Oglala Light at Pine Ridge High School, or Oglala Community High School, where I graduated in 1983. I thought I knew a lot of things back then, but as I grew older and even now realize, I do not know as much as I thought I did. My quest for knowledge continues to grow.

I read books and articles to keep up my learning. I have spoken and debated with some great minds in the past thirteen years. So let this be my opening statement, these are the ramblings of a Lakota man and not the end all word on anything written about in my columns or on my blogs. I hope you judge my heart as well as my words.

Family is the strength of our Lakota people. I loved sitting with my mother and listening to her talk about her youth on the Pine Ridge. She would share with me about growing up in Slim Buttes and then moving into town. I loved to sit and listen to my aunts when they came and visited.

My mother taught me where I came from and the identity I needed to succeed in life. She taught me that I was from Wounded Knee, and she spoke of my grandparents, Al and Pearl Matthews. Grandma Pearl was from Standing Rock and came to Wounded Knee where she met my grandfather Al.

I did my first burial in 1996 at Wounded Knee. The coldest day in Minnesota history was the next day, and I was in minus 36 degree weather doing a burial. It was beautiful as the People honored me by telling me they were my relatives. I felt more connected to my identity.

9

The very next day I would be stuck in Minneapolis on the coldest day in history. I was on my way to Atlanta where I would be participating in a walk of 168 miles. It was called No More Broken Treaties. It was from Cherokee, North Carolina into Atlanta, Georgia.

I was finishing up my two week trip, and I thought I had been gone from Pine Ridge far too long. I was standing before forty-five thousand ministers and priests on stage. I tell people I was at the top of the world. I was on my way to National Leadership. I was back stage, and all of a sudden I heard the inaudible voice of God, "Go Home! You do not belong here." I was stunned because it was so powerful to be in such a huge place in front of so many influential people. I asked some questions, and God continued to tell me I belonged with my people. I could have gone the wrong way, but I believed I needed to follow the instructions of God, so I went back to Pine Ridge.

I still travel some. I have been around Asia in Japan, Korean, Thailand, and India speaking about Native issues. Some people talk about free will and having choice; others talk to you about determinism and how we are bound by a previous circumstance.

I believe I am in Pine Ridge because my mother taught me who I am. I am a member of the Oglala Sioux/Lakota Tribe, and I am related to the Martins, Red Shirts, Matthews, Her Many Horses and Hillmans.

Wow, I just realized I am related to lots of people. I am truly sorry if I did not mention your name, but I know you are out there. I love it when the elders come and share with me about being my relatives. I chose to live with my family on the Pine Ridge because it is home. And, we have some of the greatest people living here.

My hope in writing is that you will begin to get to know me, and I can get to know you. I have had many people come to me and share with me the issues of our Tribe. I hope to write about some of those in the next few weeks. We are faced with tough times again. I realize the greatest generation went through the Great Depression and survived. We, too, can survive, but it will be family that gets us there.

REZ LIFE

Everyday life on the Pine Ridge

The Village on a Saturday Morning

This morning I woke up and went to the post office to get my mail. I did not have any mail. I had some errands to run, and as I was thinking about my day, KILI radio was playing in the background. A familiar voice was playing songs about God and Jesus. It was good and I listened closely. The host was talking about prayer, alcoholism, and raising your children. Teach them to be nice to each other and do good things. When they are older they will return to those ways. What a powerful message for our Lakota nation. I would like to thank the host for such encouraging words. You can catch the show on Saturday mornings.

I like to be positive, but sometimes I am not as positive as I would like. We seem to be bombarded with negativity in our lives. I remember being carefree when I was a boy, looking to explore different aspects of life. Life in the city was exciting, but it did have its moments of boredom. If I ever told my mom I was bored she would find something for me to do in the house. I guess I kept myself busy while growing up. I loved to play baseball in the summer heat. After we played a game of pickup baseball we would go swimming. Sports and other events are great for the youth.

This past week we had village days. My hope is we can begin to build on this late summer event. It would have been great to have a concert and other family events. I think we should have a chili cook-off next year and just see who has the best chili on the Rez. John Mousseau, one of our tribal council members, has a great chili. It was so hot. I could only eat two bowls, and I could not eat any more frybread. Frybread spikes my sugar, and I could not let myself eat more than two pieces. Nevertheless, I believe we need to have a cook-off some afternoon.

Tiny D, Henry Brown and crew put on a great event on Saturday night. I even laced up my sneakers for a little three-on-three basketball. The weekend was great. I hope many of us can participate more next

13

year. It was a positive weekend for many people. I talked with the new principle, Robert Cook, and thanked him for coming to Pine Ridge High School. He has always been a pleasant person, and I am sure the students will find him to be a positive influence in their lives.

It was great to talk with Wayne Weston. Did you know I enjoy listening to Wayne and Chris and others on their radio show called Wicasa Hour? Man hour…. now that is great because men need encouraging.

I thought it was time to let our Lakota people know we can encourage each other. Life is difficult, but when the times get hard, you will see character come out strong. We need to pray for ourselves and each other every day. It is my commitment to pray for our people because it is hard to live as humans. We have so many wonderful things to live for in Lakota country, and it is time to start helping each other become successful. It is true when we hear the only person we can change is ourselves.

A few weeks ago, I gave a message about Jesus asking a man who could not walk if he wanted to be healed. It applies to our emotional health as well. Think about it. If God asked you if you wanted to be healed in your emotions, what would you say? The man in the story said, "Yes," so Jesus said, "Well then, get up." Immediately the man got up, picked up his mat and walked away. I believe God wants us to get up emotionally and start walking. I will say it again and again; forgiving others will set you free. You need to forgive yourselves as well. Then you will find peace in your minds and hearts.

Hairspray Alley
….*from 3-30-10*

I remember working on computers in high school. You had to load the program via a floppy disc, which was truly floppy. It was not very fast. When I was in college I had a typewriter to do my papers. We had a computer lab but it did not seem convenient to run down to the lab to write and print a paper. My friend, a computer wizard, sold me an XT Windows computer for about two hundred dollars. I think this is what changed my life in college. I could now type my papers from my living room, save them to a disk, and print them at the school. I heard rumblings of the Internet but really did not have time to explore the early Net. Information can change your destiny if used correctly. I believe I was one of the first to get on the Net when Golden West started the Internet service in Pine Ridge Village. I could hardly wait for the Net to hit Pine Ridge because I knew it would mean change to the Reservation.

I have gone through a few desk-top computers and a number of laptops; I enjoy being mobile with the laptops. I am ready to write where ever I can find a hot cup of coffee and a table. When I was in high school I wrote about many things, and I remember the green glass all over the alleys of Pine Ridge Village. I wrote about change and what we could do about the change. I can assure you there has been change when it comes to the Green Lizard or Muscatel bottles that once littered our back alleys. One change that is visible is that many of our relatives have moved to White Clay, Nebraska where Malt Liquor is sold very cheap. So the high alcohol content is preferred over the Muscatel sold thirty years ago.

If you go to the alley between the Lutheran Retreat Center and the Catholic Church you will find hair spray cans. It is said a hole is punctured and poured into a gallon jug and then mixed with water for consumption. I believe life on the Pine Ridge has changed over the last thirty years. The Village or the Tribe needs to send the stores in our area a letter; hopefully the selling of hair spray can be curbed. We have a tremendous number of issues facing our young people. It would great if we could start dealing with the issues our children are faced with in this new century. Dealing with the root causes of our addictions can help us confront the real problems.

Now that the snow is almost gone, we should pick up the litter around our businesses. Take a walk or when you are driving look around and see what people passing through our village see as they travel on Highway 18. Our people deserve more when it comes to the basic needs of good food and clean streets. Information can change our way of life and hopefully we can curb the high incidents of cancer and diabetes.

This week marks the Easter season, and I am grateful for what it means. We celebrate the death and resurrection of Jesus. Jesus was a great leader when he walked the earth teaching people to love and pray for your enemies. He was a revolutionary force like none other the world has never seen. He healed a man one day on a Saturday, or Sabbath. When the Jewish Religious leaders heard about it they were upset and worked with the Herodians to plot his death. They were jealous of Jesus because he was gaining power with the people while living a servant's life. He did not have a home. He required his disciples to deny themselves and take up the burdens of following him. Not many people are willing to deny themselves and follow a man who would eventually be killed. Almost all of the disciples were killed for their faith. John was the exception; he wrote the book of Revelation when he had a vision.

As I have lived for forty-four years, I have learned a lot about the Lakota people, and I see our struggles on a daily basis. I have tried to understand what it means to be a follower of Jesus, and I have struggled to understand the European/American approach to the faith of Jesus. We, Lakota, have seen forced Christianity fail because it was not done with the Spirit. Instead, it was supported with federally funded religious people. Jesus lived a life oppressed by an outside people group. He continued to live for the people and sought to help people even though it would eventually lead to his death. A follower of Christ trusts Yahweh, the God of the Bible, and believes the death of Jesus gives us forgiveness of sins and eternal life. I am no longer bound by my wrongdoings. I believe Jesus died for all of my sins, pure and simple. A child can understand the concepts of salvation. I invite everyone to the Gospel Fellowship as we worship Jesus and share a meal on Easter Sunday. Bring your family and pray for the Lakota Man because he was a target for a long time.

Rated R on the Rez

I have thought about the issues of the Rez, and I have come to a conclusion. If we do not change the way we live, it will be devastating if we are faced with a disaster. I believe many people will die if we have some financial or natural disaster because we do not live for the future but we live for now. I am tired of people making bad decisions for their families and for themselves. I believe we have to choose strategies that will change our lives. I fear the meltdown of the American economy and what it will do to our people living on the Reservation. We have survived through some of the worst conditions on the plains, but we need to look back at the way the Government destroyed our food source. The Creator gave Tatanka, or the American Bison, for sustenance. The Lakota used every part of the buffalo and did not waste. Today we have moved in the opposite direction. Our lives waste away as we live the way of life on the Reservation.

We have an elephant in our living room, and no one talks about it. We have a severe drug abuse problem, and it is destroying the people from the inside. In a previous column I mentioned we had over fifty people go to jail for the distribution and sale of cocaine. Their customers are still on the Rez and most likely have not gone without their drugs. I know people who have done drugs since the seventies and will continue until the day they die. Cocaine is a drug that is highly addictive and when it is cut with certain chemicals it can be a huge money maker for the dealers.

We have people who are not trying to make a better life for themselves. There are a few people who seek to build for the future, but the vast numbers of people are just trying to medicate with alcohol and drugs. I know what it is like to use alcohol to not feel a certain way, but I believe we need to make personal choices. Ultimately it is our personal responsibility. We all have siblings and relatives who we can talk sense to when it comes to destructive lifestyles. This brings me to a point. The point is there are supernatural forces trying to kill, and there are people who seek to use these spirits to help. We as a people need to understand there are forces that seek to destroy and act accordingly. I have experienced these evil forces myself and through others. I really do not want to have anything to do with them, but I sense we need to pray against evil. We are a spiritual people, and I am talking about humans. It is harmful when we do not know there are forces outside of our natural realm. I believe our issues originate from spiritual challenges. We are

17

only humans and do not alone have answers for most of our problems. It is through the spiritual that we can find answers to our problems.

What it's Like for Rez Kids

I received some encouraging words about yesterday's blog, and I wanted to add a few thoughts of what it looks like on a Saturday morning on the Ridge. There is not much traffic on the streets, and a few dogs barking. A child is waking up after a restless night because of the party that kept going until the cops were called. On most nights the cops do not bother you because they are overwhelmed with the house parties that get out of control. Last night the child was sleeping close to his or her little siblings to make sure they were safe. The child wakes up to see everyone has left, but the carnage is still there. Beer cans and mud are everywhere. There is a pile of dirty dishes and one adult who never made the trip to jail for some unknown reason. Maybe it was the grace of the officers because they could not leave the children alone. By now it is nine o'clock in the morning, and the mouse is not even stirring. Maybe the mouse drank the spilled beer all around the house. The child looks in the refrigerator but there is likely no food in it. Looking around in the cupboards the child might find some stale bread or crackers. But in the end it looks like empty cupboards and refrigerator means empty stomach and a sad day until the parents come home and make empty promises.

While growing up on the Rez is hard and you can see it in the children, there is very little help because of the overwhelming pictures of this way of life. At least during the week a child can wake up, go to school, and be fed there. But how is the child expected to learn with all of the stress of his or her home life? We have seen many young people get tired of it and try to end his or her life by suicide. There is a cry and this cry is for help because life is spiraling out of control everyday on the Rez. When I grew up I found myself in this way of life. Now it is 30 years later and the same way of life is being lived. I remember parties that lasted for days because they would wake up and start drinking again. The empty promises of my own mother were there, and they left me feeling empty.

18

The parties are fun at first. Then they turn into fights and issues of unresolved grief. Loss of life means more on the Rez because of the destructive ways our ancestors and relatives were killed. I have vivid memories of parties and the anger that would come out. I know we need to seek resolution, but it seems impossible with the make-up of the leadership. We have bitter people on the Rez who seek to gossip and destroy others because of their own unresolved bitterness and grief. Looking for a few dollars to cure a hangover has now become an everyday occurrence on the Rez. Children are growing up seeing this behavior in their everyday life, and it is heartbreaking. "How can we help our people?" is the million-dollar question.

We have issues but we can overcome
....*from 7-7-10*

It is with great sadness I write my words this week. While I have been very busy with friends and groups from different parts of the country, it has come to my attention we have lost some people to suicide. In my training I have learned we need to talk about it and expose the issue. We have lost some of our people to suicide, but we have also lost many who have just checked out. Checking out is a way we cope with our issues, and I have experienced the feelings of this way of life. Because human beings are by nature relational, we hold to our experience. I guess I do not feel I am clear enough but I hope to work on this through my writing.

While I have been home I have seen many things change in Pine Ridge. When I was a teenager I saw many "Green Lizard" bottles broken in Pine Ridge; this has changed. The alcohol of choice has changed from wine and beer to a new drink called Malt Liquor. If we dig a little deeper, we understand it is a cheaper way to get drunk. People who have less to regular beer find it easier to buy the Malt. I am frustrated with the view of alcohol because every expert will tell you it is not the alcohol but the reason beneath the surface that destroys. We need to understand what is happening to our people. Not be afraid of the effects, but try to realize we can overcome.

19

I have seen the effects of drugs and alcohol in my family. A few short years ago I went to my mother's funeral, and we as a family had her cremated. A funeral for your mother is not easy. I bought some KOOL cigarettes and laid them on her body. I opened a pack of cigs and took a couple out because I knew it would be the last time I took some from my mother. I realize we have many issues among us, but I put the tobacco out there. Just before we were finished I also took some and realized it was the last time I would smoke without my mother's cigarettes. For better or worse, I did what I did and will never apologize, but I offered that for my mother. It was scary but done in a good way because I LOVED my mother, and no one can change this fact.

Because you are reading this book I want to encourage you. We have struggled with many obstacles in our lives and know we have our people in our mind. Lakota people have had the Europeans in our lives throughout the last 200 years. Medicating is not a way of life we should be seeking especially when seeking a Lakota way of life. Alcohol and other substances we medicate with are harmful to our lives. When we stop medicating, we will be left with real issues. I am sure we have medicated our belief system into believing what is false, and we have followed what we believe is true. Our lives have developed into what is right and wrong. I have many friends in Native America and throughout America, and I believe we can overcome the pain, real issues, and struggles we live daily in our lives. We can overcome without drowning and medicating.

Much is written and many try to persuade people to believe what they would believe in American Indian life. I want to share with you.... we have hope. Bottom line, we can overcome the life that the American culture and its influences have and still exert on our lives. What can the Lakota life lead to? I believe we can overcome the life the evil one has left us too. It is a hope when you understand fully.

As a tribe we need to understand what is happening and the power of the tribe. Deal with the real issues and start looking to help the people. Hope is what we are looking for on the Reservation. We need hope, hope of a better day...

Newspapers.... the Power of the Pen
....from 4-15-09

The newspaper is great way to know the current affairs of our community. I read newspapers and magazines almost every day. When I was a student at Oglala Community School, I was part of the Oglala Light Newspaper. We had free reign on the stories and were taught the basics of reporting styles, the difference in editorials and news reporting, by our mentor, Bob Mayne. He was also the senior English teacher. He was my all-time favorite teacher. He was more like a friend, but made sure we were respectful. He could have taught anywhere, but he came to Pine Ridge. He wore a brown leather jacket which could serve to dress him up or to keep him warm. If he smoked a pipe, I would not have been surprised. Corrine Mesteth was the brilliant young editor and I was an assistant editor. We went to all of the events and took pictures. Bill Hotz would develop them in the dark room. How times have changed, with digital cameras and software to lay out papers.

Lakota Country Times has served the Pine Ridge and Rosebud Reservations very well over the last few years. I was asked to write a column for their newspaper and it was an opportunity to be a part of a positive influence in Lakota Country. It took about two years for me to begin my writing, but in the fall of 2008 I made up my mind to begin writing my views and thoughts about living on the Pine Ridge; I wanted to be a part of the positive news.

We have good stories across both reservations where people are making news. Our Lakota people are involved in many areas across the state of South Dakota and throughout America. Our nursing school in Pine Ridge is said to be one of the best in South Dakota. Economic development is slowly progressing with new national chains coming to town. Pine Ridge added Subway, and they serve a great sandwich. I am proud of the development they are making.

We are on the upswing even as the world economies are struggling. New building is on the rise in Lakota Country and the Lakota Country Times is at the forefront in their reporting. I know people are reading because I am getting good comments from friends, even from Texas. My desire is to continue to write and develop my ideas in the paper and to let people know what it is like on the "Rez". The combined population of the Rosebud and Pine Ridge Reservations is comparable with that of the Rapid City area with regard to population. If you have news, I would suggest you call the paper and let them know about your story.

Here is an idea about tribal government – we need our tribal leaders to step up and begin to share what is going on in our tribe. We need accountability and checks and balances in Lakota Country. Our development is dependent on the understanding of trust. At this time I do not believe the majority of our people trust our own government. And if our own people do not trust them, how can others trust them as well? We need in-depth articles to help us understand our surroundings. Just walk into Big Bat's in the morning and see how many people are reading articles about the Pine Ridge. One of the things that bothers me is the articles are poorly investigated. It would be a great idea for a reporter to be working on the articles we want to read.

If you are wondering who reads these articles, you can bet your EBT Thune, Johnson, and Herseth Sandlin are reading what is happening in Pine Ridge and Rosebud. The power of the pen is one of the most powerful weapons you can use to change your condition. If you consider all of American Indians in South Dakota, we form a powerful voting bloc. The leaders would begin to listen because we could change their future. This can be done through the power of Lakota Country Times.

A Stronghold
....from 10-13-10

Pine Ridge is a stronghold for the Democratic Party. During the last election we had a number of people on the radio that were easy to recognize, and people were stopping in to rally for President Obama. We have Kristi and Stephanie battling for one congressional seat and the opportunity to represent the values of South Dakota. I am undecided on who would represent my own views. A couple years ago I found that I was tired of the same politics and chose to travel to Hot Springs. I changed the "R" and put an "I" behind my name. When I turned eighteen, I registered as a Republican because I thought they best represented my views. Of course, it took almost twenty-five years to understand the two parties are the same. I am a registered Independent. It is a better fit.

On one hand I believe we need to be open to more programs and the Democrats seem to work on poverty issues. There are issues that come with poverty, and I believe we need to address them. But, I am a Lakota person with different views, and I do not like dependency. I would hope for a candidate who would like to give the Lakota Nation its due because the United States has stolen the majority of the wealth from the Great Sioux Nation. While this was being done, "Christians" were working to civilize the "Indians". I believe we need to hold people accountable for the action that was taken against the Lakota people. Of course we have politicians and leaders who get excited when they come to Pine Ridge for votes. I remember one person who was not afraid to ask Tom Daschle the hard question about our water rights, and they asked him about his supporting some Anti-Lakota legislation. Of course the question was ignored, but it was asked. This man is now running for Vice President of the Oglala Sioux Tribe.

I have seen the politicians come and go, and I have to say things have become worse over the past forty years. Outside of the Civil Rights movement, we have seen aspects of our daily lives only become worse on the Pine Ridge Reservation. Poverty is a mentality that breeds apathy, and apathy takes the heart and soul of men and women. It is very difficult to overcome when the political environment is ill equipped. I believe we need to stop believing the two political system works for the good of our people on the Reservation. We need a movement where people come together and show the candidates we stand in solidarity. It would be a great day if the Lakota Nation rose from the ashes and began to make changes in the political landscape of South Dakota. If we came together as one, we could have a great impact and change the future of our Reservations.

We do not need people in office to promise change and to make false promises of fixing our problems. We need people who can change themselves. Stop doing things for selfish reasons. I have the luxury of sitting on the sidelines, but I realize and hope everyone else that reads these words would understand we need hope. Hope comes from feelings of a brighter future. Everyone needs to ask themselves if the candidates offer industry and change or just more of the same. We need to work on the issues we can change and not the change that never comes. Our people have become dependent on the government and this is unfortunate because the government cannot meet all the needs of the people. Some people will not be in office again because they did not help enough people change the amount of change in their pockets.

Someone asked what social justice looks like in Native America. I believe it is making things right, and the way to do this is to restore the people to pre-Reservation conditions. Before the buffalo were slaughtered, Lakota people lived in true freedom and lived a powerful life. I believe the United States needs to be held to their treaty obligations. I have been called a welfare Indian like most of you, but it is really sad the people of America are mostly ignorant when it comes to what the United States owes the American Indians. We have lost our way because of the political leaders and their inactivity when it comes to making our treaty rights the primary focus of their two years.

I would hope the next administration would begin to fight for the Oglala Oyate and seek to bring the treaty obligations to the table. So the next time a candidate from the Republican or Democrat Party comes to Pine Ridge, I hope someone will ask them where they stand on the treaties. Keep this focus. When social justice is achieved, we could begin to bring our people hope and a future. You can solve the suicide and gang issues if you build our Nation. The foundation must be the treaties, and we need to keep up the pressure. Change must start from within. True change comes from the Creator. Seek the Creator with your heart, soul, and mind.

Not Smart Enough for Council
....from 9-22-10

Fall is upon us and like the cycles of the earth we humans also find changes in our lives. I believe we can make great changes in our lives; hopefully they will be healthy changes. I have decided to continue with my weight loss and get to my goal by Christmas. I have a couple of months to get to my goal and am hoping I can resolve some of my health issues while eating healthier. When I started to think about how our ancestors lived two hundred years ago, I thought about the high protein and low carbohydrates they consumed. I have many thoughts about changing and beginning to make some life changes. My diet is probably the biggest change, and I am full of hope after losing as much as sixty pounds. I want to eat a more balanced diet when I get to my goal so I can keep my blood sugars under control. More walking and exercise is important to help balance my life.

The fall season also brings American football to the front of people's lives or at least to Sunday and Monday. I was talking with a friend recently, and I said I did not care for the Steelers because of the Steel Curtain of the seventies, and yet time healed the wound. Then the quarterback controversy and the handling of it were difficult to understand. I am not really interested in the Steelers either way because I have one team. The Denver Broncos is the team I live and die for when it comes to the gridiron. In 1977 I was in downtown Denver welcoming the runners-up of the World Champions. Denver lost to Dallas that year and to this day I cannot stand the Cowboys. Of course, I am Indian and when the Red Skins beat the Cowboys in week one I was very happy. Oh, and the ex-Denver Broncos' quarterback beat the Cowboys last week. Again I was happy. It is great to be passionate even about the team that beat you thirty-three years ago. I am a part of the Broncos because the fans have a great power of influence. One last thing about football, I like the Red Skins because Shanahan is at the helm. I believe someday he will be back when owner Pat Bowlen gets a clue and brings him back to Mile High.

There is a lot of controversy surrounding mascots of American sports teams. The Fighting Sioux are the latest to drop their name

25

because of the NCAA and some Native American people wanted the change. I like the Haskell Indian Nations University Indians. I also liked the Spear Chuckers with Marcel Bull Bear, and the housing basketball team that would travel to Denver to play against other high school students who were Indian. We cannot forget the Fighting Whiteys in the Colorado school's intramural basketball program. I went on Native American Calling a few years ago and was speaking about the reason we need to focus on our own back yard before going to great lengths trying to change our image. I know Tim Giago is against mascots, but I believe the Red Skins and the Chiefs have great followings. They honor those sports teams. The Vikings do not think badly about Northern Europeans, and they are not making fun. Instead they have chosen a fierce, competitive, and honorable name for a billion dollar industry. We need to focus on developing our communities and invest energy in positive change for our homeland.

Oh, I have not forgotten we are on the verge of a change in the leadership of the Oglala Sioux Tribe. We have many people running for office and looking to make decisions for a multi-million dollar business/organization. Someone asked me why I did not throw my hat in the ring. I told them I did not believe I was smart enough to be on the Council. I would be a one term councilman because I would not be handing out money and paying light bills. I like to be close to home so I would not travel but work to bring people to Pine Ridge. But I understand I would not be able to make change. We as a people need to begin to change our thinking because the future of our tribe is at risk. If we continue enabling our people we will have no future. Our everyday lives need to change in the coming few years because if the economy completely collapses, our people will struggle the hardest.

We are developing a forum for Pine Ridge Village, and we hope you will come to ask questions and hear what the candidates have to say. Our time is short, and we hope to come up with some guidelines for the forum. We would like to invite the Pine Ridge Village candidates and the Vice President and Presidential candidates. Look for the posters and announcements on KILI Radio for further information.

Election 2010

So it begins on the Pine Ridge, elections. And now I hear we are going electronic. I heard this morning about the Florida election of 2000 and how the Supreme Court decided who would run the country for eight years. I don't have a strong opinion about how that was decided, but I hope to not have the United States Government or the Oglala Sioux Tribal government intruding in my life. I believe in social justice, and yet I am a strong proponent of smaller government.

I do not know if it was a mid-life crisis, but I left my lifetime affiliation with my party a couple of years ago. When Democratic Senator Tim Johnson came to Pine Ridge the first time, I listened to his words and thought he made a good case for himself. He had strong family values and, at the time, I felt he was the best candidate for the job. I was moved when he spoke in Pine Ridge Village. I spoke with him and asked if he would come for a Wopila, a thank you dinner, when he won the Senate seat. He told me it would be an honor. He never did come for a dinner, but I figured he became too important. I realized after talking with a Senator from Indiana they watched out for each other. I was a nobody, but I do have a vote. Of course my feelings were hurt, but when I received a personal note from Senator Johnson it made up for any wrongdoings. I know I am easily offended and full of being HUMAN. I apologize for my shortcomings and hope to become less sensitive, or maybe not.

I do not regret my leaving the party; I love being Independent. It makes me feel like I can make better, informed choices. I need to be inspired to complete my work. I will find a way to get control. I was talking with God over the weekend and He told me I need to complete the work He has for me.

Cell Phones and Missing Cell Towers
....from 2-19-09

There are many people walking around today who cannot

conceive a life without the cell phone. I remember a time when a car phone was a big deal. You would see people driving around in their Lincoln Continentals talking on their phones and it would seem a bit surreal. Now we have young children talking on phones around the reservation. There are still questions lingering around the idea of having cell phones in our ears. It is too early to tell if we are going to have medical issues as a result of using these phones.

To be honest, I do not even remember when I got my phone. It has travelled many miles with me, and I try to always answer when my wife calls. So where are we today with our phones? They are one of the greatest economic factors on our reservations. We have the ability to get business deals done because we can communicate.

Of course, if you live in Pine Ridge or some of the other places you cannot get a good signal. I get frustrated because of the dropped calls. I was told by the carrier that if I bought a smart phone to access my email, it would be just a few months before we would get a cell tower in Pine Ridge Village. That has been at least three years ago. I have asked people in charge of this project and no one seems to know what is happening with the cell tower development.

If you were going to build commerce or business in your town, it would be a good idea to establish lines of communication with technology which will bring industry to the economy. In my opinion, Kyle and Pine Ridge should have been the first places to receive cell towers. They have the largest populations and need them to start and keep commerce in their communities. I have been in Denver doing business on my phone, and the person on the other end did not know that I was in Colorado. I have been in Rapid City doing business over the years and the cell signals are great.

We need to be calling our elected officials and people in charge of the cell tower project. If we are going to get things done in Pine Ridge and Kyle, we need to have the best possible communications for our people. It is imperative for our people to be able to talk on their cell phones for emergencies and for business. I know that we can get some of the calls, but we need to be able have conversations the other party can hear.

These may seem like small steps, but I know if the Two Bulls administration would take this on as a project, something could get done. If they allowed other phone carriers onto the reservation, they could make the money back in a hurry. We have many people coming to the Pine Ridge Reservation who cannot use their phones. I believe it is a monopoly, and yet no one seems to mind that the cows have better cell signals than the people of Pine Ridge and Kyle.

Potato Chips and Soda Pop
....*from 10-06-09*

The leading cause of stress is doing things we should not be doing and knowing we should not be doing them. Stress is a silent killer, and I believe it has caused a lot of suffering among our people. Having scruples is a good thing when you live in this world. Having a conscience is what makes us human. The ability to know the difference between right and wrong is vital to our communities. I was sitting down, having a cup of coffee, and thinking about the last fourteen years. I came home from Minnesota where I was attending Christian College. I started out in the Pastoral Ministries tract and ended up with the Christian Ministries program. My reasoning was I needed a better understanding of the Church as a whole. Pastoral Ministries is a great program, and I have enough knowledge to understand hermeneutics which is the science of interpreting texts. Hermeneutics is primarily used in the interpretation of the Bible, but can be used with any text. I believed I needed a more rounded education, and to this day I am thankful for a better understanding of the Church.

Honestly, I believe the years I have spent developing the Church of Pine Ridge has been fruitful but it has also had its difficulties. There are people who are anti-Christian and fight against the message of Christ. I even know of a person who said there are no real Christian Churches on the Pine Ridge. Of course this comes from a lack of understanding in what the Church actually is according to scripture. The

29

Church is not a building; it is a group of people worshiping the Messiah through the Holy Spirit. This is a basic understanding of the Church but it is important to know the Bible does not make it overly complicated. If there are only two believers together, there is a Church.

I was visiting with a couple of guys about the church groups that come to Pine Ridge. One of the guys basically stated he was tired of seeing these groups come, because all they want to do is save our souls. I thought about this for just a moment and wanted to expound on this conversation. I began by telling him he needed to understand what Christians were all about. Jesus in his last words told the disciples to go throughout the whole world and make disciples, teaching them to obey the Commandments, which are to love God and love your neighbor. These last words are what Christians should live by in their daily lives. I do not mind people coming to Pine Ridge; it is good for our economy, and if people stop traveling to Pine Ridge it will hurt our development as a community.

We have enough people on our Reservations to create our own distribution corporations. You see the potato chip van going around and the wholesale vans taking products to our stores across the Reservation. What about the soda pop trucks who keep bringing their products to the Reservations? We have a large enough population to build a small city. My desire is to see young people rise up and begin building our homeland. We need to dream dreams and envision a better life for our grandchildren. I think back to the 1890s and wonder what my great-great-grandfather prayed for me. What was his ideal lifestyle for me? I liked what Vic Glover said to me; he said he was a man of questions not answers.

I remember my mentors and thank them dearly for the wisdom and strength they gave me. Uncle Roy taught me how much of a friend my dad was to him. He was a good brother to his family. He loved his family. Reverend Hedlund answered the hard questions for me about the faith. I asked him many questions, and he was able to teach me about our Lord and His church. My mentor and friend, Chris Eagle Hawk, taught me what it means to be Lakota. When I had questions, Chris gave me words of wisdom and continues to be one of my heroes.

I know I have been rambling for a couple weeks, but it is Called Rez Ramblings and Reasoning. I started thinking about my words and just wanted to get many things off my chest. The last fourteen years have been overall good, and I would not exchange them for anything. I live among our Lakota people with great pride and want to thank all of you for your kind words. We do not live forever, and I hope we can learn to make a better life for our children.

Taste of the Rez

I was paying an electric bill today and was a witness to life on the Rez. First, I went to get my mail, which is at the post office because we do not have any street addresses or mail delivery. It makes life inconvenient, but it is the way it is. Well, I checked my mail, and then it was off to the grocery store to pay for the electricity we consume on a monthly basis. Oh, before I left the post office there was a lady who had a handful of mail. She dropped a letter so I bent over and picked it up for her. I was thinking it is important to be nice and be a blessing to others. She looked at me a little shocked, and I went on my way knowing I was being spiritual. So next, I was on my way to the grocery store and paying bills. I needed to use the restroom so I went to the back. I found the key and made my way through to the restroom. I washed up and went out into the store where there were many people around. The workers were busy with their duties, and the customers were all around buying the high priced food. The Pine Ridge Village supermarket is like going to a subpar grocery store and shopping for goods at convenience store high prices.

I went to the counter where the ladies were doing their bookkeeping, and I showed myself. One smiled and came over to take my check. I was writing the check, and I noticed a young lady next to me asking for a phone to call the police. A guy apparently took her cell phone and her food stamp card. She tried to fight him off but he succeeded and ran away. A jailer from the Public Safety facility saw the whole thing and told the lady behind the counter to call the police because the lady standing next to me assaulted a man. She asked the lady

31

what happened and asked if she was drinking. The lady said, "Yes," and told her story of the man stealing her property. My heart broke because not only was her food stamp EBT card and phone stolen, but now on top of all of that, she was going to jail. Life on the Rez!

Death and taxes are sure things, but we do have choices
....from 4-13-10

We have endured many tragedies in our lives. With spring and summer come more accidents and incidents. Our lives can be marked by the death of our loved ones, as they are cataclysmic. In the movie Joe Black, the only sure things are death and taxes. We can see this on the reservation. Pine Ridge has a death rate second to the island nation of Haiti where poverty is rampant. Eighty percent of Haiti's population lives under the poverty level, and it is said to be the poorest country in the western hemisphere.

I have learned that some visitors to Pine Ridge believe we do not pay taxes, which is only partly true. We pay income tax, but we do not pay property tax. Our land is held in trust by the government. We have many issues facing our people when it comes to the length of our lives. We have poor diets which is one of the biggest causes of our low life expectancy. We have a high alcoholism rate among our people. We can change these issues if we put our minds together and begin to see reality.

I am trying to change my lifestyle when it comes to exercise and healthy eating. It is difficult because of the poor food selection on the Rez, but it can be done if you pay attention to what you are eating. Sometimes I like to grab a corndog and some chips. I just enjoy having a quick lunch. There are lots of choices we make in our lives and eating healthy should be one of them. Also, we need to get out and walk. When you walk you can actually lower your blood glucose levels. It is good for the heart and for burning a few extra calories from dinner. Choosing family activities is a great way to get involved with your children and extend your lives. This summer I hope to hike Harney Peak and do a few more hikes in other places. My goal is to go to the Teton Mountains and climb for exercise.

As I was walking over the weekend, I noticed more youth out in the Village of Pine Ridge. It saddens me when I see young teenagers walking around town without supervision. We need to watch out for our young people and help them to make better choices. One of the things about parenting is it is important to know where your child is at all times. We need to make sure they are safe and within a safe environment. Life is full of surprises, and if you know where your children are spending their time you will be less likely to have surprises. There are a number of groups your children and youth can be a part of as they grow up around the Reservation. We need to utilize these groups to keep our children in school and graduated.

We are still dealing with the White Clay issue. I went to White Clay last week and spent a little time there talking with the Relatives. I met a couple of the ladies up there who went to school with me at Oglala Community High School. I talked to them about people considering me a nerd in high school. It was funny because you never really know the way others thought you when you were young. I thought I was a cool kid, but I guess I was just weird. It is sad when I think about some of my classmates ending up in White Clay or other places where they are stuck and cannot get out. I heard them say they just like to drink and hang out with their friends.

Often times we see people stressed out. This is difficult because it is hard on the body and soul. We need to start changing our communities and start allowing our children to be who they are in a healthy environment. We can talk about things and have meetings, but in the end it will have to be people doing their best to live the life the Creator gave them. I choose to live where my grandfathers lived, and I want a better place for our grandchildren. It will take work. I know we come from a people group that can work because fortitude is a value kept. When I visited White Clay last week I reminded the people up there they were not forgotten. I told them the Creator loved them and cares for them. You must also believe the Creator cares for you and wants to bless your grandchildren. It is our future that is important and we need to begin to think of the Lakota who will come after us. Simple changes in our lives can have huge effects on our lives. We can move forward if we are willing to give our lives to God. My hope is we can build a stronger Lakota people and develop all areas of life on the Rez. I believe change is coming and with change comes responsibility.

What to do with a Million Dollars

If you make money and live your life with all the world has to offer, you are looked at as a sellout. But I do not know many Indians who would turn down financial success because they feel it takes away from the Indian Identity. This past summer a question was posed to me and I have had great difficulty answering the question. "What would you do with a million dollars, Leon?" Then and now I have the same answer; "I do not know!" Funny, when a simple question hits you right in the face and there is no simple answer to such an easy question. I could have said I'd spend it, or give to the poor and create a fund to help people with their needs.

I have a friend who talks about empowering people because it really is the answer, but we see what 20 million dollars does to the community or Reservation of Pine Ridge. I was involved in the early part of the Empowerment Zone for Pine Ridge. I hope there are more success stories coming, but very little has changed with $20 million. I know people can say we were promised $40 million, but I do not know if even $40 million would have changed much. Time will tell if we see some growth, but there were never any big businesses that came to Pine Ridge. The Cellular phone system came, but it has changed hands many times since the beginning. No one knows what has happened in lost revenue. I would guess some people know, but it is hard to pick through all of the years to know what actually took place.

So do we have an Indian problem? I believe the system that was instituted over 100 years ago has caused great loss of life and culture. The westward expansionism has destroyed many lives over the years. Now we are faced with picking up the pieces. I have been working on developing

34

a book because I believe it is important to write. I have a friend who told me something extraordinary. He has his PhD. When he came a thousand miles to meet with me, he encouraged me to write. It was to be the next step in my development. I believe he empowered me to begin writing from my experience. I have a unique story and thoughts because of my unique experience of being alive; no one can write that book for me. I have some great people who encourage my writing because they like reading the Ramblings. Of course, I like to just write it down, but I am actually getting faster on the keyboard which makes it easier. I have been writing my column for about two years. I hope to use them as a springboard for me to complete a book about life as a contemporary American Indian. I believe I have been empowered to complete this through encouragement and prayers.

We have many issues of poverty that affect us in a negative manner. Peoples' lives revolve around surviving. The survival mode does not allow for growth. I have seen people who are gifted choose to make the same mistakes over and over without thought to changing their lives. Synergy should be a great way to raise oneself out of poverty, but when everyone does not pull their own weight it can be overburdening. We see people lose hope after a while. I have been working for fifteen years in a ministry that struggles to develop, but I have hope we can pull things together.

My plan consists of a Talking Circle to talk about the issues of Reservation life. I know we can overcome with what Jolene stated in a reply to my blog. Coping mechanisms are needed for us to survive. We need to share our hurts and pains with others so we do not have to carry them alone. Now is the time for all of our people to become healthy. We need to care for each other and do the work our Creator has given us. I believe there is movement in the Spiritual realm, and people are waking up and remembering the Lakota people. We need to be empowered!

A Modern Pow Wow and the Wisdom of the V-8 guy
....from 8-11-10

Alright! The Oglala Nation was a great success! The parade went by for a long time. It is always great to see the people lined up on the side of Highway 18 and Main Street in Pine Ridge Village. We walked down to the Pow Wow on Saturday evening. It seemed like we were walking faster than the traffic was moving. I had Benny's Big Indian but had to share it with my wife. It seems like I cannot eat the whole thing anymore. It was nice to share the two all-beef patties between the pieces of fry-bread, with all of the fixings of course. I wanted to eat more but my appetite has changed since I lost around sixty pounds.

As I enjoyed the Wacipi or dancing on Saturday, I noticed another part of the Oglala Nation Fair and Rodeo, the festivities at the YO Park. There was basketball and volleyball, with a fear factor and burgers and hotdogs. I was impressed by the number of the youth at the park "hanging out", watching and playing basketball. I understood there are competing cultural events. The Pow Wow culture and the basketball rap culture are two distinct cultures in our contemporized Lakota culture. The athletic ability of the dancers, basketball players, and volleyball players is something to see. We have many world class athletes in our tribe and throughout Indian Country.

I had a great time both nights of the Fair. Chris Eagle Hawk told me that the spectators of the Pow Wow are participators as well. I enjoyed visiting a little and, of course, I enjoyed my meal. I went to Gup's Hog Heaven and had a great pork meal. I went to Denny's and had some roasted corn. I also finished my meals with Rudy's great Colorado Green Chili burrito; it was amazing! I see how the culture has changed over the past 150 years even through the food.

The last thing I experienced at the YO Park was getting beat by one of last year's best high school basketball players, Lars Backward. I do not like to step on the court feelings that I am going to lose, but to tell you the truth, Lars is an amazing shooter. My son Brad and his other teammates really made me feel old at forty-five. Lars' parents should be very proud of their son. I was also able to introduce my friend Humphrey to one of the best girls' high school players in the nation, Christian Janis.

When I was growing up on the Eastside of Denver, I knew what danger was. If you dissed people, you would surely get yourself in fights. When I was down at the park I experienced a lot of vulgar language through the music. Even in the rap contest people seemed to be cussing each other out on the microphone. I realize our Lakota culture is dealing with a push to become more Urban American because of Hollywood and the vanishing elements of humility in our lives. In our past, young people were taught to think of others before themselves, and now the urban culture teaches to take what you can for yourself. In Denver we had people who would come from the gang cities, and we as a family or community would take care of our own. I believe our Lakota ancestors took care of their people; they surely would not be cussing each other out. We need to embrace who we are as Lakota coming from a great people.

I was talking to a man I will call the V- 8 guy. I know he is taking some time out but he is a great asset to our Lakota people. I know we are a great people because we have come from a strong people who lived with respect for the earth and themselves. V-8 was telling me of how the white man brought alcohol as a way to destroy our people through chemical warfare, to make our warriors lose their way. I know what alcohol does to families and have battled the hopelessness of this way of life. I am here to tell you I believe Jesus can empower our people beyond belief. I came to Pine Ridge to share about Jesus and came into contact with severe hopelessness. I believe there is hope in what Jesus has to offer. When you can be made right and understand you are a child of God it is liberating to the spirit.

Lakota people can live a life of hope, but when you put poison in your being, whether it is alcohol or destructive lyrics, it will bring despair and hopelessness. I know we can overcome these issues, but it must include the Creator. My understanding of the Lakota way of humility, fortitude, generosity, kinship, and wisdom is the way I try to follow Jesus. These do not contradict with my being a Lakota or a Christian. So we can find hope in Jesus. I know it might be hard to understand, but I believe the Creator is seeking us. We need to understand what he has offered us as a people. Life is hard. We need to build hope in our community. I am asking for people to step forward to come together in unity to build hope in our youth. I am calling us to prayer in the centers of our communities.

Rez Ball
....from 1-15-09

Over the years I have watched young basketball players come of age. I have watched young players grow to maturity and become the best they could be in a very competitive sport. Hedlund's is a small basketball court, but when you are in Pine Ridge it is the place to see some of the great players. I grew up playing basketball there, and it was awesome. People would gather in the summertime and play against each other every night. Today we see players compete in three on three games throughout the summer.

Over the years I have seen my play peak and now go downhill. Of course, the young men like to beat up on me whenever they can. I had to start lifting weights so I could keep up with the ability of these young people. So if you are looking for a game, come to Hedlund's court.

The history of the court is great. I started playing on the dirt court that was there before they built the concrete court in 1982. Some men came from Huron and laid the foundation with reinforced steel. I was amazed the day they were putting it in. I did not know how much the court would mean to me over the years. The vision Reverend Earl Hedlund had when it came to the basketball court changed many lives. There are too many names, and I would feel badly if I forgot someone, but I assure you there have been many great players over the years at Hedlund's.

Last Friday I decided I wanted to watch some "Rez Ball". I thought the best game to watch would be Pine Ridge against Little Wound. This was going to be the game to see because it could be the district championship preview. One player was on my mind. Over the last two summers I have watched this young man grow and become stronger each year. While playing against this young man I have felt the power of his game on the court. One day he hit me so hard my glasses flew off my face. I have to tell you, this young man is unstoppable in the low block area.

During the game Friday night he was in foul trouble early and that meant he spent most of the time on the bench. But the third quarter was a sight to see as Little Wound only scored two points. Roman Leftwich was power rebounding and pumping up his young team. Roman is a sight to see when he is playing up to his potential.

It would be wrong to not mention the sophomore guards, Dalton Buckman and Orie Brown. They reminded me of some other super sophomores a few years back. I look forward to watching them play in the next few years. When you think of reservation basketball and how powerful it has been over the years, I hope you are keeping your eyes on these young men. I have watched these young men grow and improve with each game they play. I saw Orie Brown after the game and told him I was happy to see him tear other people up beside me.

I would also be remiss if I did not mention Spur Pourier. Little Wound has a lot to look forward to because of this young man. He is only a sophomore. He scored 31 points in about three quarters. I was shocked as I watched this young man take his team to a 16 point lead and then unfortunately lose the lead to the Thorpes.

If you are looking for a good game, I would suggest you travel to Little Wound High School or Pine Ridge Thorpe Country. You will not be disappointed.

I look forward to seeing the Lady Thorpes. They are truly one of the best teams in the state. District 14 is great to watch in both girls and boys basketball. I am looking toward some great b-ball in the coming months. Come out and support your team.

Forty-five Year Old Clarity
....from 8-04-10

This week I have decided to begin the process of figuring out the rest of my life. I turned forty-five on August 2, 2010. It does not feel any different from forty-four, but maybe I need to get further into the year before I can judge the two years. This week we are celebrating the Oglala Nation Fair and Rodeo. I would like to welcome all of the visitors, and especially the relatives, who have journeyed home from the cities and faraway lands. I hope to be visiting with many people at the pow wow. Of course I will be involved with some friends from Minnesota. I like the Oglala Nation time because we usually celebrate and worship on the Higher Ground deck. It is really great to be able to create traditions in the midst of so many people coming into Pine Ridge Village. I know people are busy, but it is always good to take time to worship the Creator. We will begin at 11 a.m. on Sunday morning during the pow wow weekend. Everyone is welcome to come and worship Jesus!

Okay, since I have celebrated my birthday this week, I thought I would try to work on clarity. Clarity is important when you are writing because the words can have several meanings, and tone is vital as well. I try not to write when I am angry because it can come off like I hate the world. But I want to share with the readers what I feel is vital to the health and welfare of our Lakota Nation. It is important we seek to bring people to our reservation. We need commerce and we need to work to make it a good experience for the people who come to Pine Ridge and the rest of Lakota country. I am tired of seeing all of the cars or vehicles drive away from the reservation. We need people to spend their money here so it will become a healthy environment.

I have a lot of friends throughout the country, but I enjoy seeing my relatives the most. I am always glad to see Chief Her Many Horses from Rosebud Public Safety. My uncle, Mike Horses, as he is commonly known by his friends, told me to write something interesting. It is difficult to please everyone, but I like to use my time of rambling to challenge people to think about what is important. If we say something is important to us then we need start working towards that end. We need to make the Pine Ridge Reservation a destination point with regard to the world. We have a strong history, and our story needs to be told. We come from a people who defeated the United States. The United States Government wanted a peace treaty. Of course, the United States Government did not stop taking the hunting grounds of our forefathers. We need to begin making decisions based on our future and not our present.

Last week I wrote about taking out the middle man. It is important for our future that we begin to build our economy. Our people need good food and other essential items. I sat one day and thought about how ridiculous it is to not be able to buy some underwear or other needed clothing items on the Pine Ridge Reservation. We do not have clothing stores! I would hope people would begin to understand we do not have a bank; banks are vital because they loan money to start businesses. Why not develop a legal bank where we could utilize all of the tribe's money? We could have our own interest and banking fees work for our people. We all need to work on our credit ratings. I got involved in the credit card schemes of the outside banks. I can honestly say I have put to rest my last credit card this year. The only loan I have other than a school loans is for a car. I decided I wanted to get away from the interests on cards because they can strangle you when you get into their clutches.

It does not take a business degree to understand that we need to start looking to provide goods and services to our own people. We need people to start businesses and develop stronger attitudes toward the economy. I appreciate the local business owners because I know how difficult it is to continue to grow and develop in a crab mentality culture. When people start to do well, we need to praise them for their fortitude. Our reservation system needs to become self-sustainable in a growing global economy. We have many people in Europe who would like to visit, but we are not oriented toward visitors. So when you see the Oglala Nation come together this year, understand that everyone is a potential customer and they help the world go around in Lakota country.

The Universe

I believe with all of the stars in the heavens we must come to an understanding the ancestors knew. Today was a great day. Our family took a trip to the Black Hills. There is not enough time to write the whole story, but our ancestors understood the beauty of the Sacred Black Hills. We took the 1995 Ford pickup and it was fun driving the truck through the hills. We got a late start because I had to fill up the pickup and get some nuts and bolts and the mail.

My cousin was at the dump. He told me about a van that burned at the gas pumps at Big Bat's. The oil company name might change, but locals call the station Bat's. Bat Pourier is one of my heroes. He built up a business, and then sold it to his sons. Last I heard they have five stores in the region. I do not know what happened at the store today in Pine Ridge, but the fire burned a pump and part of the canopy.

I was helping an older couple find their way to Hot Springs and thought about the way road construction is slowing things down. Then I saw one of my favorite all-time policemen; he would always tell me he was an outlaw. Rick Mousseau is the first old guy I saw make fouling on basketball court an art form. It is always a great to see him. He encouraged me with his taking care of his diabetes. He was on his way to play softball with his grandkids.

Then I went home and got everything together for a day trip. It was fun as we headed toward the hills. Driving for about three hours was a great time. We stopped at a rock shop and picked out some rocks for the garden. Then we got a latte and drove by Mt. Rushmore on the way to Hill City. We drove into Hill City at three o'clock. We went to the Alpine but they told us they stopped selling lunch at 2:30 and we would have to wait until five for the dinner.

Well, it was time to move along, and we saw a guy making arrowheads. I thought it strange he resembled Billy Jack the Martial Artist but a lot younger. We went to the pickup and when I was almost ready to start it up, the Billy Jack guy waved me over. I got out of the vehicle and went up to him. He asked me where I was from. He told me he was from Rosebud and told me his family names. It is an Indian thing when someone tells you about their family. I told him to not feel bad about being from Rosebud. After all we cannot all be from the Oglala, or the Pine Ridge. We laughed and he gave me a piece of the arrow heads. It was special because it was a gift from another Lakota. I told him I'd see him later. I got back in the pickup, and we drove down the road. On the way out of town I saw my friend Rick and gave him a quick call. I told him I was in the hills, but our phones did not work, so he could not understand me.

We took the last half an hour very fast as we drove to Rapid City enjoying the scenic views and the drive. We stopped at our favorite restaurant. Belle had a salad and I had my steak. Of course, I was enjoying my day in the hills. We went to a horrible movie and I cannot remember the name. It is probably better to live and forget. I think I am too young for that movie and only older people would get it.

Afterwards, we drove into the Badlands where cell service is terrible. We were able to see the stars and a thunderstorm rolling in around ten our time. It was breathtaking! I could only imagine others looking into the stars, but I believe our Lakota Ancestors knew how small they were in this Universe. One of the things I love about Pine Ridge is the views. I truly believe it is a battle to understand where I fit in the universe. One person asked, "Can we ever be 100 percent sure?" That person must have been thinking of me. I truly want to know for sure where I need to be, and I want to move without fear. When I do find fear, I hope I can have people move with me through those unknowns. I believe God is working to make me a better person. It is sometimes slow, but when I think of the magnitude of the Creator, and that he loves me, I realize, love never fails.

TIWAYE

Family

Grandparents

Children become parents, parents become grandparents, and
life continues its cycle. I remember my maternal grandparents because
my mom took care of me most of my childhood. I met my grandpa Al
Matthews and was taken by his green eyes and wavy hair. I remember
him smoking outside of the old Catholic church in Pine Ridge village.
My mom took us over to our grandparents in North Ridge in the
seventies, and I remember my grandma Francis. She made a bed for us
in the living room and made us go to sleep. She seemed tall and thin at
the time, and I remember her long hair with streaks of gray. My grandpa
Wallace talked about Mongolians. I thought this was strange, but he
was an older man with lots of information. One day he was eating some
bread and started to choke. I came in after school and saw what was
happening. I gave him the Heimlich maneuver. The bread came out and
everything seemed to go back to normal.

I asked my mom about my grandmother Pearl. She told me she
came from the Standing Rock Reservation and was visiting Wounded
Knee where she met my grandfather. Grandma Pearl was a Demaris, so I
have relatives in Sisseton and Standing Rock. I loved sitting on my deck
listening to my mom talk about our relatives. My grandma Alma spoke
at a Christian event. She talked about when she was a little girl. She
went to church as a little girl. When she grew up, she left the church and
then returned to the church when she was older. Then she said she was
very proud of me for becoming a minister. I appreciated Grandma Alma.
Her words made me feel stronger in my life work. Grandparents give
us hope and identity. I learned from another grandpa that my grandma
used to bring my dad to the Gospel Fellowship when he was a boy. It
was called the Gospel Mission back then.

We seem to lose so many grandparents, and it is very sad.
Sometimes all of the weight seems to fall on the shoulders of one of the
family members. When we lost our mother, I know the weight of the
family issues fell on my sister Sue. We talk on the phone and I try to get
to Denver often; but I know it is not enough. Family should be more

important in our lives. We need to realize what a wise man once told me. He said, "When older people die there is always someone to take their place." I know it is hard to replace our parents, but I assure you they have given you everything you need. It is the memory of our relatives.

There is a story in the Bible where a young man asked Jesus, "Who is my neighbor?" Jesus talked about the Good Samaritan. It is a story about a man traveling on a road where robbers would lay in wait. This man was on his way to the next town when he was stopped, robbed, and beaten. They left him for dead. Some religious people came by and walked around him. But, the next person was a Samaritan man. He stopped and bandaged the hurt man and took him to an Inn. The Samaritan told the Innkeeper he would return to pay any unpaid debt on his way back through. You see, the young man asked Jesus who his neighbor was. The point of the story is to let the young man know, he is not to look for neighbors, but to be a neighbor. We talk about our relatives, but we need to be relatives to all people.

Young people need us to be their relatives. Our people need all of us to take care of each other. We need to engage our people in order for change. The Great Lakota Nation is a powerful place, and we need to encourage our family and relatives whenever we can. I am trying to greet people and let them know I appreciate them. We all need to do this and stop the fighting. Forgiveness is a gift worth giving. People close to us can hurt us the most because they are a big part of our life. You will be happier if you are not full of stress and hatred.

Blunt Horn and Sitting Bull Run through Me

Blunt Horn fought at the Little Big Horn and then came home to Wounded Knee. It intrigues me to know James R. Walker used my great-great-grandfather as a source. Walker was an M.D. and took great interest in the societies of the Lakota, in particular the Oglala. John Blunt Horn is mentioned in the three main books by Walker, and it is good our grandfather was listened to when it came to the understanding of Lakota culture. Blunt Horn came home to Wounded Knee, lived out his life there at the creek, and had children. Suzie was John Blunt Horn's daughter of whom I am a direct descendant. Suzie's eldest son is Aloysius, my father's dad. My grandparents had two sons and two daughters. Pearl, his wife, came from the family of Sitting Bull. She joined the Matthews and was a part of their lives.

I have some great experiences in my life. I went to Chicago and found some people who knew my uncle Tommy. I heard what they knew from being in the city. I come from great people; one being John Blunt Horn and the other being Grandma Pearl Sitting Bull. Our heritage is powerful when you begin to understand the realm of being. I believe our people are powerful and can be whatever they decide. My family history is rich, and I found my great-great-grandfather was a minister in 1890. I thought I was the first minister in the family, but I am not as much an anomaly as I thought. My great-great was a minister of the Gospel of Jesus!

Living and Healing through our Ups and Downs

I have made a decision in my life. I need to get this book out of me. I am telling people about it and they say, "You should just do it." I believe I have a message and before I get too busy with life, I want to focus my mind and my spirit. Sometimes life gives us up and downs. I have tried to live my life fully. I believe God desires to give life and even says he wants to give us life more abundantly. I have had the opportunity to meet some great friends over the years. These people care deeply, and I believe they are God's way of letting us know he has not forgotten. As much as I believe I have tried to live life with passion, I believe God has more passion for me than I could ever imagine. I suppose that is God's way of letting me know I mean more to him than he could ever mean to me. I know that I fail as a human with my love and passion when it comes to God. My friend Humphrey spoke some truth in my life this summer. I felt his conviction and as he spoke with love and truth. I understood a little more of God's will in my life.

As I move in this life I believe my mother left me with a great gift. She taught me there are no strangers, just unmet friends. I think of the way she lived her life. I know she had some pain and difficulty in her life. By observing her living, I understand that she lived out her challenges. I have to share a story. One night great aunt was with my mom, and they were going from bar to bar celebrating. My mother told me they wanted to change so they stopped at the house. My mother went upstairs and changed her clothes. She went downstairs and in the kitchen there was man sitting at the table. She asked, "Who are you, and how did you get here?" He replied, "I am the medicine man, and I came in the taxi with you!" She went on to tell him medicine men do not drink. He told her, "Ah, you should see _____ _____, a famous Holy Man of the Lakota." They had a great laugh and went on their way to celebrating. I share the story because it was one my mother told me, and I believe she lived with great passion. I believe I get that from my mother. She was a wonderful, intelligent woman.

We live with hurts and pain, but we need to live in healing. I desire more healing in my life, and I hope to find it in God's hands. My fear is not that I would not have loved, but that I would have failed at being loved. No fear, living with passion, and great love. I believe we are a people in Lakota Country who have struggled to find this love. We live with lots of pain and heartache and I believe our people are seeking this love and passion. When I have come across people who are struggling on the streets of White Clay, Nebraska, I believe they have not had the love. What does all of this mean?

I believe the powers that be made an attempt to systematically destroy our family structure. We are struggling because of this attack on the Indian family. Boarding schools and churches were used as weapons to destroy our way of life on the Pine Ridge and in Lakota country. The FBI came and talked to me about the gang issues on Pine Ridge. Their solution is to hold the offenders in jail for three years instead of just one. I was fascinated because the Feds know what they did to the family in Lakota country, and yet they are at a loss for what to do.

Well, as I continue to ramble on in this blog I hope to finish my book. Yes, life is difficult and we will have ups and downs, but I hope and pray we can find a love we all deserve.

You're Beautiful

"Shared a moment that will last to the end", comes from the song by James Blunt. "I see her and realized it would never be." I guess I am a romantic when it comes to love songs. The one thing he shares in the song is they shared a moment, and he believed that one moment will last to the end. So here we are in a world full of life, and in an instant, just a blip in the reality of life, he sings the song, "You're beautiful." All he saw was her face, and he did not know what to do because the reality is he will never be with her. I believe we can search our whole lives for that one moment. That one moment may never occur, but we can search for it. Okay, I need to get some different songs in my life. I need to change the subject; sappy love songs can wear you down.

I am sitting in a coffee house listening to some music and writing. I love the coffee house in Lawrence, Kansas. Dunn Brothers is a great coffee house we first came to in Lawrence. It is close to Haskell Indian Nations University and an all-around great place to share an experience. Today, it is all about work. I am getting some words down on the computer while Belle is working on grades with Tammy. I think she does the teacher/parental thing very well. She understands education; me, I just want to write and listen to some music.

Oh, in case you were wondering, Belle asked me if we had never met what I would do if I saw her in a crowd. My response was, "I would still be searching my whole life for her.", and I finished off with, "I would be flying high." Of course the reference is to the song, and him being high on red wine. I thought it was a nice exchange. My heart sometimes needs to be reminded of what it desires. I believe we need to share the experience with others and know we can have great moments in life.

I am working on developing my life. I know I have lots to learn, and I hope that the mistakes I have made will make me a better person as I grow older. Some of the songs are good to develop thought and reflection. We live in a world where we can be in many places and still accomplish the goals and work we need to finish.

I think of my friend, Jason. He works all over the country,

51

and I like to visit with him when he comes to the Higher Ground Coffee House working on his scheduling and ideas. He accomplishes his work in Pine Ridge even though he is all over the country with scheduling events. I hope people begin to see what can be done through communication.

We have one of the best companies in the telecom industry waiting to get into Pine Ridge for the purpose of developing their network. Communication is vital when you are a developing nation. I believe we have the opportunity to develop our communication; it can be world class. Business is dependent on being available through the phone systems and the internet. We are on the threshold of success, and I believe we can reach the world with a product and a message. I believe we can go global and create hope for our people.

The Lost Art of Visiting
....*from 11-10-09*

The lost art of visiting needs to be brought back into our lives. Facebook, Bebo, and other forms of communication have taken us further away from visiting each other in a personal manner. I remember my aunts coming over to our house. It was so awesome to see them visiting around the coffee and cigarettes. Time would stop, and it was always a blessing for my mom. My aunt Agatha was my favorite because she was a passionate woman. I remember my uncle Roy who would brighten our days, and my mom would be very excited to see him. Of course I love all of my aunts and uncles the same but there is my cousin Ted; he is a blessing to our tiospaye. I love visiting with people because it is truly the way God made us. One thing aunt Pearl knows that I know is how great a cup of joe and cunli taste when you are visiting a great woman. If you think I am speaking in code I will say it, my mother made the menthol cigarette and cup of coffee taste so good.

I am talking about visiting because it is passion I love. I have one friend who is a rocket scientist, activist, social worker, pastor, director and the list goes on. I even have a DJ friend who moves me with his ideas and his willingness to not agree with me. I love life and hope to visit more people in my life. I love talking with my wife because she is very intelligent and wise. In less than a month I will have my silver anniversary. Life has blessed us with many friends and a place of ideas and hopes. I found out this past week Lloyd's of London was started in Edward Lloyd's coffee house in 1688. When you realize how powerful Lloyd's of London is in their area of expertise you will understand we all need places of ideas.

Lakota people and other people have been visiting for centuries. It is an art form that must be cherished and built upon. While shopping over the weekend, I met some Lakota from Standing Rock, and I told them about my relatives from their Reservation. I also met my first Ute Indian. I like to talk with people because of my training and because my mother told me there are no strangers, only unmet friends. Sometimes I do not get things done because of my visiting, but I believe I may be getting more done by visiting.

I know many people around Pine Ridge and love talking with them. There are a couple of people I have been visiting for fourteen years. We just carry on the conversation, and it is great. I asked some people from the east side of our Reservation if there were any presidential people. I was intrigued by my cousin who was talking about running for office. It is never too early to start thinking about political office. I like it when we are in election time, and Tom Casey is reading results in each district. It is truly amazing to see what is going to happen. I was told by one person that I was not put here to change the political system. Of course I had hopes of becoming a council person. But, to tell you the truth, I do not think I could handle political office. Hats off to our people who run for office, and know I will pray for you.

I am still waiting for a leader to rise from the ashes and lead us into the future. Can you imagine Crazy Horse leading us? Or any of the great leaders we have seen in our history? I want a revolution and I believe someday we will see a leader, not a politician but a leader, rise up and lead our Oglala and Sicangu into the 21st century. I try to follow Jesus in my life because he leads by serving. I love to serve people and to cook for people. We love our people, a beautiful people. Jesus fed thousands and visited with many people. It is mind blowing when you understand how much Jesus communicates to our culture and holds the key to our being.

My words are not always perfect but I will continue to write
....from 6-09-10

For some people battling apathy is a daily struggle; others just do not care. While this summer will mark 15 years of completed ministry on the Pine Ridge Reservation, we as a family believe it is vital we refocus our lives and start to think about the next fifteen years. When I arrived home in Pine Ridge Village in 1979 I knew life would be different from that point on. I lived in Denver most of my life, where I learned from the streets. Brutality was a way of life and I was excited to get out of the city because of the violence. When I was young I remember thirsting to be in church and listening to every word. Sure, I was ridiculed for going to church but I felt like it was the safest place for me. When I lived in New Crazy Horse in Pine Ridge Village, I woke up early to get to church. It was a vibrant place with a powerful message of my Itanca or leader.

I was taught who my people are by my mother and she would ask us where we came from on the Pine Ridge Reservation. I would tell her Wounded Knee and my paternal grandmother came from Standing Rock. It has been my dream to go to my people north and get to know them. We walk in our ancestors' footsteps and I believe life will not be complete for me until I meet my relatives.

I appreciate my mother's family more and more because of the way my uncles treated my mother. They had a great love for her and she was their sister. Our lives have been devastated by inaction and not developing our family or tiospaye. My desire is to continue what the Government wanted to destroy and that is our way of life. We can start by having a family reunion and meeting our children's children.

Now is the time we begin to pick up the pieces that have come from forced poverty and assimilation. Many people have heard of assimilation but the true culprit is enculturation. I am sure people have not used this in their writings, but I will begin to study it more because I believe this force has played a huge role in the destruction of a people group.

I want to complete some of my thoughts in the next few months and move toward a work that would be more complete. I have thought of closing down my column but I think it is important to continue writing about the Reservation. I have done radio, television, documentaries, and newspapers and have enjoyed all of them, but it has been more difficult to sit down and write out my thoughts. I was told not to write by a person and I felt like it gave me a writer's block. I thank God for my Uncle Mike because he told me to write. At the same time I was talking with my mother and she told me I should write. I miss my mother and have a greater understanding of her loss of loved ones. These two people are responsible for me and I believe they have a great love.

When I was doing radio a few years ago, I must have made some people angry. I accept that my words can be misunderstood and misconstrued. An Itanca came to me and was pretty upset. I did not want to offend him anymore but I wanted to speak with humility. I said, "Itanca I know my words are not always perfect, but I would hope that you would judge my heart and not my words." I still believe this today. I am not a perfect man and I surely find more faults in myself than anyone else can, but I am for the people. Not just my relatives, as some politicians operate, but all of my relatives. The Oglala Nation, we are a great people with much to offer the rest of the world.

This week is when we as a tribe honor our Veterans and I wanted to encourage everyone to come to Pine Ridge Village and express their gratitude for the service of these men and women. And when you do, you have to try Benny's Stand. He serves the Big Indian and by far the best fair food you can possibly have at the Oglala Nation and Veterans Pow Wow. Benny is in town and ready to serve up some of the famous two all-beef patties with all the fixins placed between two pieces of frybread. I saw Benny (Lance Benson) at the Alltel office in Pine Ridge

Village. He was happy to see me and told me he would hook me up with a Big Indian. I told him I would see him at the pow wow and would bring some people to try his stand. Best lemonade in town when Benny is in town. My wife Belle makes me stand there for hours waiting in line for ice cold lemonade. Summer is truly one of the most blessed times of the year.

Uncle Floyd Hand

One day I was at the bank doing some business and in walked Looks For Buffalo, or Ginny Hand. He walked up to me with a cane and asked if we kept records at the church. I told him they did not leave me with records so it was never part of my work at the church. He told me he remembered going to church with his mother and siblings. Then he shook my world; he actually said my dad came to the Gospel Mission as a boy and remembered my grandmother Pearl. Of course I believe my grandpa Al was a strong Catholic so he was not mentioned. I was surprised at the idea that the Gospel Mission ministered to my family before I was ever born. The Gospel Mission was started in 1948 by some Mennonites. Interestingly enough the original pastor, Arthur Unrah, is still going at 99 years old. He still prays for us, and I have to believe we need all the prayer we can get. Of course, the second pastor, Earl Hedlund, will soon celebrate his 90th birthday. One of my friends told me I was gonna live to be in my nineties. Wow, these men of faith leave huge shoes to fill!

Back to Looks for Buffalo; he stopped in today and yelled out my name. I like the way the old people say my name, Lee On. He wanted to talk to me about doing a dinner for his mother who was one of the faithful. I told him to let me know and I would be available. He went on to talk to me about my dad and them drinking down on skid row in Denver. It was "the big Swede" who must have come on around 6 p.m. because he would chase them off the row. I told him I remembered shining shoes down there. We made some pretty good tips. Some women would want their strap shoes shined. It was a good way to make a few bucks. I think I told him since he knew my dad so well he knew

I could be a crazy guy too. The Matthews blood runs through my body. Of course, we had a big laugh and it is good medicine. I think God sends someone to help lift you up when you need it most.

Collecting Fossils
.... from 4-27-10

My sister cousin Cyn sent me an article about aliens and what British astrophysicist Stephen Hawking says about what alien contact would mean to the earth. It is really interesting because it talks about what American Indians faced with forced colonization. An alien invasion might be just like what happened when Columbus ran into the Americas. He did not discover what he was looking for; he miscalculated and basically bumped into two continents. He was looking for faster trade routes to the east. The Europeans were seeking resources. The Euro-Americans are still seeking resources, or at the very least, seeking to ensure access to resources. There are between 700-800 military bases around the globe to keep their interests safe. There are around 70 countries where US military bases house over 200 thousand military personnel.

The analogy Mr. Hawking used to understand an alien invasion is a group of glowing lizards becoming nomads. As they use up their resources on their home planet, they would eventually come to Earth, and that would not be a good thing for humans.

It is important to understand the reality of what took place in the Americas. I have been in dialog with some people about the history of the Americas. I gave an explanation of colonization because it helps us to see the United States of America and its beginning. Three components need to happen in order for the colonization to take place: colonies of people, trading posts, and plantations. I was thinking about White Clay, Nebraska. There is a trading post and if you remember the fort on the west side of the village, it surely looked like they had a colony of people living there. For a lack of a better plantation, you can find farming on the south side of the village. If you remember there was a trading post in

Wounded Knee before they burned it to the ground.

My mother told me she would look for fossils west of the Wounded Knee gravesite. She would collect them and then ride down to the trading post and trade them for cigarettes. My dad's family came from the Wounded Knee community. It was great when I came home in 1995 and was able to go to Wounded Knee. People would come up to me and tell me they were my relatives. It is a great feeling when you know people claim you. It means something when people remember your family. Well, my mother and father were staying out in the country west of the grave; that is where my mom used to go looking for fossils. She told me she found a brass ring one time. My Grandfather Al took it and threw it back because he did not want anything to do with the history of the ring.

My personal understanding of colonization is it has not and does not serve us well. But in order for us to decolonize we need to build our territory. We have sovereignty, but we do not exercise it properly. We need to establish our own laws and not adopt the federal or state laws to govern our people. It is time to take a Warrior's stand and take back what belongs to us. One of the people I look up to (and there are many of them) is John Yellow Bird Steele. He would go to our border and not allow the state patrol to come on to the Pine Ridge. I believe it is time we begin to take the federal and state governments to task. We have the Self-Determination Act of Congress or PL93-638. We can see the intent was to give us the sovereignty the treaties accomplished.

By contracting services with the government, we could possibly end many of the social ills of our Reservation. It would require risk. I know it would be difficult for many of our people to trust the Tribal Government with more responsibility. I am a believer in our people yesterday and today. I believe our ancestors were right when they fought the U.S. Government and signed a treaty for their grandchildren. We are their grandchildren! As a sovereign people we have the responsibility of enacting our own laws of government. Because we were made dependent on the Federal Government, we find ourselves stuck in a rut. We must get out of the rut and begin to move forward in social and personal responsibility.

The first act of sovereignty should be to challenge the fact that we as sovereigns need to make a contract with the State when it comes to casinos. If we are sovereign, we can govern ourselves. I am not a big fan of casinos, but it is our only real economic resource at the moment. This makes me think that we need to further develop our economy in order to our people feed themselves. We as Lakota know what it means to have no food. We come from a people who are strong, and we need to exercise our Treaty Rights.

I was asked a question about my faith in Jesus and how all of this affects me as a Christian. It is good to have people question your words. I believe it is part of the idea that we had termination written on us for so long. It is not hard to be upset with the injustice. I believe we need to seek justice because so many of our people are struggling. It is sad when I think about the Reagan years where unemployment rose from 40% to 70% because programs were cut. If we were able to get what the government owes us, it would be an astronomical number. At one time we were the richest people group, until the Black Hills were taken illegally.

Seasons in the Sun in Denver

When I look at an old photo my mom gave me, I see the drab clothing of the seventies. I remember wearing brown plaid pants and a button shirt with short sleeves. Of course it is what I am wearing in the photo, but I remember other clothing I wore back in the seventies. I remember being a dreamer and a lover of the love songs. They were easy to listen to and to dream about the person that I did not meet. I guess it was becoming a real issue because by the time I hit my teen years my mother thought I was a bit of a sissy. Of course by this time I had many fights, and I was beating guys up for just looking at me. I was a tough guy, but I loved the love songs of the era. I had older brothers and one younger. I fought through the middle child syndrome. I became distant and would stay away from home most of the time.

I grew up in the inner city of Denver. At the time it seemed to be a good-sized city, but I would later learn it was not as big as I thought. Now it is a growing city with the suburbs growing by leaps and bounds. There was a ten-mile distance between Golden and Denver when I was growing up. A family by the name of Supers was a family I used to visit in Golden. This is where I first learned to swim underwater. It was like going to the country. They had an adopted child from Southeast Asia. I remember them as a hippy couple; they were really nice to visit. I met my cousin's wife whose name is Holly. She was a flower child back in the seventies. I remember her flower dress and long golden hair. She was from the west coast, and I was intrigued by her presence.

I was a little boy who had a whole city as his back yard. It was dangerous, and we understood we had to watch out for each other. Life in the seventies seemed to be full of freedom. I thought the summers were the greatest. I loved school as well, but it was a lot of learning and hard work. I had a speech impediment so it required more school time with a therapist. I was picked on a little, but in the end I believe it gave me compassion for others who would be picked on for similar shortcomings. I remember one girl who must have felt my pain as I was being picked on in the school yard. The kids were African American, and they would not leave me alone. It was do or die in the school yard, and I was being bullied by a lot of kids. This girl stepped up and told them to stop! It was a great day as they never bothered me again. I lived across the street from the school. I do not know where my brothers were, but I thank God for the girl who saved me.

I missed school the day they taught about prejudice and racism. Many of the Chicanos did not get along with most black people. I did not mind and had a greater view of race and ethnicity. We were part of the melting pot of the seventies. By the time I got to college they were teaching about the tossed salad in socialism. Assimilation and the melting pot was a politically correct approach to understanding that America has distinct culture and that is what makes America great. If you are reading this, I hope you have more of an idea of who I am. You must understand where I have come from; it is similar to the movie Patience. I do remember the bad growing up in the city, but I also enjoy remembering the good times. I do not believe my mother had the training to bring up eleven children, but she worked to make sure we ate.

Mothers are special even when they see their children grow up and head to college. I believe they continue to remember the goodness and not so much of the arguments or disagreements.

So, I do remember my childhood and try not to forget. Mostly, I choose to remember the good times. I have to share my all-time favorite song. I hope you will listen to it on YouTube. Seasons in the Sun by Terry Jacks is a song that I believe helps me to remember the good times. It is about friendship and memories. I think it is a powerful song because it is about change of seasons and newness in our lives. Being a student of philosophy, I have come to understand we must in the very least know who we are in reference to the cosmos. So who am I? I believe I am the little boy with very little in his life who wore hand-me-downs from his older brothers. I believe I am the one my mother thought was a sissy but was fighting in the neighborhood and making sure people did not pick on my friends. I was a little brother and big brother who knew my position in life. When I was fifteen years old I left my mother's home. I learned rather quickly life is difficult, and I thank God every day for the love my uncle Roy gave me. I am sure I have failed him and succeeded for him in many ways. I am an adult now, and I must not fear the unknown. The unknown was something I thought I would never have to deal with, but I realize in the end I must be willing to give up everything in order to attain me!

Lights, Giving, and a Birthday Party at Christmas
....from 12-25-09

It is always refreshing to see people give during the Christmas season. We celebrate the birth of Jesus on December 25th. It is a great time to see the houses lit up with different colors. We drove up to the Pine Ridge campus last week and saw a couple of nice houses. We even drove up to Crazy Horse housing and saw at least one house with lights. When I was a child we used to go to the Civic Center in Denver, Colorado to see the lights at the courthouse. It was amazing to see so many lights and such beauty. Of course, we do some decorating but I get excited to see people give.

When I was a boy my mother called me by middle name, Barry, and everyone else called me Lee. Now, I don't mind being called Lee or Barry. One time it worked out that these nice church people were getting gifts for our family. The woman, Veronica, came to our home. She was dressed fancy. Now, I don't know what an eleven year old boy would consider fancy, but this woman seemed to have nice clothes and looked dressed up to me. My mom kept talking about her children, and she would mention me by my middle name. When she gave a list of her children to the lady, she put me down as Leon. Well, when it came time for the gifts to be dropped off, I received double presents. The woman took my middle name and my first name and counted me twice.

Well, that is a great little story about giving, but I want to share with you about Christmas on the Reservation. It is not the darkest time of year, but for many it can be the saddest time of the year. For our Lakota people, we understand family means everything. I believe this can be the saddest time of year because Christmas is a family celebration. We go through life understanding our family is vital to us. I look around and see that I am older, and the older ones are no longer with us. Life is a cycle, and a wise man once told me, "When older people die, there are always people to take their place." He is now gone and I hope there was someone for his family. He was a very loving man. I would guess he did more for our family then I will ever know.

Sometimes people misunderstand and miss the true reason for the Christmas season. We try to have a party for our little church. We call it a birthday party for Jesus. I told a high school classmate; I see Jesus through my being a Lakota man. I ask this question, "Is it necessary for one to suffer for the many?" It is true of our Sundance. We have dancers who are not supposed to dance for themselves but for the betterment of the people. This is a principle that is vital to understanding what Christmas is all about. Jesus was the gift to the world. He is the Creator and came to suffer for us. He is known as the Suffering Servant. As a grandson to my ancestors, I believe I live as a Lakota because their blood runs through my veins. I accept very plainly what Jesus did for me on the cross, and His coming into the world needs to be celebrated.

I feel that is important to say because so often we forget what Christmas stands for in a consumer based society. In the next couple of weeks we will see the Lakota Nation Invitational and a New Year. 2010 is almost here. We as a Lakota Nation need to start developing ideas and implementing them. We need to develop our economy in a way so that it will be able sustain our people. We need to look at new ways of getting people to spend their money on the Rez. I was thinking about Pine Ridge Village, and I realized we have three grocery stores serving us; one in Pine Ridge and two in White Clay, Nebraska. We do not have a clothing store or an office supply store. I see the trucks that transport goods to our Reservation because we do not have a distributor on the Rez. We have lots of land, but we do not have any warehouses except for the Commods (government issued food) and other tribal entities.

Just a few thoughts as we seek to tackle the suicide and other problems we face in Lakota Country. We are on the threshold of great things in our area. We need to bring our minds together to hope and pray for the betterment of our Lakota Citizens. I was sharing how I define success with a Chinese gentleman. It is being able to feed and clothe your family. Everything else can be fabricated depending on your belief system. There are many families that are two income homes, and they are doing well financially on our Reservation. It is the ones that do not have income and are just scraping by in our society where hope fading. I came from extreme poverty; I used to eat beans and homemade bread. I remember some days there would be nothing to eat. Many of our people remember these days. Education changed my life, and it will have the power to change yours as well.

Life Lessons

One day we were in Pine Ridge village as children or young boys. We were a carefree bunch as we, the three little brothers, were hanging outside of our grandparents' home. Some other boys from up the road had some fishing poles, and they were walking by us. They saw us and immediately challenged us to a fight. I suppose coming from the city we looked awkward and strange to the Indian boys. We had fought

63

many fights in the city, and we could run pretty fast if the odds were overwhelming. I remember a group of about 20 black kids chased us down the street in Denver. I was a little faster than my older brother or more afraid; I do not know which is truer. I had to slow down and turn around to help my brother fight off some of the faster black kids. We did pretty well that day as people were screaming to catch us and beat us down. I do not know why they chose to chase us or why they seemed to dislike us. We were Indian boys in the city, and I would bet we looked awkward in the city as well. Being awkward makes you one thing or another, really fast or really tough. I do not know if I was all that fast. I did become a fighter, and would often find myself beating someone up. Back to the Rez....As the Indian boys from the Rez challenged us, I saw they had potential weapons in their hands, and I picked up an ax. We walked toward the boys. Their eyes got huge, and they took off down the street. We had no intention of fighting that day so we let them run away.

My brother Wally is one year older than me. He reminded my mother of our uncle "Skooter." I do not know why they called him this name, but he seemed to be a really nice man. He walked with a cane and when I inquired about it, he told me it was to keep the dogs from biting him. I will speak about the dogs another time. One day we saw Uncle Skooter walking away from our grandparents' house. We ran up to him and asked where he was going. He said he was going to work, "gonna go pick speghetts". It was a magical moment, and we ran to tell our mother where our uncle was going. She laughed, but I did not know why. Later I learned a life lesson; spaghetti does not grow on trees or bushes. He was a great uncle to have as he would be a chipper man if you would have described him to anyone.

When I visited with my mother as an adult, I would often listen more than talk. I know for some that is hard to believe. She recounted the days of the old place north of the Slim Buttes. They had a spring on their land, and my mother said people would come from far away to get water. Getting water was a chore for many. I remember traveling in a brown Ford pickup to get water from a school or church that had an outside faucet. Well, my mother remembered people coming in a buckboard with a team of horses. Her life seemed vivid as she retold some of her stories. She told me people would stay a day or maybe a week camping out and visiting her parents. I know life must have been hard, but we as children seemed to make the best out of it, even when it was difficult.

Thankful on Thanksgiving
....from 11-27-08

Thanksgiving is a wonderful time of the year. I remember my mom cooking everything imaginable at Thanksgiving. We have many things to be thankful for as Lakota people. We have family. Family is the greatest gift given to us by the Creator. As a young man, I remember one year when we had guests. My cousin Marv came and I was happy to see him. His girlfriend was a real hippy. How many times do you get to see a real live hippy? Of course now they are yuppies, but I believe his girlfriend is still a real hippy. I remember this because my step-father was a butcher at the time and kept his knives very sharp. I remember Marv looking to carve up the turkey to get some meat from the carcass on the table.

My step-father said, "Be careful, the knife is sharp," and as soon as the words came out of his mouth, Marv slipped and it seemed like half of his thumb came off. I was shocked and turned away. I was pretty young, do not even remember how old I was, but I remember the time the hippy came to Thanksgiving. Those were good days!

In more recent times, I have had the opportunity to spend Thanksgiving with my wife's family and it has been awesome. We have been able to eat great meals with family. Food is such an important part of culture. I can write with all truthfulness, I have not gone away hungry in the Thanksgiving season. It seems there has always been enough food and I have seen the wateca (leftovers) leave the dinner table. I know there was enough food for everyone.

My job is the mashed potatoes. I do not know how I came upon this job, but my experience being in a large family has taught me to peel many potatoes. My wife is a master at pies and gravy. Frybread is one of the things that have changed from my mother's dinners. It is a part of dinners with my wife's family. My mother didn't make frybread; my wife's family does. I love frybread as it mixes well with everything I have ever eaten in my adult life.

This year will be different as we are having dinner with friends from Colorado at the Pine Ridge Gospel Fellowship. We will have enough food for 250 people. So everyone is invited to come and get a meal at the Gospel Fellowship in Pine Ridge.

I am excited because it is a radical move when the European Americans bring the American Indians food. America feeds the world. Wheat, corn, and other dry goods go around the world. Tomatoes are the best food in the world, and they originally came from America. The food of America is truly a gift to the world. Corn, being one of the best foods originating in America, can even be used as a fuel that runs cars. How can you beat such a great source of energy?

I am most thankful for the family of God. I have many people who I am thankful for, mostly the Hedlund family. They took me in and helped me see what it means to be a Follower of Christ. I spoke with a few friends at the coffee house this past week and explained to them that I am not defined by what I do. Rather, I am defined by the fact that I am a radical follower of Christ. Look, I am not the buckle-wearing Puritan, but a person who seeks to live by what Jesus put forth as a person who walked among men. Jesus confounded the world when he sat with sinful people.

The judgmental "religious" people did not approve of the people Jesus dined with while he was on earth. I am one of those people that these "religious" people would not have accepted. We need to shake off the idea of perfection and instead cling to the hope we have in becoming one of the friends of God. My hope is that people will see the Church as a family. That is truly what it is, especially when it comes to Native American Christianity. When you understand family, you will truly understand the faith. In the coming weeks I hope to explain what this means to us as Lakota people.

Kay's Story
....from 3-2-10

I would like to share a story of a young Lakota woman. When she was a little girl she would often take care of her siblings with loving care. She also loved babies and adored them with love. She would find babysitting jobs when she was a pre-teenager. You would see her love and care for children. She would also be stern and fair when the children were being naughty. She loved children and would often find children to care for them if the adults were visiting. She had a wisdom not known to most young people her age. Our people believe children are the sacred ones. She lived up to the model and was kind and compassionate.

I will call her by her Lakota name because it is how we know her, Wankiyan Ohitika Wi, or Brave Lightning Woman. She loved to chase the storms and watch them come from the land of her grandparents, a place called Slim Buttes. She would beg an adult to drive her to the top of the hill west of the village of Pine Ridge. If you ever get a chance to see the storms come through Pine Ridge, look to the west and you will see one of the greatest light shows on earth. Brave Lighting loved the storms; she loved to hear the thunder and see the bolts of electricity crackling the skies.

When she was a student at Red Cloud High School, she tried to encourage her friends as much as possible. She went to school and loved to befriend the shy students. She would often look after the one who needed a helping hand. She never let her own health become a crutch, and she lived life like a healthy young lady. She was a heart patient, and by the age of eleven, she had gone through five surgeries. Her life was full of suffering and pain due to the heart condition, but she would seek to help others.

When she was out camping in Minnesota, she was watching her little sister play basketball and had a heart attack. She was flown to Minneapolis and some of the best doctors were taking care of her. The heart attack came in the summer. By October the doctors felt Brave Lightning should be placed on the list for a heart transplant. March came and it was clear now that she would be waiting in the hospital for a transplant. June came and it was getting more and more difficult, but she was still an inspiration to many of the staff. One man who brought her food called her Princess.

I believe he saw Jesus in this young lady; it was powerful to see the peace in her room. The power of the Spirit of God was evident in her room. As you may know by now, this story is about our Kayla Lou. She lived a short, powerful life, and she touched a lot of lives. The morning she left us I was sitting with her. She woke up and asked me this question, "Daddy can you tell me a story or some jokes 'cause I keep having this same dream." I told her some jokes and a story. She laughed and thanked me. It was my moment that stopped time as I cherished our last story on this earth.

The story does not end here. The night before she left this earth, people say the most powerful lightning storm hit the city of Minneapolis. We stared out the window at the University Hospital and knew that God the Father was celebrating the life of Kayla and welcoming her home.

We have cried many times for our baby girl, and it's her life we celebrate. We believe she is in Heaven with Jesus. There are more stories to tell, and I pray God allows me to share more of her life. This week we celebrate her 25th birthday, and we are looking forward to the day we will meet in Heaven. The illusion is that we are all alone, but the Spirit of God is here to comfort us. I pray that our people will find healing because the loss of a loved one is difficult. Wankiyan Ohitika Wi lived a powerful, short life. She lived for Jesus, and her suffering made her strong.

Speeding with an Expired License

While I have been in deep thought and seeking to be inspired, I realized it is timing that is important. I was traveling to Kansas last week, and I was pulled over by a state trooper in Nebraska. I was doing 66 mph in a 55 mph speed zone. I was asked to get out of our vehicle and move to the patrol car. I did so, needing a stretch as it was around 1 a.m., and I was a little tired. I got back to the patrol car and was told I had an expired license. It was interesting. I was talked about the full bar back in the little village. I asked if he was going to check on the people drinking and getting into their pickup trucks. Of course, I was polite but I wanted him to know I was not in a good mood about my being pulled over when the drunks were getting into their vehicles. Well, Belle had to drive a few miles, and I wanted to live through the night so I took over again. Belle doesn't see well at night and driving is not her cup of tea at night.

As soon as we got home I went to get my credentials straightened out, but I did not know where my birth certificate was. I had lost my social security card a few months back. I have not had the best of luck with my credentials. So our planned trip to D.C. has been postponed, and I do not have a valid license so I cannot legally drive anywhere. I was hoping to be able to get on the plane, but there are new laws. In addition, it is difficult to get an ID from the state. Well, needless to say, I had to order my birth certificate from the state of California and wait. Yes, I was born in LA County. It seemed like it would take forever to get a copy. Well, today I received it in the mail. Now I can get my social security card and my driver's license. We will postpone the trip to D.C., but I am planning a trip to Minneapolis to be where we saw our Kayla go home to heaven.

Belle has not been back since that time. I hope we can find peace and comfort where we started our education. Our love of the cities is awesome because Kay spent most of her years there, even when she was diagnosed with a heart condition. My prayer is we can begin to put all the pieces back together in a place of such great memories. I choose to move on and hope we can find God's care. My plan is to be away until Monday and come home refreshed from a trip well worth the time it will take on the road. Life throws us its curve balls, but you can still hit the ball. To follow the Spirit is a powerful way of life.

Living with Regrets

I was thinking about regret. It is a part of life, and it will stay with you throughout your time on this earth. I told a friend I have only one regret, and I wanted to blog about it today. When my daughter was a baby she had chicken pox, and she was miserable because it seemed like she got them really bad. Her head was full of the pox and her body was miserable. She had socks on her hands so she would not scratch, and she was not sleeping well. I remember being so tired, but I was walking her one night. Every time I tried to put her down she would start crying in pain. I would pick her back up and walk her through the night. I remember being exhausted from walking her back and forth. She was amazing and grew up to be a beautiful young lady. Her heart had so much love for people, and she seemed to be older for her age.

I guess I knew I should have been with her during her surgeries, but I let my wife make the decision for me to stay home and watch the place. I visited Kay when she was waiting for a new heart, and she was full of life. The University of Minnesota Hospital Staff was great, and they really took care of my princess. I remember seeing her sick in her bathroom. She looked up and said, "Daddy, help me." I could not help my baby and it broke my heart, so I knelt down and began to pray for her. It was real, if anything has ever been real; the pain and love and the heartache were real.

She loved her daddy, and I knew it by the way she looked at me. I would have hoped to have her longer, see her finish college, and have children, but God did not have it that way. He called her home. When she wanted a certain food I would go out and search for it with all my power. One day she wanted some earphones that cover the ears. I told her I would look and did some, but I am sure I did not search with my whole being. So it is this burden I carry; that I did not do everything to help my baby. I miss her dearly and hope to be a better daddy. I always knew I would do anything for my children within my power, and I failed one time. So when my daughter Tamara wants something, I do my best to help her. Sometimes it is difficult because other family members do not receive my help. But I am a daddy and I love my children. Should have gotten those dang earphones!

"As you grow older, you'll find the only things you regret are the things you didn't do."

~Zachary Scott

"Do not brood over your past mistakes and failures as this will only fill your mind with grief, regret and depression. Do not repeat them in the future."

~Sivananda

"Falsity cannot keep an idea from being beautiful; there are certain errors of such ingenuity that one could regret their not ranking among the achievements of the human mind."

~Jean Rostand

"Forget regret, or life is yours to miss."

~Jonathan Larson

"Get correct views of life, and learn to see the world in its true light. It will enable you to live pleasantly, to do good, and, when summoned away, to leave without regret."

~Robert E. Lee

FOOD

Culinary Arts

Once in a Blue Moon

Developing ideas for weekly columns can be difficult, but there are many every day experiences that help me find just the right words. Last Friday I was on the hunt for a couple of items. We traveled to Rapid City, which is normally ninety two miles on the Red Shirt Road. I love to travel this way, but sometimes I need to go the other way just to shake things up. I wanted to get a pair of pants for my uniform I am putting together. I have a cook's jacket that was a gift from my daughter Tamara and a chef hat as well. It is always nice when you get some recognition and mine is for being a cook. I have a number of items I cook. I have created Italian, Chinese, Mexican, and American full course meals over the past few years.

Many people ask me where I learned to cook so well. My only answer is I knew what great tasting food was because of my mother. When I was growing up I remember beans and potatoes and these were part of most meals. I remember trashcans full of beans and potatoes and we learned to clean beans and peel potatoes on a regular basis. I left my mother's home when I was fifteen years and spent the rest of my time with the missionary couple known as the Hedlunds but I also spent a little time with my uncle Roy. My uncle Roy would make soups and they were great, so I guess I was inspired by his soups. But, not all of my formative years were great as I tasted green Jell-O spinach, I try not to remember that but it was part of my upbringing. One day after going home to Denver my mother was cooking Stir Fry and Italian and it was amazing. I already knew she cooked Mexican but the dishes were amazing and I watched my mother cooking a grilling and it was amazing as it seemed she always invited others to eat with us. My mother was the biggest influence of my cooking.

I have traveled across the country eating Chinese meals and

75

trying different foods because I had a love affair with the food across the country. Unfortunately the food I ate out there could not be found in our Region of America. So the next best thing is to start cooking but the quality needs to be the same of the foods I ate traveling the country and in Asia. I once fee one hundred and fifty youth during the Youth Opportunity years and they could afford to pay me. We made smothered burritos and many of the youth wanted seconds so that was a good sign. I also catered a meal to Alltel for one hundred meals as we served fifty smothered burritos and fifty grilled chicken on a garden salad. I thought I communicated how the meal was to be served but when the first fifty people came to get their food they took the salad and the burrito.

I love Italian, spaghetti is the best meal in the world but the red sauce needs to be perfect for me to enjoy the meal. I love to have mine with meat balls and I personally blend mine so I can get a great flavor. I had to buy a meat grinder so I could grind my pork because not every store carries ground pork. I like to make my meatballs with sliced bread because it does not make the meatballs fine. I have also brought chicken parmesan to my recipe repertoire and will add a chicken cordon bleu in the couple weeks. My first real job off the Reservation was at a five star restaurant washing dishes. I started with the dishes and was able to help with banquets and I was moving to salads and I believe the next steps would have been to cook and on to chef. That was my plan but things changed as I moved back to Pine Ridge. I would never trade my time in Pine Ridge for anything because it is truly home but the food is lacking so I have chosen to change the present for the a better future.

I have also cooked a few Chinese meals like fried rice, Mongolian beef, sweet and sour chicken, and egg rolls. I have a few other things I stir fry but those are my favorites. I traveled in many major cities and tasted some great Chinese meals. My favorite was in Los Angeles in China Town, I heard they had better Peking Duck than Peking, China and you had to order it 24 hours in advanced. Of course I have also made some Korean food but that is another story. So my cooking skills were severely lacking something. I had a cook's jacket and some head gear, thanks to Tamara, but I still needed something for my job at Higher

Ground Coffee House. I am getting ready to start making soups and pizza and breakfast and many other things but I was missing something.

So I traveled to Rapid City and bought a pair of cook pants and now I have a complete uniform. I enjoyed the trip but was turned around about for miles north of highway 18 and then across Cuny Table and then south by KILI radio and two miles north there was an accident. Belva was tired of being in the car but saw Arlo Iron Cloud and he would be our Indian guide. He thought there was a trail on the eastside of the road so we followed him and we went through Uncle Chub Thunder Hawks place and made it back to the road. So I figure it is only happens Once in a Blue Moon we travel back from Rapid City and it takes us almost two miles. We will pray for the victims of the fire and the accident.

Eating Chinese all over the World
....from 10-30-08

Now we are fully into the political season and people are getting ready to vote. It is time for a change. Since I have been doing my "Rez Ramblings and Reasonings" column, I have enjoyed every word I have written. So if you have been following my Ramblings you know I have written about the state of our Reservation and have introduced myself. I realize many people would like to know who I support for the upcoming election. It is vital that we all vote and then support the person who gets elected. I am interested in seeing what happens on election night. I will be listening very closely to see who wins. I hope you are listing on KILI radio for the unofficial results on November 4th!

This week's column comes from the heart. If you know me, you know that I love to eat. My favorite all-time food is my mother's. My mom cooked everything, and Bessie Red Shirt Matthews was a master of everything she decided to cook. I only wish I could cook like my mom. I ate Chinese, Italian, Mexican, American, and a combination of these foods during my lifetime. My mother made Indian Tacos at the March Pow Wow in Denver, and everyone loved her bread. Grandpa Boob told me how he looked up to my mom at the March Pow Wow. He is a blessing to me and an encouragement to all of the Oglala Lakota people. I once asked my mom about my wife's fry bread, and she said there was nothing wrong with the bread. Of course I love my wife's cooking too. An approval of the daughter-in-law's bread is great for everyone.

In the early nineties I started eating Chinese food. I fell in love with this food and decided I would try the Chinese in every city I visited. I went on a trip to Atlanta and ate Chinese at the same restaurant two weeks in a row. It was great! I still remember the trip because of the fine food we ate. In 2000 I traveled to Korea and ate at a hotel. This was the fanciest place I had ever eaten at before. The linens were as white as could be and the service was awesome. I ate escargot (snail) for the first time. I told my host I loved to eat Chinese. He took me to a very posh place where the chef was from China. I will always remember this hotel because I could never imagine a place so perfect.

After eating Chinese in the Orient I had the opportunity to eat my favorite food in Los Angeles. I ate Peking duck at a place in China Town where they said the duck was better than in Peking. It was very good, and I loved the opportunity to have such an awesome experience. Shortly after this time I went to New York City and ate some great Chinese there.

As you can tell I have eaten Chinese food everywhere and anywhere I could in the last 20 years. So, where is the best place to eat Chinese? Chadron, Nebraska is at the top of the list. I have had great food every time I took my family to dine at the China House. Mike is a great host and if I had to pick an all-time favorite it would be in Chadron, great service and great food. I usually judge by the crab Rangoon and they serve a great Rangoon.

With the election coming up this week I hope you all go out and vote. Voting is a powerful experience and you can truly change the direction of our Tribe. My mother use to say there are no strangers, just friends unmet.   I hope you can begin to experience what I feel is important to me. Food is the greatest way to experience a culture and people; there is something about the way you can enjoy your food with company and company with food.

Vote for the person you think can bring us jobs! Jobs will change our lives and young people will begin to experience the world through hope of a better tomorrow. You can make a difference. Until next week!

Omelets

I am trying my hand at making omelets over at the Higher Ground coffee house. I have eaten them because I was practicing, and they are very good. I have eaten omelets while traveling. The last omelet I had was in Arkansas, and it was burnt. I vow to not serve a burnt omelet because the flavor can change drastically.

I remember when I left the Rez back in 1984 for Denver, Colorado with my then girlfriend, Belle. We found jobs and were working hard to get a little money. I remember we went to breakfast at Lou and Mary's for breakfast. The table was full of food. I have to say it was the best breakfast I have ever eaten, except for Thailand (I will get back to Thailand). I remember we had some biscuits and gravy and the usual sausage, eggs, and hash browns. I remember not being able to finish my breakfast that day because I was so full. Of course, now I know better than to just eat to get full. The restaurant was on First and Broadway by the Mayan Movie Theater where you could actually see a movie for a dollar. The area had a supermarket and some other shops where you could by odds and ends. I enjoyed my time in Denver, but I was ready to go back to the Reservation and see what I would accomplish. I do remember a great breakfast.

In 2004 I was traveling in Thailand. The first place I recall was the Holiday Inn International Hotel. It was big and clean, and I remember they offered water at the front desk. I drank the water and asked where I could buy a calling card. The guy at the front desk directed me out the front door and to my left. I headed out the door to call home. I was walking across the street and was immediately approached by a man a picture book of prostitutes. Bangkok is known for human trade and I was smacked right in the face with it. I kept walking across the street, bought my calling card, walked outside looking for a phone. I walked down the street and saw people lying in the doorways of offices. I thought this was strange because it seemed I was in a nice area. It took me a while to find a working phone. Eventually I was able to call home and let my family know I was now in Thailand.

The next morning I woke up and went downstairs to meet with the rest of the group. We went into the breakfast room. It was a huge hall and there were lots of people. There were chefs and many people busy with the breakfast. I saw every breakfast food imaginable with stations for omelets and fried rice, yes fried rice for breakfast. I thought I'd died and gone to Breakfast Heaven.

So you have heard my two favorite places to eat breakfast. Lou and Mary's in Denver, which was closed down a long time ago, and the Holiday Inn International Hotel in Thailand. I do not believe I will be in Thailand again very soon, so I am left with memories. Now I make my own omelets. If you are interested in an omelet and you are in Pine Ridge Village after eight, stop in at the Higher Ground. I will throw together an omelet for you.

Fried Chicken

When I was a boy I found being close to my mother brought me peace and comfort. I would watch her cut different meats and make bread with ease. My personal favorite was to watch my mom make fried chicken. As I go through lists of food to eat I can see certain foods are an art form. Not everyone is comfortable with making items passed down through the generations. My mom would make her liquid, with what I do not know, but it always seemed very good. She made a simple salt and pepper mix. Then she would dunk and dredge the chicken, and put it into the cast iron skillet. I watched her turn the pieces of chicken with expertise. It would come out golden brown and cooked to

80

perfection.

I use a deep fryer. I use more herbs and spices than my mother used, like cayenne pepper for my flour coating and depending on my mood I will add red pepper flakes. Fried Chicken is a food you should not eat regularly even when using high quality oil. But, when the family is asking who made the chicken and Belle says, "Uncle Leon" it brings me a smile. Belle loved it as well, and I thought I did a pretty good job. Now I am on my way to do another round of dieting moving toward my goal. Sacrifice and freedom will be the keys to staying strong on the Pine Ridge.

Tuscany Zuppa

I have had a busy couple of days because I was making Zuppa! Soup is loved by the Lakota. It has been a main meal in the life of Lakota people for centuries. I have eaten the dried meat and wild turnip soup of my people; paba and timpsila is the name. I also like the wajapi which is made from berries and lots of sugar. I think I may have overloaded my sugars a few times. Fry Bread is a food I just cannot digest well, and I feel guilty every time I eat it. So I have developed a few of my own recipes for my family. I got a new stove for our home, and it has a griddle in the middle. It was the perfect size. My friend Ata put it together, and I had to try it out. I got out the meat grinder gadgets and went to work on some steak I had for a rainy day. Of course it was not raining, but heck. I had a new stove. I told Belle I was going to make some steak burgers and would have some friends from Idaho over to have some homemade food. They brought me a blanket, and I trusted them because I know they would never give me a blanket with small pox (no offense intended to my white readers).

I ground the meat and took it to the house. I had my friend Henry run to the store for some fries for the burgers. Funny thing is he brought one little bag, so he had to go back and get another bag of fries. I put some burgers together. It was great as they cooked evenly on my new stove. For the second batch, I put some pepper and salt in the meat and continued to make my burgers. They were a bit hot but I thought the steak flavor came through with flying colors.

Earlier in the day I went to the Higher Ground and put my hat and apron on. It says Grill Sergeant on my apron and it has a camouflaged print. I was feeling cool. I got my Italian sausage and ingredients ready, made my soup, and went to town for a two hour meeting I had with Job Corp. I finished my meeting and went back to the coffee house. My Zuppa was gone. Sold out! I love it when people like the food. Some older Lakota men wanted to know if Belle made the soup, but she told them I was the cook. They wanted to meet me because they loved the soup. We had breadsticks, salad, and soup; it was a great way to have lunch, and a big success! I am now growing my own herbs, and I hope to have some fresh herbs for the winter months. It is exciting to see people eat great food. I love living my dream of making food and making money. It is ok to make a little money while doing things you love.

Cooking great food comes easy to me. I like to try my dishes at home before I take them to the Higher Ground Café - your latte heaven. I prepare a great variety of food, but some really stand out from the pack. I love to share my Chicken Fried Rice and have had Chinese try the dish only to find they love it. We sell lots of fried rice on Mondays. My favorite soup is chicken and rice, and it does a body good on a cold November day. Lo Mein is great. My noodle dish is a bit spicy for the novice, but I try to keep the heat level down for the newcomers. Of course I make pizza with homemade and our own bread; it is great to share the New York style. I love to make red sauce for the pasta and have developed my own sauces with mushrooms and garlic.

It is important to develop recipes that can be prepared quickly and have great taste. I have never been a big fan of chicken and prefer beef over birds. But I have developed my own Chicken Parmesan, and it is mind blowing. I like to spice up everything. When you put a slice of provolone on the top it makes for a great meal. It can be cut with a fork and enjoyed with pasta or placed between some bread for another awesome sandwich experience. Chicken Marsala is also a new dish and the sauce is wonderful.

One last note food, I mentioned earlier I traveled to Korea. I could not figure out the smell on the buses and trains but then realized it is the Kimchi, full of garlic and flavor. I need to share this story with you because it is about the best meal I have ever had in my life. While in Korea I was up early. My friend, Mike Ahn, was taking me to have breakfast. We walked and traveled around corners until we arrived at our destination. It was on a quiet street. The building had a huge front window and in the window was the biggest soup kettle I have ever seen. They had beef strips with the bones in the soup, and it was boiling. I went in with my host, and he ordered for us. They brought out the soup and it was steaming. Kimchi was placed around the table and a bowl of rice. I was told to put the rice in the soup and to try the different Kimchi. Of course the broth was excellent and the whole meal was perfect. That was the greatest meal I have ever had in my life.

Bread Making, a Spiritual Experience

Okay, the quest for the ultimate Italian Cheese Herb Bread is on today. I have been working on developing a great loaf of bread because we do not have a bakery. The store has their bread shipped frozen to save on money. So bread is a great way to use my time and talents. When I was in Minnesota I worked at Cub Foods. They had a full bakery with everything, and it was cooked in the walk-in ovens. You could actually walk around in these ovens and a couple of grown men could fit in them. Well they did make some nice bread. When making bread I approach as an art form instead of a scientific method and I end up with a great taste. I am experimenting with larger loaves today, but I am sure they will be perfect. I will make sure I get a picture to go with the article.

It is a great pleasure to see God's magic powder, yeast, at work. You know it may be you, but also a whole lot of God working to make that bread rise. I was afraid of bread because I did not fully understand the process, but now I make loaves of bread. It is fun. I always think of the followers of Jesus when he broke some bread and drank some wine to symbolize his body and blood. He was willing to sacrifice himself, and yet when he did give everything he gained the Universe. I think this is

83

what trips people up when they think about the cost of following Jesus.

We can look at the negative effects of Christians, but I do not believe Jesus can be blamed for what was done to Indigenous people around the world. I thought to myself, what are the effects of Christianity around the world? What would drive me to continue in a faith that has brought the Crusades and oppressive rules to people around the world? I guess I believe many of the ways of Christians are not the way of Jesus and his caring for the poor. Often times we see churches become more corporate than spiritual in nature. People want to control the gifts by quarters rather than rely on the Lord to meet their needs.

I met a guy named Charley today, and he has traveled the world. I shared the idea of the Creator leaving his imprint on each human being. I believe it is very powerful when you link this together with the power of God. We shared video and laughter. We actually talked about the Detroit Lions and what a bad team they were. I baked my bread and it came out pretty good. Life is good at the coffee house. You never know who you might meet as they come in to have a latte or smoothie. Charley can be seen at www.explore.org with many videos. He does grants and education philanthropy work. Charley came to see Russell Means and stopped in at the Higher Ground.

Pizza
....from 5-6-09

Here I sit in the lobby of a hotel in New York City, what I call the greatest city in the world, New York, New York. "I love NY", is a great slogan, and it is everywhere in the city. Even the van driver from the airport told us you can go anywhere in the city and be okay or safe. I am with my wife Belle, and it is a great trip. Growing up in a city, I can assure you that it is not safe everywhere.

I grew up on the streets of Denver, running, walking, and playing all over the city. Half of the guys I grew up with are dead or in prison.

We had to fight for survival because there was always someone looking for trouble. I guess you develop an extra sense when you are walking around the city. I had the opportunity to grow up fast and learn the ways of the city life. I am happy I can be among our Oglala Lakota Oyate. Do not get me wrong, I enjoy diversity, and the many types of languages, but I prefer home to anywhere.

We are in the "Big Apple" for a Christian Conference. I am looking forward to seeing how the conference helps me to develop our own church back in Pine Ridge. New York City is the epitome of Western Civilization, and central to the economics of the world. It is the greatest city in the world, and it is one of the most diverse cities you can find on the earth.

My goal this week was to find the best New York slice of pizza. My first day I found a slice, but it was lacking. My second day, I found the perfect slice of pepperoni pizza. It was the pleasure I had hoped for ever since I left New York in 2000. I vowed to return to find the perfect pizza slice. I asked around because research is vital in every scientific study. One reply was interesting because he said you can't get a bad pizza in New York, but I knew he was wrong.

Millions of people walking and riding the subways is a sight to see. We went to the Statue of Liberty and Ground Zero at the World Trade Center location. I told a few people that I wanted to go to the Empire State Building and offer some tobacco. They asked me why the Empire State Building? I told them it is where King Kong lost his life. If you go to New York, go to the 102nd floor; it will be worth the extra fifteen bucks. I know I appreciated the height of the 102 stories as the buildings and surroundings seemed closer. We saw so many buildings or skyscrapers that there were too many to count. The Manhattan skyline is one of the greatest, but the people are what make the city.

It is said Red Cloud, Red Shirt, and other great Leaders of the Lakota Nation went to New York and Washington, D.C. But, did you know disco, salsa, and hip hop had their origins in the Big Apple? It is true that there is worldwide culture that follows the New York experience. I believe it is the greatest city in the world. In just one day

I have talked with someone from Argentina, Spain, Netherlands, and beyond. I say beyond because there are too many people groups to count, and I would be remiss to not name one of the groups I met today. The accents alone make it very challenging to bridge the language gap of English. More people around the world are trying to speak English than any other language.

English is the language people are trying to develop, but the Chinese are the biggest people group. There are over 1 billion Chinese speaking Chinese and not that many English speakers. Actually, like I said before, there are many English speakers, but we are spread out and not concentrated. We are looking at around 50 thousand Oglalas and the countries of China and India have over a billion each. Does that blow your mind? It has shattered my understanding of the Oglala and Lakota Nation. We need more people on our side.

Sovereignty is not a game or just a word; it is the epitome of who we are as Oglala Lakota. The whole world is moving in commerce, trading, and developing, even in difficult times. The Oglala have their hand out and are waiting for the U.S. Government to give when we should be taking.

People may laugh and ridicule the cell towers, but they represent commerce around the world. It is a way to develop economy. I would like to say, call your representative and congress people, and tell them you want to talk on the phone. This is an easy step, and people need to get the idea. Communication is our way of life. And the cell signals will help develop our communities.

Crazy Horse and the King of Beers
....from 2-9-10

Okay, I have written about many things over the past couple of years, but I have something very important to share with you. It has been one of my lifetime goals to find the perfect piece of pizza. I have sought this slice of pizza in all the major cities I have visited. I even had a slice of Korean pizza in Seoul back in 2000. When I heard there was a slice of New York pizza in Chadron, Nebraska, I made a mad dash for pizza in Nebraska land. On a cold February afternoon we loaded up the dogs and left the Reservation on the quest for great pizza. We braved the snow packed roads and the bit of ice on the highways. It seemed to be a perfect afternoon for a slice of New York pizza. Of course we had to buy a whole pizza pie; I believe it was called The Eagle. Mel and Lisa Adams have a great pizza parlor. When you enter the dining area, you know you are in for a treat. My advice to all of our readers is to take a trip to Chadron and get a pizza pie. Go down the stairs right behind the post office and you will find the new business, straight outta New York.

I believe we Lakota have some of the best warriors on this earth. Crazy Horse is known to be a great tactician and is studied in War College. I believe the Lakota were a force on the plains and the stories of old tell of the bravery we had on the battlefield. Leksi Joe Brown Eyes tells of when he was in Vietnam, and they would make the Lakota the point in the offensives. Hey, if I were going to war I would want the Lakota on my side. We have been told of the warriors who would stake their ground and fight until the death or until all the foes were gone. That is the warrior I love to hear about as I have listened to and read the stories of the Lakota. It is the desire of my heart to use the Lakota spirit in me to live my Christian life as a true Lakota Warrior for Christ.

I was discussing the Fighting Sioux issue because the case is in court as I write. I do not mind being called a Fighting Sioux. I am an Oglala Sioux tribal member and that means a lot to me. I read in one blog last week that this is how the world knows us. They know we are the Sioux people, and they respect us because of our fighting spirit. Yet many people would try to change the perspective and say we were a peace loving people. I know this is controversial, but it is important to know the United States made treaties with the Sioux. Once upon a time, we had the GREAT Sioux Nation. It has since been stolen, and now they want to take away the rights of our people.

In thinking about the issues of the day, it is clear we need to begin to fight for our people in the boardrooms. An update about the White Clay issue and something I think is important to our understanding of who is really making the decisions; Anheuser Busch went to the capital of Nebraska and gave testimony about the tax issues in the 30 mile radius area surrounding White Clay. Let us just say the King of Beers does not want to be singled out. They are a favorite among many people. They want to maximize their profits and control what is being done with the taxes. Think about this put in this perspective – if you were in office and you were building your donations for re-election and the King of Beers comes to you and says, "We do not like what you want to do with the taxes in the northwest part of Nebraska," you will listen because these corporations can donate tons of money to help you win re-election. I hope you understand what is being done in regard to the beer business in White Clay, Nebraska. Just when you thought there were people thinking outside of the box, the corporation comes in and messes things up. Every dollar spent on the Reservation helps with 4% coming back to the tribe. This is vital for us because we need to be business friendly. I tell people if you needed a pair of pants or shoes and you could not leave the Pine Ridge Reservation, you would have to go without clothing and shoes. All of the towns around us have clothing stores and we have around forty thousand people. But we need to keep looking up because after all we do have two Subways.

The Philly Cheesesteak
....from 10-27-10

I am always ready for a great sandwich, and it is hard to get one out in South Dakota. A few years ago I took a trip with a great group of people to the City of Brotherly Love. It was an amazing place. We found a basketball court and played when we took some breaks from workshops about community organization. It is memories like these that I believe will stay an eternity.

We took the train downtown. That was amazing in itself as I thought about Will Smith growing up on the streets and in its poverty. I saw the depths of poverty and the heights of wealth all in the same breathtaking trip to downtown Philadelphia. We were walking down the street and saw a man in a long coat and hat the resembled Jeepers

Creepers killer. I think it was some famous founder of the city or someone well known. We were downtown and went to see about going to a game. Luckily for us there was a nice gentleman that had extra tickets outside. We purchased them and were set to watch the Phillies against a Florida team. I had a great time at the game with the three others, and I thought it was a great moment. This year the Phillies made it to the end but just missed the World Series. I am happy I was able to see some great baseball while I was in the City of Brotherly Love.

On another trip with my associate we walked to a place called Gino's for a Philly cheesesteak; it was mind blowing and everything I hoped a cheesesteak would be like. I have tried the Philly cheesesteak and I now make my own version of the Philly. I would test mine with any other in the country. While I was on my way to a birthday party for my 90 year-old mentor/adopted father, I felt it was important to get things right and test our regional favorite cheesesteak. We arrived in Rapid City, South Dakota and checked into our room. My plan was to take Belle out for a nice meal but bring it back to the room. We walked across the street, dodging a pickup driver who looked like he was trying to run us over. I know a good sandwich, and I ordered the cheesesteak with green peppers and grilled onions. I like it this way because I have eaten a few before.

I felt like I should try Philly Ted's. Belle got the Packer; yes, the Green Bay Packer cheesesteak. Three cheeses - if you love cheese this is the sandwich for you. Oh, I got some tots to go with my meal. We got back to the room. When Belle was a couple of bites into hers, she started looking at mine. I knew I had the superior cheesesteak, and as much I did not want to let her try mine, I did. She liked mine better, so I ate half and we exchanged sandwiches. I must say at this point, knowing a good sandwich is a testimony of culture. So my advice, if you want a Philly cheesesteak, travel to Gino's in Philadelphia; you will not be let down. And the experience of Philly will have a great impact on your life and your dreams. If you do not have the time or the money to travel to the City of Brotherly Love, then I say this with sincerity. Go to Philly Ted's in Rapid City, South Dakota and get the cheesesteak with green peppers and grilled onions. You will not go away hungry. If you happen to take a date make sure you order her some tots to go with her sandwich. We were absolutely satisfied and felt a great evening was complete, except she ate up my tater tots.

I will be in Denver in the morning and Missouri by noon. Should be a great time seeing my daughter. Oh, the city of Philly makes me want to travel again for a sandwich and more. I thought Ted did a great job giving the experience of East Coast hospitality. He is working the counter even late into the night and is very nice even though it must be a long day for him. Plus his baseball Phillies lost, and I know he is feeling badly about the loss. I hope you can try a cheesesteak. Take my advice and enjoy every bite. Unless you want to share, and in that case your friend or date will enjoy it too.

The Big Indian

The stores are busy with customers and product is slipping off the shelves. While driving around Pine Ridge Village, I get the feeling there is a lot of money circulating around the Reservation. Tonight you will most likely see people walking around with chips and pop. Benny is down at the Pow Wow grounds offering specials on the grill. I am sure you can find a "Big Indian" down at the grounds. A few years ago when I was doing radio on KILI, the local Indian owned radio station, I was talking about the Oglala Nation, or as we like to call it, the "Og Nash". A time when all of the Oglala are invited back home for the annual pow wow and rodeo. It includes the softball, basketball, and horseshoe tournaments. And yes, there is also the notorious carnival. Food stands are abundant and you can even find some Chinese stir fry around the circle at the pow wow grounds. Oh, back to the "Big Indian." I was doing a radio show, getting excited about the pow wow and seeing all the people, and I started describing the "Big Indian". It is two all-beef patties with all the fixings between two halves of frybread. When you take a bite it is juicy and the grease slides down your jowl. You know there just has to be at least one Big Indian in heaven. Well, Benny called the station and after hearing me on the radio. He said I could have one Big Indian any time. Those were my super heavy weight days. I am waiting for August to try another. These days I have been buying them.

Second week of June we will have the Veterans Pow Wow, and it should be a great event. People are gearing up for the local pow wows all across the Reservation, and you can see people really are having a great time around the Rez. So if you are in Pine Ridge or some other bigger Pow Wow, look to see if Benny's is in town. They serve the Big Indian with curly fries and the best Lemonade you can have on a hot summer day.

Late Summer

Summer is slowing like a turtle crossing the road. After the Oglala Nation Fair and Rodeo it seems like people get ready for school and things start simmering down. The Sundances have completed their yearly obligation, and now the Reservation turns to its fall schedule. There are many who like football and volleyball, but I believe it is something that passes the time until basketball. I know some believe I must worship basketball as much as I talk about it and still play. The competitive edge is dulling with each passing year. I mostly want to get up and down the court so I can burn some calories and work on my conditioning. Funny thing now is I think I am ready to start jogging. I am going to try and get a little running in this week because I have lost many pounds.

I was closing in on 300 pounds a couple years ago. Yeah, I was eating myself to death. I enjoyed lots of food whenever I would travel and it was killing me slowly. When I went to the doctor he told me there was nothing else to do but put me on insulin. I was shaking my head and wondering if I was going to have to do the needles. I went home thinking about it. I tried to button a shirt Belle bought me for Christmas and it would not fit. The buttons were almost popping off my present. It was time to make some changes in my life because I was killing myself with food. The diabetes was out of control and pills would not do the trick. I was determined to lose the weight, and fifty pounds later I feel better than most of my years I spent in my thirties. I am forty-five years old this year, and I have reached the life expectancy of the Native American man. How sad is that, when so many people are living

91

well into their seventies.

I talked with a nutritionist today. We spoke a little about what our people go through living on the Reservation. Poor diets, I believe, are the biggest contributor to death from diabetes. People here do not have enough money to buy proper food and have lived on junk food for far too long. It is easier to eat heavy starches and quick carbs then it is to buy good produce. I have thought of the Lakota way of life before the coming of the White Man. The people lived on a high protein, low carb diet and thrived with strong bodies on the plains. It is as simple; we need to go back to our way of life before the invasion. Of course, there are a lot of issues concerning the coming of the white man, but it is clear the food source was slaughtered almost to extinction. Our diets consisted of bison, some vegetation such as berries and wild turnips, and an abundance of small game was eaten. I remember my uncle Manuel brought some prairie chicken over to eat. It tasted like chicken just in smaller portions.

I have been out looking for what we call timpsila. It is fun because you have to look for a flower in the month of June. Not only are they good to eat from the ground but you get exercise while searching for them. Our lives were full of finding these types of foods.

Losing 60 Pounds

While many people come from all around the country to visit, I also get some world travelers. People ask me about traditional meals and I think of fry bread and soups. You must understand fry bread came after our people lost their freedom. Tonight I was reminded of my friend from Arkansas who he told me he wanted to be a warrior. Ata Jack said, "Who, Brave Heart's William Wallace?" Then I remember my friend telling me he likes running in the fields. I wonder if he stops and yells at the top of his lungs, "YOU CAN TAKE MY LIFE, BUT YOU CAN NEVER TAKE MY-----FREEDOM!" I do not know, but tonight as I was watching some television, I had to take a breath. Not that there was anything on the television that prompted this, but I was trying to get my thoughts together and I yelled, "FREEDOM!" Then I walked to the coffee house. Our afternoon barista was coming out and I said, "You can take my life," and then yelled, "BUT YOU CAN NEVER TAKE MY FREEDOM." Of course, she thought I was pretty funny but she was at a loss for words. My wife Belle was laughing and one of my nieces got up and said, "I am out of here."

Oh, about food….. frybread is not a great food for me because my body does not digest it fast enough. A lady from the outside was telling me she gained a lot of weight while staying on the Rez for about three months. I told her she needs to stop eating everything they put in front of her and do not eat fry bread at every occasion. I love the taste of fry bread. Belle makes great bread for popovers and Indian Tacos, but I cannot eat them every week. But soup is another story. I saw my aunt at the store and it brought back the memories of my Uncle Roy. He made bread and soup. Uncle Roy was an all-around great person. He would doodle on paper when he visited and it was pretty cool to see his artwork. His life was full of helping people. I remember he would do his best to get people to stop drinking. What a great legacy to have and hold on to when remembering a loved one who has passed on to the next life. He took good care of his friend's son. He was also my mom's brother. I could always count on him for advice; it was straight and to the point. I miss him very much and realize I need to live an honorable life for the lost loved ones.

I found in my research that American Bison is a very lean meat. It is a great protein source. But when I would buy a buffalo burger, I would ask for bacon because of the leanness of the buffalo. And I remember searching for timpsila, or wild turnips, and finding wild berries to have in the late summer. You had to harvest them at the right point so they are sweet. I see our historical diet as being a high protein, low carbohydrate diet. I found a high protein, low carb diet on the internet, and I lost around sixty pounds. My sugars have started to be lower, but I then my blood pressure and cholesterol numbers went up. My goal is to get back to college weight. Keep off the weight and live a healthier life. I was getting a fifty pound bag of dog food out of the van tonight. I threw it over my shoulder and took the twenty yard walk to the house. I thought to myself, man I lost a lot of weight and my knees must be thanking me. I encourage people to eat more of a traditional diet with some modifications such as vegetables and fruits. Your body will thank you for your weight loss. I have another twenty pounds to get to my ideal weight. I believe I will get it done in about two months.

OYATE KIN

The People, Meaning All People

The Reservation System
....from 6-02-10

When you see death all around you, it becomes a norm. People forget dying young is not natural. Sometimes death is sudden and before you know it, there is no time to regret your actions. Most of us have cousins who have committed suicide and/or have attempted to take their own life.

While I was in White Clay looking to visit with Bruce BonFleur about some private issues, I came across some people who were feeding the people there who seem to be lost. It is always nice to see the people as they greet me and seem to be happy to see me. I have been in White Clay where some people did not know me, but then someone always tells them who I am.

Back to the group feeding... there were four women and at least three men. When I was waiting I overheard a conversation one of the men was having with some of the locals. He was telling them, "If you don't want to go where your ancestors went, to hell, you need Jesus." I was disgusted by this man, but I did not feel the need to say anything. I do not believe the man had any right to say this about our ancestors; maybe his ancestors are in hell. The audacity of these people trying to help is devastating.

To a Lakota person, family means everything. I went in and sat down hoping one of the women would help out with an event happening on Wednesday of next week because she is a millionaire. They started asking me questions so I tried to help them understand. Honestly, I don't believe they understood my words.

We have been working at home for fifteen years. We have seen death and pain, but our sustainer has kept us strong. One of the areas I want to develop is a better understanding of the Tiospaye or extended family. I have heard of the way churches came together and celebrated together as a family. It was easy because of the Tiospaye system in place.

Today we see many people struggling because of the Reservation system; it is both bad and good at the same time. We are able to feel at home on the Rez, but at the same time we can see struggles at every level.

My desire is to see more people involved in positive events. As we move toward the election season, we need to see what our leaders have accomplished. Our people need protectors and providers, as it was in the old days. Look at the leadership today and see how they are protecting and providing for all the people.

At the end of the meeting I asked one of the women if she had children. She said she had seven. I then asked, "What if the government came in and took them all away and didn't allow you to see them at Christmas?" She said she would be devastated. Tears came to her eyes, and I explained to her that she had just experienced empathy. Until the white people understand what the Indigenous people went through over the last five hundred years, feeding people who have chosen to end their lives by standing in Nebraska drinking Malt Liquor is not helping. But, if they begin to understand the devastating effects of boarding school on our people, I believe we can begin to make progress.

We recently had a young Lakota man killed in Rapid City. The lethal force used here is the real issue. Of course to the people in charge of policing, it is not a question. The officer could have shot him in the legs but he did not. He made sure there was absolutely no threat; he killed him. We have people who live around us who do not know any of the history of the treatment of Lakota. They assume we are all drunks and thieves. Of course, they sit on the land our Grandfathers fought for in the nineteenth century. Most of us have non-Native friends; we need to begin to change their understanding.

The United States Government set out to destroy a whole people group, and we need to come to a healing. When you see people having a hard time, you should have some empathy. If you do not have empathy, then I would question your humanity. It is one of the qualities I believe sets us above animals. Everything has a purpose, from the trees to the rocks. It is part of our purpose as humans to have compassion for our fellow human beings.

Good Friends are a Blessing

My night ended about 1:45 a.m. last night. My day had started around 5:10 a.m. as I shook the cobwebs out of my head. It was a dark morning as we drove the ninety-two miles to Rapid City for hair appointments. I don't care if they walk on four legs or two legs; if you have to get up that early and then drive for a 7 a.m. appointment, I'm gonna call it a hair appointment. Shadow and Oreo, the Cockers, were going to get groomed, and it was an early morning. I was able to get my social security card, and we had a great time seeing our son Brad.

On the way home, I was driving through the badlands and all of a sudden two deer ran across the road, then another trailing behind. We moved right through the herd. I never knew what it meant to run through the herd, but now I do because we did. I know it was God showing his grace and mercy.

Russell Means had called and wanted to meet with me about a project. I was rushing home because I did not want to be too late. I was very careful as I listened to talk radio and heard the latest topics. I had a couple of errands before I could get back to the Higher Ground, but hoped I was not going to keep them waiting long. I walked into the shop and told Mr. Means I was not old enough to be getting up at 5:10 a.m. Jason, the young entrepreneur, laughed as Russ told me he got up at 5 a.m. It was funny because only old people should be allowed to get up before the crack of dawn. I know I may get into trouble, and I suppose bakers and other notable professions should also be allowed to wake up early. But really, for dog hair appointments?

Russell Means, "One of the biggest, baddest, meanest, angriest, most famous American Indian activists, of the late twentieth century..." -The Washington Post- This is on the front of the book, Where White Men Fear to Tread, Russell's autobiography. This is a book I get to live because whenever I have a question about something, I just ask him if it is true or not. He often tells me to read the book, but I just shake my head no because I want to hear it from him. I told him today I would have made a great American Indian Activist, but they had already finished up what was needed to be done. He then said, "You can change

99

the tribe." I thought, funny he should say that. Jason and I were talking about the political system the day before, and I wanted Russell to hear the words of the young brother because I believe we could possibly change the structure of our own government. Howard says different generations are coming together to make one mind! Howard quite often is listening in the background. I am sure many people would love to be a fly on the wall like Howard.

Howard runs SingingHorse.com and supplies artists with hides, beads, and other things the local artists need to do their handiwork. I am proud to know him as he has taught me a few things about business and gave a great compliment to the coffee house. A lady commented there were lots of people coming into the Higher Ground one day. Howard said, "You can tell by the first word on the board up front." The lady said, "Higher?" Howard told her it was LOVE. On the message board it states, "Love Never Fails." Howard continued telling her to look around; everywhere you look you will see love. She agreed, and we continued with our visiting. I think Howard understands the love one must have for the business you are involved in. If you do it with lots of care and good advice you can become successful. Of course, there have been many great people in my life, but I count Howard as a great friend and mentor.

Many ideas were talked about around coffee and soda on this day. I wished I could have been more engaged because the ideas were flowing. I believe our people can teach the world about relationship and how important it is to get to know people. I have found I am somewhat of anomaly in my life, or, as some would say, unique. I accept it and have brought my understanding to a place where I am at peace. Many people know me because of different things I have done in my life, but most of them are from the sidewalk. They can tell you where I live, who I am married to, and a whole list of other things, but they have not taken the time to really get to know me. Drink a cup of coffee, visit around lunch, or just come and engage me with thought provoking ideas. Yes, I have some great people enter my life all the across the country and some of the lessons learned are the ones learned sitting around open in conversation.

Everyone should meet Russell, Jason, and Howard. They have a lot of knowledge. Jason has some great ideas, and I believe the heart to complete whatever he sets out to do in life. I love the fact that he has moved home to be closer to his girlfriend, when most people would be living in Hollywood or some other rich and famous place. Howard is doing his business, meeting with clients and helping where he can with their daily lives. Russ has become an elder and is seeking to build a school. It will be a great tool for the Lakota language as it is full immersion. No English allowed. I am fortunate to have their friendship. Each has their own role in life and I am blessed to know them as good friends.

Here is something very interesting about Jason. He told me we need to have a party for change, not the Donkey or the Elephant, but a party for Change. He told me we need to start today and work for two years. We can change the future of our tribal government. And you know what? I believe it could happen; we just need to sit and visit and see where the talks will take us. Me, well I want to call it the New Lakota Nation because we have great core beliefs that be built upon. Every builder knows how important it is to have a strong foundation. I guess I am really excited because even Lloyds of London started as a coffee house. Until tomorrow. . .

Humility
....from 11-20-08

While getting a fountain pop one day I was startled to run into a Canadian aboriginal. He did not even greet me properly as he seemed upset. He was coming from a committee meeting at the tribal building. The thing he told me was, "Do you know what the Oglala Lakota problem is?" I said, "What?" He then went on to tell me it was our ethnocentric idea that we were the center of the Universe. I thought to myself and realized this was not a problem at all because most people around the world live within their own cultures. He was more than upset. I laughed and this encounter has stayed with me for some time.

Being Lakota is great! How many times have you run into another Lakota while traveling across the country? We have traveled the world while being some of the poorest people in the country. When you run into other Lakota it is like a family gathering. We have people who have done many things and will continue to influence others around the world.

We have operated and lived our lives throughout the region but people still do not understand us. While traveling through the panhandle of Nebraska I went into a convenience store and was waiting in line. A man was more or less in my way, and I thought it rude. I looked up at him, and he was glaring at me. I looked him right in the eye with intensity. He turned away. I said, "I bet you never had an Indian look you in the eye." He said he never did. I taught him about the Lakota way of respect, that to look into the eyes of another was a sign of disrespect. Of course if you were trying snag a girl that would be another lesson. I told him about our ways and he seemed a little more understanding. I struggle when I go down to Nebraska because I know sometimes people treat our people wrong. We need to strive to teach our neighbors.

Humility is the ability to treat people like they are better than you. It is not just acting, it is real. When you encounter this characteristic in others it makes you feel so great. I have had the opportunity to see it in a number of places. One particular place has been in my everyday life as I have lived here at home on the Pine Ridge Reservation. Kenny Morgan was a friend who will be truly missed. This man was a hero to many, especially to his grandchildren. I have to admit it is rare when you see such greatness. He was great in the little things and those little things made you feel so good. When I ran into Kenny at the post office or somewhere else he was always so happy to see me. He emphasized the "on" in Leon and so it came out as Le-ON and it was such a great feeling when he said my name.

My tribute to this Grandfather will surely fall short, but I want to encourage the family with this bit of information. Yes, he was in the Air Force, the 101st Airborne, but where I believe he made the biggest impact was in his family. You can feel the love and for this gift to me I am truly thankful. I pray Ate Mapiya will wipe the tears from your cheeks and touch your souls. Another will rise through your tiospaye (family) because his legacy lives on through you. Many people have gone on to the next world. We must strive to live honorable lives for them.

Humility will help us to make the changes we need. Crazy Horse was a man who lived for the people, and the people honored him by following him. With the new council set to take their seats, our hope is in the ability of these new leaders to not just care for their own families, but to care for the whole tribe. A solution to some of our issues will be solved when people think and act with humility...to think of others better than yourself.

Russell Means Meeting

On Tuesday I received a call from Mr. Russell Means. He stated he wanted to meet with me at 9 a.m. on Wednesday. I was moving around slowly at 8:30 a.m., getting ready for some coffee. I received a call from Mr. Means. He told me something came up, and he would be at the Higher Ground at 10 a.m. I watched some news and prepared myself for a long day. Around 10 a.m. Mr. Means called and said he was tied up with some issues. He would be in town at noon. I was still okay with him coming at that time and I went about my business. Well, noon came and went and it was 12:45 p.m. when the activist turned actor came in and ordered Rattlesnake coffee with no room for cream. He uses honey as a sweetener and likes the dark roasted gourmet coffee. I think it is our best seller, and people seem to like the name. Although some Easterners do not seem to like the name, many locals know we have many rattlesnakes in western South Dakota.

Many people do not fully understand Russell, but I believe I have spent enough time with him that I more or less enjoy listening to him recount the history of the American Indian Civil Rights Movement. We finished up around 4:15 p.m. It seemed like the day passed very quickly. It reminded me of other times spent with good friends when the hours turn to moments and the time becomes no more. We talked about the Lakota Treaty and Immersion school he wants to start on the Ranch in Porcupine. There is a need for a tractor, and I am working to help him find people to help with this project. Then we talked about everything that came to mind, including the passport he used to travel to Switzerland. He said it was a piece of rawhide, and he actually was able to get back and forth into the country. I do not believe that would fly today, and he agreed.

There was a couple who came into the coffee house looking to engage, but they were careful not to interrupt our conversation. I noticed the woman was moving closer to us looking at books and pictures. I finally asked, "Where are you guys from?" She answered with somewhere in the northeast, but originally from New Jersey. It made me think of some other people with eastern dialects, but that is another story. She was visiting some people here, and I thought they might be interested in taking on the project of trying to help the treaty school. So I asked them if they were learning about and interested in American Indians. The lady was very interested and had read many books about American Indians. I asked if she read In Spirit of Crazy Horse by Peter Matthiessen, and what she remembered about the book of the 70s. She said, "Lenard Peltier, Dennis Banks and Russell Means." I smiled but did not let her in yet. Of course, I thought she looked a lot younger than her husband and teased a little bit so they thought I was a funny guy. The husband was just a little older than his wife, and he told us he was a 65 year-old retired gym teacher. He looked like he was in good shape for an elder. Remember, old is a good thing in Lakota country.

Well, I then introduced Russell Means and they thought I was still joking around. Of course that did not make Russell too happy when they did not believe me. She said to Russ, "Turn so I can see your profile," She said, "I saw a picture of Russell Means and you do not look the same to me." Then she made the ultimate mistake and asked to see identification. That was funny, but Russell held it together. He then went on to teach them or prove to them who he was without an older picture or identification. It was so funny; I was just shaking my head. Russell said, "All White Americans hate us because we are Indian." They were offended because they did not hate us, but Russell told them that because they did not believe me they proved it.

I know there were cultural issues involved and these nice people were shocked that they were able to meet Mr. Means and Mr. Matthews while getting coffee. Russell mentioned Vine Deloria Jr. I wanted to give them a gift, Custer Died for Your Sins. I went to my house to grab it for them. They wanted to pay for it so I let them, but it truly was a gift. Another cultural difference they did not quite understand.

One thing about the day, I would never say it was wasted because I spent time with Russell Means. Many people have different opinions about him. But, it is like I told him today and times before, I would have made a good activist but they accomplished everything they wanted and more. We have freedom of religion and self-determination; the list of things they did for our people is immeasurable. I am honored to count Mr. Russell Means as a personal friend and, yes, even a mentor. My opinion is mine alone. I believe he will go down in history as the greatest American Indian in the latter part of the 20th Century. And my time spent with him will be well remembered. Just another day living on the Pine Ridge Reservation where time seems to slip away in moments…

Summer Over

Enjoying the afternoon would be easier only if I was in a hammock on some island reading an interesting spy novel. Of course, I have not had much time to read my espionage genre for a few months. I have been really busy, but the mark of the end of summer is this weekend. Families will head to the beach and to the cabins up north with the idea this weekend ends summer. Being out of school makes the years go around and around. I remember starting school in August and even in September, but when you grow older the years turn into circles. I try to encourage the young people to enjoy their years in school because when you have to start looking forward to vacations it will get a lot tougher. This week we said our farewells to the Haitians and Germans. The Haitians were not very friendly, but maybe it is the Voodoo they do. Wait, it was probably the shock they were going through when I asked them if they were Christian. They assured me they were not followers of Christ. My assumption is they practice some other forms of spirituality or service to spirits. Whether they are family spirits or some form of

105

magic, I do not know.

The Germans were all women and they were talking bad about German men, but I am sure most of them will get married. They made the point German men do not grow up; they stay boys. I met one of the Germans last year, and she told me she would return next year. I have seen many different types of people come to Pine Ridge, but I have to say, the young 18 year-old girl was interesting. Wow, it scares me to think of my 23 year-old daughter in another country. I asked the young German how she felt when she arrived in Pine Ridge Village. She said she got off the bus at the local gas/diner and said it was a little difficult. I believe she was in shock. Then the people started asking her if she needed anything. It was good that her English was improving, and she was very nice. Going to study art at the University was her goal in life. I believe someday she will return to America. This trip seemed as though it gave her greater perspective. I would love to have read some of her writings.

It is almost 4:30 p.m., and I am ready for a long weekend. Now five but more later...

Indian in the Cupboard

When I travel on planes I like to just kick back and get into my zone, the Leon Zone of No Visiting. It is a treat to just relax deep into my own thoughts. There was one flight where I was initially seated next to some Mormons. I was not happy about this because of the differences in our belief systems. I figured they might want to talk so I dreaded the time, but all of a sudden my name was called. I was moved to first class; saved by the ticket counter person. I enjoy having my own space.

Another time I was traveling from some distant land via an airplane. I cannot really recall where because I've traveled many places. I saw this big Indian. He was about 350 pounds and 6'2. He said, "Hey Bro, where you from?" I told him Pine Ridge, and he told me his bro wanted to talk to me. I walked with him and his bro was the Indian in the Cupboard. We greeted each other, and I told him where I was from again. It was real nice and I walked away.

Well I got on the plane and made it to my seat. Who was I sitting by? It was the Indian in the Cupboard again and his bodyguard. He started talking to me about what he wanted to do with his life. I was nodding my head and listening. Then he told me he was the next Crazy Horse. At this point I was thinking to myself, I do not believe Tasunka Witco, or Crazy Horse, would have been saying he is the next anything. But, I guess I was not shocked that the Indian in the Cupboard had some issues with who he was with regard to his Island.

Meet with Hollywood People and French Photographer

It has been fifteen years since I came home from Minnesota. It seems like a lifetime since the summer of 1995. We have seen our children grow up, and now we are working at developing a Coffee House. It is a good way of life, drinking coffee and meeting the weary traveler or the local smoothie drinker. I have met many people at the Higher Ground. I met a witch or two, a Reiki Master, the recruitment officers, the FBI, and Drug Enforcement Agency as they have come through the doors.et in the world of Reservation life. I enjoy meeting the authors and the photographers.

I sat and talked a movie producer, writer and photographer from France. He had the spaghetti dinner and thought the sauce and noodles were excellent, but of course Belle's bread sent the meal over the top. He was a photographer from France who worked for a food magazine. The producer did the movie Rez Bomb, his name is Steven the Scotsman, or that is what I call him. We have some people who just stop in for muffins and others who buy the specialty coffees. Life is difficult on the Reservation and, more often than not, a place of hopelessness. I have felt this same ugliness and oppression of darkness. Some people say they understand, but until you are in the depths of the darkness, you will never understand what the Lakota people go through on a day to day basis. That is why I have referred to it as the Culture of Death.

Obama at the Fire Station

I met Obama in Rapid City, and I thought he was a person wanting to do good. I have no idea of what that means, but I believe Barack Obama's heart was right for that moment. I was driving down Main Street in Rapid City and thought I would drop in on the party at the Fire Station. He was there and I talked to him briefly as he was seeking to become the President of the most powerful country in the world. I am not a future teller by any means, but I believe it was a great day when I met the next President of the United States of America. No photo ops were necessary that day, and I do not believe in coincidence. I am left to pray for our President and hope for the country, that he will do what is right in the eyes of God.

A Men's Fraternity
....from 10-20-09

I was enjoying a beautiful Saturday afternoon and thinking about my common cold. I was hoping to get some vitamin C in my system. I drank some orange juice and thought about the Indian summer we are enjoying, the change in the landscape around the Reservation. I thought about my afternoon and was thinking it is quiet with not many people out and about the town of Pine Ridge. I saw a few people walking down Highway 18, and it seemed like an enjoyable afternoon. My wife and I decided to take the garbage out so we loaded up the cocker spaniels and headed out to the dump. It was a warm, sunny day, and it seemed like there were a few more people near the center of Pine Ridge. We stopped for gas and saw my cousin "Takoja" or Verdell Red Cloud Jr. He was selling a couple pieces of artwork, and I looked at them but did not have any money. He showed them to my wife but she could not hear him because the dogs barking at my cousin.

We got back to the house, and I thought I would check out my laptop and see the headlines online. I finished up with the news and started watching my movie, Code Talkers. Adam Beech did a great job in his role as Yazzie. Nick Cage is my favorite all time actor, and

I enjoyed most of the movie but I had to get dinner started. Belle, our niece Kelsey, and I walked down to the market to pick up some hamburger and fixings. We walked back, and I started my prep work for a late supper. I made our family some burgers with marble jack cheese cooked into the meat. I also made a couple steaks with mushrooms, green peppers, onions, and garlic. It is amazing that you can cook a meal for less money than taking everyone out to eat in some of the restaurants around the region. Of course it is very special when you can go out and find some great food and service.

I received an email about Willard Varnell Oliver who died last Wednesday down in Arizona. He was one of the famous code talkers from World War II. I appreciate the service of our veterans and know the Spirit of the Warrior is strong in Native America. I had many relatives go into the service and know of many friends who served the United States of America. It is with great pride that I look at our Lakota people and know we have been in all the wars including the world wars. Sometimes it is important to remember we come from a powerful history of men willing to stake their ground, fight, and not run. When the times get hard and you are battling with different issues such as depression, hopelessness, guilt, and sorrow you can know you are not the only one dealing with these issues. I hope I can offer you a solution to many of the issues you are dealing with.

My thoughts have continued to be on the men and women who find themselves in White Clay and places like the border towns of Pine Ridge. I have seen many terrible things in my life but the one thing I do not want to stop seeing is the people who are struggling. My fear is some of our people suffer from the inability to forgive themselves and others. You may know some bitter people who seemed to never overcome their own bitterness. I told a guy this past week I want to get a shirt that says, "Forgiven because I need to forgive as God has forgiven me." It is clear there are people who hold things against their parents and the Church or boarding school. You can hear the rhetoric when you listen to many people, and it becomes clear people have issues of not forgiving.

I am starting a Men's Fraternity which will focus on being restored as men. Manhood is important to any community because it affects every aspect our lives. If you would like to become a member of the Men's Fraternity you can come to the Pine Ridge Gospel Fellowship on Mondays at 6:30 p.m. All men are welcome. We hope to build trust as we struggle in our lives together.

Adam Beech

If anyone knows Mr. Beech, let him know I want my thirty-six dollars back. Most people do not know Adam Beech, but I am a fan and enjoyed watching Code Talkers because he played a role with Nick Cage. Nick Cage is my ultimate movie star; yeah, I like Sean Connery, but when it comes to my favorite all time actor, it is Nick because he is a cool Elvis dude. I know he admires the King of Rock and Roll. August 16, 1977 will be a day of great mourning for years. Yeah, I know some of you believe the King is alive and well, living a quiet life, but I believe the King would never lay low and therefore is gone. I remember the day he passed on; it was a sad day. People were wailing in the streets of Denver, Colorado. People were very sad because when the King died it meant an end of an era. Time seemed to stop on the late summer day. I, too, was a bit down, but I got through the day, but people in my neighborhood were pretty upset.

Back to Adam Beech, he has been on SVU, and he played the doctor in HBO's Bury My Heart at Wounded Knee. But, I did not watch the movie because the guy owes me money. I am willing to let it go, but he needs to at least acknowledge that he owes me money. Adam has some family around here, and I even took some pictures. I have to admit I got lost in the Hollywood persona. I am sure I would be okay, but I have often dreamed of catching up with him and getting my thirty-six dollars back.

Indians have had things stolen by other tribes, but now it seems that family members are stealing from each other. Times have changed over the years. People need to know, nothing is for free; somebody is going to pay. I have often thought of the way the Black Hills were raped and how all of the gold would be gone when they were finished.

Homestake Mine yielded 10% of the world's gold in its one hundred and twenty-five years of mining. The homesteaders came illegally, but General Custer went into the Black Hills with a thousand men to see if "there was gold in them thar hills". Of course, before he went into the hills it was illegal for white people to trespass on Sioux land because of the 1868 treaty. When gold was discovered, the Army changed from keeping white people out to now protecting the white people who sought to make their gold strikes. Often times I think about the way the Lakota were ripped off; I know the Government can never repay what was stolen. They have stolen land and have taken everything they possible could from the Lakota or Sioux people. So when it comes to people stealing, I know some are seeking to survive, but many people are just greedy.

Back to Adam Beech. It was late in the day, and I was getting ready to close the Higher Ground. Who walks in? It was the Hollywood guy from a few movies. He was in Smoke Signals and some other films I do not know, but he is an actor who has been on the big screen. He had a bunch of people with him and they ordered lattes and smoothies. Belle took some pictures with him and then he just kind of walked out the door. I don't know, maybe he thought pictures were pay enough. When I see him, I think I will at least have a few jokes with him. After all, it is not like he stole 10% of the gold in the Black Hills, right?

Katrina, The Kid

Okay, so I was a day late with my column. I would guess I probably was not the only writer to lose a day with Labor Day. I was determined to get some writing work completed. I was also training a new barista at the Higher Ground. Katrina is doing well, but there are a lot of things to learn when you are running a shift at the coffee house. Drinks are just the start of it as there are many things you need to know, like how to do a refund if you over charge someone.

It was funny because a family of three came in to the shop today

111

and wanted an Oreo Frappe and a Banana Rama with three brownies. The wife sounded like she wanted a Snickers Frappe and the new girl charged it so I thought they ordered the three. The price seemed a bit high so the man says, "That much?" I jumped in and named the three drinks, but, of course, they only wanted two drinks. I said, "Oh, he is from Red Cloud High School and they are good in math!" The man said, "He has good ears," and she said, "A good mouth." I just more or less ignored it, but it was really shocking.

Dealing with customers can be a chore. I have extensive training in customer service and was trained by the best. I say the best because the man I was trained by started at the bottom and ended up being worth more than a $100 million. I do not aspire to be worth a lot of money, I just want success. Yes, I realize success can be somewhat relative, but in the end I believe it must be something you love. Doing what God intended for your life is the ultimate success. Because of life's ability to throw us a bit, we constantly need to be searching out wisdom from God.

It was a great day, but being busy, serving drinks, and trying to write can be a bit burdensome. I was referring to my trip to the National High School Journalism Conference, and a friend was trying to talk to me. Of course, I was writing, "It is not good to talk to crazy people." Just when I was writing about not talking to crazy people, my friend Arlin was trying to talk to me. I mentioned him in the column and I told him about it. I was a bit out of sorts because I was writing what he would eventually read. It was a moment, but a great moment to have with writing and trying to listen.

I have to admit I am not all that great at multi-tasking, but I finished and now I am basking in the sun. Not exactly, but I get to blog and develop my thoughts. My desire is to be blessed! Just a little part of my day is a bit pleasure and work; I actually made some Italian cheese bread. My sister-in-law said I need to be a baker! If I had an oven I would do more bread making for sure. It is a great compliment when your in-laws like your cooking. More about my mother-in-law later, but it was great to become her son-in-law.

Russell Means, a Gentleman

It was a great Monday at the Higher Ground. I was putting together a prep table. We were reorganizing the office and storage area to be more efficient in our work place. Mr. Means was excited about his youngest son killing his first buffalo. The Omaha people were going to send elders and do something special as it was a great deed for the young Means. I was excited for him as he seemed be in a vibrant state. Well, he was on his way to the tribe to give them a heads up of coming events.

We sat down and talked about the world. It's status along with the local tribal elections coming up next week. Primaries will cut the number of candidates for the General Election in November. Time is closing in for the candidates to get out and make sure people know their names. Of course, it comes down to be a popularity contest and people seem to only want to vote for their relative so they will have power and access to crumbs.

Jason, a young Lakota man, was also there. We had a great time talking about different issues from gold to basketball. Of course, you have to throw some basketball in there. I hear Russ was pretty good in the 70s, but I did not ask him about that. I did ask him if he did his own stunts in Last of the Mohicans, and he said he did all of his own stunts in his movies. Jason made the action of the "over the head wild baseball swing".

All in all, I thought Mr. Means did a great job in that movie. He walks away as the last of the Mohicans. It was a great movie about a young Indian man falling in love with a white girl. There was also Hawkeye who falls in love with her sister, another white woman. They had the forbidden love fall off a cliff, and Hawkeye and his lady lived happily ever after. Ah, a love story in the midst of total annihilation. Other than that, I liked the running in the hills of North Carolina, but it makes my knees hurt just thinking about the running. Great movie! We had a few hours visiting, and then I was called away to move a desk to my sister-in-law's house. Funny thing, my wife is pretty strong. She got the light side of the desk, but Russell made fun saying, "Yeah right, that's the light side." We made it to the pickup, and Russell insisted on helping my wife out. He bent over and picked it up. We put it in the truck together.

Russell Means inspires me every time I meet with him. He truly is Lakota, and he fought for the rights of his people. It is great to know there are men like Russell who live with such passion. No one person is perfect, but you will never know a person until you sit and visit with a cup of coffee or a meal. We need to let people know they are appreciated because of the sacrifice they have given for the rights of our people.

For the Love of the Net

While traveling to the south and ending up in the Ozarks of Arkansas I have a greater appreciation for civilization. I say civilization because if you go without an internet hotspot and have a low cell signal you will know you left the civilized world. I was happy to get back into Lawrence, the home of the KU Jay Hawks and a great basketball program. I was able to connect to the internet and send my article into the paper last night. Now I am online at Borders blogging away and spouting off my ideas about the Tea Party. I believe the Tea Baggers are a group of people who believe everyone has a choice. This is hard for me to believe when I see our people who grow up in an environment that makes it difficult for us to move forward. It is a system that was developed to kill the Indian. The American Indian is going to develop as a people in America, but we will always be First Nations.

While I have grown up out of poverty and my family is not completely out of the dire surroundings of the inner city, I know I have been able to go to college and become what I set out to be in the 21st Century. I know I am not the best and brightest thinker in my field, but I made a choice to go to college and work three or four jobs at a time. I then made a choice to move back to the Reservation. The Reservation is a very difficult place because of a lack of housing and development. If you do not have housing lined up for your family it is very difficult to set up your life. So what follows is many people move off the Reservation hoping for a better life. But eventually you have to be ready for the racism in the border towns.

This morning I met a young lady who said she was Spanish, Mexican, Dakota and Ojibwe. I mentioned my relatives from Sisseton. She knew the name, Demerris. I encouraged her and thanked her for knowing who she was back home.

We have many people who will not move back to the Reservation because it is too difficult to live there and raise your family. We have people seeking to help, but it is difficult because we do not have enough progressive people to overcome the issues of the Reservation. The Tea Baggers have very little compassion. I know there might be some people out there who care. One of my favorite saying is, "What if people do not have boots when someone is saying they should pull themselves up by their boot straps?"

I have heard the Republican Party is the party of greed. When they are exposed to truth it is difficult to deny this. Some believe George W. Bush was giving freedom and democracy to the Iraqi people. But, it has always been about oil. They struggle and get angry when confronted with a different opinion. The wars have cost many lives of women, children, and elders. In the last few weeks we have even seen killings for sport in Afghanistan. No one is crying about this issue, yet we have people believing the Gospel of Fox News. I do not believe we can be of either party. I like what a brother said. John told me it is not about the government helping the poor because it should be the church. He is working at this and I applaud him for his work with the poor.

The poorest people in America are the American Indians. This is ridiculous when you understand how much was stolen from them. I am supposed to believe America has done enough good to cover up the evil they do in the world. Okay, I am done for now. It is good to be back in civilization.

A Mother's Love
....from 1-08-09

Life is like a bowl of wojapi, pudding but not really.

Some would say life is all mixed up without knowing the future. Someone asked me last week if I was in the movie Skins. I thought that was funny. I replied to him very quickly, "No."

I was with Chris Eyre on a plane a few years ago. He was going to Japan and I was going to Korea. We were on our way with the first stop being in Denver. He asked me what I was doing and I told him that I was going to present a position paper on the ethical treatment of American Indians. He told me he was a producer and was working on some movies that I would probably like when they came out. I was impressed with him and his ability to share a vision. We never know who we are going to run into when we travel around the country and the world.

Another time, I was traveling home from some distant land. I do not remember the place, but I was hanging out, waiting for my flight. All of a sudden, this big "Indian" came up to me and said, "Where you from bro?" I told him Pine Ridge. I believe he said he was from Oklahoma. He was traveling with Lightfoot, the guy from Indian in the Cupboard. Well, we had a great time joking around and visiting in the airport. I said my goodbyes and boarded the plane. I was amazed these two young men were out sharing a positive message and trying to represent the People in a good way. I was even more amazed when I sat down in my seat and these same two young men were next to me. We spent the rest of our time on the plane talking, and I thought I had a better idea of who Lightfoot really was; I was impressed.

I have met many people across the country and throughout the area, and I truly believe what my mother taught me: there are no strangers, just friends unmet.

I met Russell Means when I was just 20 years old in the old Rapid City Airport. Of course, I have mentioned famous people related to movies, but my favorite pastime is meeting people everywhere. I have enjoyed meeting people in coffeehouses, stores, restaurants, malls, and every place imaginable. I have met some amazing people.

I have to share a beautiful story of "Rez Life." I used to do radio, and one of my long time listeners was Angie from Angie's Burritos in Kyle. I saw her at a store in Rapid City, and it was so great to see her. Before I was on the radio, I would travel the fifty miles for her burritos. Her customer service was first class. It was always a pleasure to travel those miles just for a burrito. But you must know it was her love that drew me. I guess I saw my own mother in Angie, because she was a great worker and an excellent cook. Angie has since left us, but her spirit is strong in her family. I made a trip this past fall to see if I could get a great burrito. I traveled out to Kyle and was amazed by her sons and other family members working hard to keep the business going. If you get a chance, or even if you have to travel out of your way, stop in at Angie's Burritos for great service and great food.

My own mother has been gone for two years now, and I appreciate what a wise man once told me. When we lose the older ones there is always someone to take their place. I know it is difficult to think about our mothers who have passed on, and to try to replace them is impossible. But I would say the great mothers leave their legacy with us. Mothers are God's miracles here on earth, because a mother's love is forever.

The Red Pill or the Blue Pill
....from 9-01-10

In a Time Magazine article you can read these words, "dryness," "darkness," "loneliness" and "torture." It is said if you want to experience cultural shock go to Calcutta, India. Well, I went to India and stayed in Calcutta for a few days. It was like walking into a 1950s film. The airport was old and dingy with fading walls and what seemed to me a fading people. I had just arrived from the state of the art International Airport of Bangkok, Thailand. When we were finished finding our luggage we were ushered out into the open air and immediately I was overwhelmed with a stench. I brushed it off and followed our leader who was Naga from Nagaland, India.

A little boy walked up to me and asked me for a dollar. He

117

reminded me of the Chinese boy in one of the Indiana Jones movies about India. He had a similar accent to the boy in the movie. I thought for a moment I was in a movie, but I realized it was too hot and muggy to be in a movie. Oh, and the words from the Time article are from Mother Theresa, but I know we as the Lakota Nation deal with these same issues. A culture of death as described by a few of my friends is what we deal with every day of our lives.

I was talking with a few people this past week, and I wanted to know about a young man who walks around Pine Ridge Village with a long trench coat and some sort of mask. I know people are different, and I like to esteem our differences. This seemed a bit out of reach for me because I just did not know anything about the young man wearing a mask and trench coat. I usually have a pretty good idea about trends in America, but the guy with the mask and trench coat threw me off my game. It reminded me what my good friend Ted Standing Soldier Jr. said while we were uptown in Minneapolis. He looked around and said, "If all of these people want to be counter cultural, why don't they just become Christians."

Another friend said, "You should ask him if he wants the red pill or the blue pill,"- a question from The Matrix. The movie is a philosophical/religious movie that shows Morpheus and Neo meeting for the first time. If Neo takes the blue pill he goes back to living a lie, and if he takes the red pill he can see how deep the rabbit hole takes him. Morpheus tells Neo the only thing he promises is to show him the truth.

There have been times in my life that I have felt like I was caught in a matrix where the truth was shielded by a façade. Over the past few years I have been watching what is going on in America with regard to boarding schools. I have talked with some elders about their experience. Their experiences were both been good and bad. Many learned behaviors have brought a significant cultural shift to our Lakota lives. Americans have been notorious for having their heads in the sand. We have many emotional and spiritual issues because of the struggles against the policies of the United States. These policies were meant to kill our culture and make us American. I believe all of us need to do an inventory of our lives. Then seek to know the negative and positive affects in our lives and deal with them.

Forgiveness is the key. Do you want the red pill or the blue pill? The truth or the illusion is what is being offered. You can keep living in a lie or you can pick yourself up and start the healing process. It is one of the most difficult journeys you will ever travel. Our lives are full of areas that need to be healed. I live as a disciple of Jesus; he offers healing through forgiveness. It is powerful to know I am totally forgiven for everything I have ever done. But the other part is God offers me a chance to forgive others. You will find it will make you a better person when you do not hold things against others. Bitterness is stressful and stress is a silent killer. This is why we need to find healing. I believe we can find a better way of life.

Just be Yourself
....*from 9-08-10*

I believe election time has arrived in the Great Oglala Lakota Nation. We are halfway through the Obama administration, and I heard there is more stimulus money to come. After the Great Depression my grandfather planted trees. I smile when I see the trees he planted by the White Clay Creek.

I like to return to Robert Grey Eagle because he was telling me one day about the conditions of the unemployed. He told me he thought our people were really well behaved due to 80% unemployment. He was intent on talking to me about this issue, and I listened carefully. Of course, it was easy to listen to a friend. He asked what would happen if Rapid City's unemployment skyrocketed to 80-90%; what would happen in a small city…revolt, carnage, demonstrations, and terror? I have often thought about the conditions of the Reservation or concentration camp. It is difficult to see how any business could continue with eight out of ten people not working.

When you are in powerful positions, people listen and want to make sure the decisions makers are involved. Okay, what does that mean? It means that when you are elected you have the power to change the lives of the people. Our people are in survival mode, and they barely get by every day. I see people hustling to get food, diapers, and whole list of items. Our government is expected to help us with every part of our lives. Our tribal government cannot run when there is very little money coming into the accounts. Jobs are a key because people will be able to spend more on the Reservation. I was telling a young person last week it is ridiculous that if you need underwear today you cannot find a place that sells those things in Pine Ridge.

When I was in high school I wrote about the issues of Pine Ridge for the Oglala Light, Pine Ridge High School's newspaper. I remember the teacher who taught me to be me in times of doubt. Robert Mayne was a really good teacher; he taught senior English. I know my grammar is not the best, but I believe he taught me a great lesson, to use in my story telling. I went on to college and did well in my written grades. I was not always a great test taker, but I could write term papers and essays. We went to the National Journalism conference for high schools in Seattle, Washington. It was my first plane trip. I was full of excitement and awe of the plane. Then the landing was a shock. I looked up to the front of the plane. It leaned down on descent and upward on ascent. Corrie Mesteth and a girl from Red Cloud went on the trip too. Corrie was our editor and super smart. I was a year ahead of her, but she deserved to be the boss.

We were able to go out alone the first day, but after the tales of our adventures in the city, Mr. Mayne stopped us from going out into the streets alone. I went to a Moonie Reading Room where they tried to brainwash me. An African American woman walked up to me and asked me if I wanted to go to a reading room and talk about their religion. She was glossy eyed and smelled like incense of some sort. Luckily, I was able to break away from the cultish enticement. I believe it was because I had already developed my foundation of proclaiming Jesus as the Messiah. The Moonies could not penetrate my mind because I was already a follower of Christ and his teachings.

When I was walking near the waterfront, a man dressed in old clothes came up to me and asked me for a cigarette. I told him I did not have any to give and kept smoking. He got down on all four limbs and started beating the ground yelling and screaming at me. I guess that is why I do not talk to mentally impaired people. The National High School Journalism Conference was a great event. Thousands of students came to learn about writing.

Robert Mayne taught me more than how to write and to develop a story. He taught me to be myself, even when I was in doubt of myself. We were eating in a five star restaurant. There was an elegant table setting. I must have looked lost because I was trying to figure out the forks. The girls were talking about it, and Bob Mayne leaned over to me and said, "Leon, just be yourself." I believe that is one of the best lessons I have received in my life. I have been to the country clubs and some of the best restaurants in some large cities. I try to stay true and transparent with my identity. We need to teach our young people to be themselves. The Oglala or Sicangu or any other Lakota is a great heritage!

New Year's Resolutions and Hopes
....from 1-01-09

A New Year to look forward to is here this week. Pine Ridge has been slow these past weeks with a great Christmas celebration and now we look forward to the New Year. Last week my column did not get in the paper. I failed to check my email sent box so it did not get to the paper until Christmas evening. I was kicking myself when I realized what happened. Technology and a forgetful mind is the culprit; I understand how important it is to be organized now. I hope to keep up with the paper this coming year. I have met many people these past few months who have been reading my columns and I want to thank you for your input and encouragement.

New Year's resolutions are here again. On the top of my list is to continue to write and broaden my areas of study. I guess I will have to place getting in shape on the list as well. I know round is a shape, as my brother-in-law, Will Peters, reminds me at local functions. I would also like to get my sugars under control as I have had diabetes since

2000. These are my top three. I would also like to stay in touch with my friends through more letter writing and emails, but these are only the start of where I should begin because I need to become a better person. I fail often, and I am grateful to my wife for her forgiveness. I once told a guy I pray to my God 24/7 because I know how much I fail. We need to know who we are when it comes to personal healing. I do not beat myself up all the time, but I know I need to become a better person.

My hope is that I can do a better job with the youth of our Lakota Nation. I believe this is one of the areas where I fail because I do not work hard enough to help them. I know we can do some great things because I see our youth and I am blown away at their potential. We need to help them get through their adolescent years so they can become stronger adults. We need more for our young people in each of our communities. I have talked with two of our Pine Ridge Village Council members and we talked about opening a place for young people and adults.

A place of hope and not despair is what our people need. A place where we can hope for a better way of life, where we can grow and become better human beings, will be the greatest place for young and old to learn from each other. Here is an opportunity to utilize the buildings we have to change the direction our people have been going. This place will be called a wellness center where we can have talking circles, games, friendships, and an endless hope of dreams coming to reality, with computer labs for our people so they can grow and learn from the vast knowledge at our fingertips. I look forward to beginning these projects in the New Year.

The air is full of hope as we see our student athletes compete at a high level. The Pine Ridge Lady Thorpes are looking strong, and it will be amazing to see them battle for the districts. Little Wound Lady Mustangs are also looking strong with their inside outside game. And we cannot forget the Red Cloud Crusaders with their high powered offense, with Carl Swallow and Mike Twiss, along with their other teammates; they will be a force. These young men were fun to watch on TV last year, and they look to be going strong again. I am sure they will meet the challenge with courage they get from their friends and family. I have many favorites and many t-shirts from the different schools. I even have one from Hay Springs where we will see Lars Backwards tearing it up in Husker Country. I will be watching Roman Leftwich; he is one of the great small/power forwards around. I have had the opportunity to have him run into me a few times on Hedlund's court.

So we have much to look forward to, but I guess I look forward to reaching my goals. I believe we are looking better as each year passes. I wish you and your family a great New Year. Know that we all need prayers.

Tom Crash

I had the opportunity to spend some time with Crash today, and it was great to lose track of time with him. I decided to hand deliver the flyer for an event I am working on to help raise some money for KILI radio and a youth group. The Walk has been around for a few years and is starting its fall schedule. KILI has been around since 1983. I remember Vern Robertson playing the latest tunes on the Voice of the Lakota Nation. Vern was smooth and knew his music back in the 80s. Of course, there was Calvin Two Lance who I believe spoke Lakota like a poet. His voice was very strong and full of vitality. I knew Crash for a little while, and he asked me to do an interview about my faith and share what was going on with our ministry. I was very nervous and afraid at the same time. I do not know how the interview went but it seemed like Crash could ask some tough questions. I remember we were in the studio live on the radio. Tom asked a question and then he got up and waved at me to keep it going. He left the room. I was shocked, but when he left the room, I kept it going. After years of knowing the Crash man I often thought of just waiting for the next question. But, like a real natural, I did not have any dead air. Dead air is a no-no for radio as things must be kept flowing. It was a memorable introduction to radio, and not just any radio, Voice of the Lakota Nation.

I appreciate the time I spent at KILI Radio because I went on to have my own show. I did a little play by play basketball, but mostly color commentating. It was one the greatest times in my life. Crash taught me that when he took a break it was my cue to start talking. So I would talk about hair and clothing styles and anything that entered my mind. My Friend Bob says, "It is like a box of chocolates, you never know what is going to come out." I call it random, but when you are on the radio it is important to not have dead air.

Our best times were spent in the car visiting and getting to know each other. We had moments on the air. I would tell people my passions, popcorn, Belva, and Jesus. And Crash would say, "Yeah, but not necessarily in that order, right?" People seemed to love the games and would listen when they could not be at the games. I enjoyed it and had a great time watching Lakota basketball.

Like I said, we had great times driving to the games, but I could not stand it very long. There is a reason why they call him "Crash". When I was at the station I thought his count was around sixteen or seventeen. It could be a lot more now. I am referring to animals, mostly deer he has hit while driving his car. I would see him driving down the road, and he would be reading! When I was going to games with him it was crazy because he drove really fast and on wet roads. I started driving myself to games and probably saved a few years because I was less stressed.

We had our Kodak moments and shed a few tears because of the depth of our conversation. We were both married to a Belva; his was Belva Hollow Horn and mine was Belva Thunder Hawk so we had that in common. But we also had someone else in our lives. Uncle Mike Her Many Horses adopted Tom, and in the Indian way, I am obligated to treat Tom Crash as an uncle. I have enjoyed our times together and learned so much from him. He teaches at the college, and I have been a guest speaker for his class at times.

But as with Bob and other friends, I have found that you can lose track of time. I went to the station and Tom Casey was at his desk reading news on the web. I walked in and he greeted me and almost three hours passed before I realized I should have brought my phone in from the car. I left it to charge and time slipped away. I realize I need to spend more time with friends and begin my networking because spending time with people is truly about the moments. Our lives become intertwined and it seems like we need each other more than we think. I left the station, arrived home and started the homemade pizzas for the youth. Next I took a nap and finished work at the coffee house. Now I am relaxing after a Nick Cage movie.

Oh yeah, Crash likes to eat soup and sandwiches and go to movies. We have a lot in common because I love those things too. Popcorn, Belva, Jesus, soup, movies, and basketball are just a few of my passions, but not necessarily in that order. I hope when I die they put my passions on my headstone, but I would also add "friends".

Our Young People Will Rise Up
....from 2-16-10

Basketball warms my heart warm on a cold February night. I started my weekend with a game in Hay Springs, Nebraska with Lars Backwards and the Hawks. It was great to see Lars dropping three pointers like rain. He was part of almost every play with steals, rebounds, blocks, and assists, along with scoring many points. Lars ended up with 39 points. I am sure if he wanted he could have had about 70. He is truly a gifted player, and someone to watch as they make a run at the State title in their division in Nebraska. That was Friday night, and I was very excited about the cross-town rivalry that ranks with the Raiders vs. Broncos on any given year. Of course, I have my favorite, and I cheer for the Pine Ridge Thorpes. So here is my Saturday.

I wanted to wake up in time to get to the bank in Rushville but found out they were celebrating Presidents Day early. I started down Highway 20 looking for supplies and excited about the day. I went to the big store in Chadron, Nebraska. I ran into Uncle Mike Her Many Horses and my cousin Dani, who I have not seen since I interviewed Senator Tim Johnson; Dani was on his staff. I also saw the sheriff of Sheridan County shopping. It was great to see him outside of his patrol car. I was in hurry, so I got my groceries and headed for the door. Then I

125

saw my classmate, Lyle Jack. I have always appreciated Lyle's leadership and wanted to set up a meeting with his office. Wow, it was a great day fifty miles away from home. I felt like I was getting some things done. I got some fuel and made a call Tom "Crash". I wanted to let him know I would be listening to every word across the Voice of the Lakota Nation. I wrapped up the conversation and headed home on the back road.

Wow, a cold soda and burger with a warm van, and Tom "Crash" along with Hot Toddie getting set to tip off the Pine Ridge Thorpes and Red Cloud Crusaders boys' varsity game. The reason I was set for this game was because the dynamics changed over the holidays. Briar Iron Cloud Cottier went to Pine Ridge High School. He is an impact player and along with the athletic young Thorpes this would make a very good game. I spoke to Coach Rama and told him I would be at the Championship game for the districts because I believe it has the makings of one of the best games ever. I believe we had the opportunity to see what the young Thorpes can do against the power house Crusaders. It is my humble opinion that the time is ripe for the cross-town rivalry to explode in Western South Dakota. It is my desire to see thousands at the district Championship game because both teams are Oglala. We need to support our teams, whomever we might cheer for in the end.

Living on the Reservation you will notice there are many activities going on throughout our communities. I have often thought of what it will take for our economy and way of life to change in Native America. Sometimes we feel all alone with our own struggles and pain, but that is a lie because we are all in our own struggles together. We are being tested and what comes through the fire will be a strong people. I have worked with young people most of my adult life, and I assure you we have a great people coming of age. They have seen life and its struggles. They can make the difference in the coming years. I believe we need a movement and it needs to come through the young people. Life is difficult and requires a resilient people such as these young people. I see them in the stores working to care for their young families like I did when I was nineteen.

I have been developing my understanding of truth and how it affects my life. There is an absolute truth, which I believe is Jesus. He spoke it when he told his followers he was the Way, Truth, and Life. I have followed the teachings of Jesus since I was twelve years old. Recently I read there are one billion Christians around the world. I hold to this one truth; He died on the cross for my wrongdoings. I never have to feel guilty. This does not make me better than anyone else, but it is a simple truth that I have been found right in the eyes of the Father God. No one ever forced this on me. I realize there have been some atrocities done in the name of the Church, which by the way is not the way of Jesus. Forced assimilation is never good, and I fight against this at every turn. Perhaps my coming from relocation and then returning home to the Reservation makes me more aware. I choose to live among our people, and I have Jesus in my heart. I will never apologize for being an imperfect follower of Christ. In my mind, I believe it will be the young people who will rise up and lead us out of the destruction of the Reservation System.

Where are our leaders; the way is there to follow
.... *from 5-18-10*

In talking with a brother this past week, I had a question and wanted to ask him what he thought. I feel like we are missing something as Lakota people. I asked who the leaders are in our generation. I am in my forties. I was thinking about leadership and the development of the cultural leadership which existed in the 19th century. We had many leaders for the needs of the day. Crazy Horse was said to be in his early thirties when he lost his life. He was full of greatness, and you could see it in the stories of his youth. He wanted people to have food so he would give it away. Even though he did not have food for himself, he thought of others before he thought of himself. This type of humility in leadership is ideal, and I wonder if it exists today.

Historically, we can trace the destruction of the Lakota Plains Warrior. If you were to search out the tactics of the United States you can find policies which were created to encourage the slaughter of the food source for the Plains Tribes. We have lost a way of life, living off the land and encouraging a more green ecology. Plastics have become the norm across the Reservations. I try not to take plastic bags from the stores when I am getting just a few items. We have seen the Reservations, or concentration camps, grow a new Warrior, and it can be debated on how these new leaders lead. Yes, I am only slightly referring to gangs. Gangs have been around for centuries but it has only been in the last twenty years we have such a strong growth in Lakota land.

My opinion is that gangs developed because of a void in our Lakota culture. Traditionally, the leaders of the Lakota were men who could provide and protect. Hunting and warfare were ways men proved their leadership. In the last twenty years, we have seen many of our young people lose their way as young men and women. With the introduction of what I refer to as the MTV youth culture, we have seen our young more Americanized than ever before. The consumer based culture of America gives our youth their meaning. There are still pockets of people living in a more Lakota cultural manner, but it is clear, we are not making enough headway with regard to developing young Lakota Leaders.

I was teasing my good friend Maypiya Maza, the DJ, about starting a fan page for him because in truth, I see him as a great person. He has a little family and is involved in what I believe is Lakota culture. Hand games and bows and arrows make for a good way. I do not want to single him out but it is good to know there are a few people out there seeking to embrace being Lakota. The twenty-first century Lakota leaders will need to adapt to the world in which we live. Hunting and warfare will be done differently such as in the board room and holding down jobs to provide for their families.

Indian Basketball in December
....from 12-18-08

Popcorn, Belva, and Jesus are three of my passions, but not necessarily in that order.

I had the opportunity to see many great basketball games played in Indian Country. I did color and a little play-by-play commentating with KILI radio. They were the best of times and the worst of times. I loved my popcorn and the best place to go in those days was Pine Ridge High School. I got into to trouble one time because I rated Red Cloud High School's popcorn poor. But I need to tell you, I went to the Little Wound/Red Cloud Girls opener and they had great popcorn. I am looking forward to tasting more popcorn around the area. Of course, Belva is my wife and I am passionate about her. I believe I've loved her since I first saw her back in 1981. As far as Jesus, well he has been a great part of my life, and I would not know what I would do if I did not have my faith in my life. Basketball is the last of my top four passions in life.

Memories of the All-Indian Basketball Tournament bring hope and dreams. I remember 1979 when Steve Broken Nose was running the break and going in strong to the hoop. I can still see "Skylab" when I looked up to him like he was the greatest player I had ever seen. He looked down at me and smiled. This all happened in the old gym on the Pine Ridge School campus. This is where the dream of playing college basketball was born in my life. I have to say, Skylab is still a great player even though he is older. I remember the crowd was standing around the court and you could hardly breathe because it was so hot in the gym.

I started playing basketball right after Christmas. I think I played for one minute my first year. I played all summer between my 9th and 10th grade years. It was not until the end of my sophomore year when I believe one of the greatest coaches in South Dakota history, Jess Mendoza, taught me how to shoot. He was hard on us, but I believe he knew the level of conditioning we needed to compete at the highest levels. He eventually went on to win the State Championship undefeated. It is a pleasure to see him still coaching because I know the intensity he brings to the game.

The Lakota Nation Invitational is more than a basketball tournament; it is a place where dreams come true. I became a fan of girls' basketball as I watched my own daughter Tami play for the Lady Crusaders. I was so excited the time they won the championship. Mary T was and is a tough coach, but I know she loves the game and seeks to get everything out of her players. Joni Mo hitting a last second shot to win as a freshman was one of the greatest shots ever taken. Ruth D led her team as a freshman like the general and was awesome. Let's not forget Sarah D as one of the finest post up players ever. I once saw her block a shot and pass the ball only to get it back and make the layup. Sunni B was an excellent player and leader. She willed her teams to win.

Playing in the LNI is a great experience. It is where I played with the legend Lyle Jack, but the most memorable events happened as a fan. I saw Mr. Basketball bring his team back from a deficit of 20 points to just come up short. It was an amazing experience to watch his turnaround jumper team leadership. George B has to go down as one of the greats.

What about Crow Creek and their high power offense? Also, loving to hate Custer as they dominated for so many years was awesome as Larry truly brought great teams to the LNI. But the greatest boy's game had to be when the Class B team took on the giants of St. Tommy Moore and beat them. Lower Brule was so awesome that year. We can truly say Indian basketball is something to look forward to in December. What other event brings Sports Illustrated to South Dakota? To have Hulkamania run wild all over the Lakota Country is a great tribute to Brian Brewer and his staff. I would like to thank Brian personally for doing a first class job. You are truly the greatest when it comes to vision and leadership. Wopila tanka.

We Are the Pine Ridge Thorpes

Dreams are made from a dirt court! Sounds like my all-time favorite player in the universe, Larry Bird. He battled because of his love of the game. Christian Janis passes like non-other, and she is every bit of the player Larry Bird was when he was her age. I know you are thinking I am crazy at this point, but I believe there is a greatness that comes with passion. I could go all day writing about the similarities, but Christian Janis is the "Real Deal". She wheeled and dealt, and took it right at the other team. I already forgot the second place team's name. It has been only a week and I realize I could look it up but, in all reality does anyone ever remember the second place team? Now, on to how this team came together.

Because of the great support the Divas, oh, I mean the Lady Thorpes, received in their summer workout; they have become a threat to the Class A division in South Dakota. Tiny D works relentlessly with these young women because of her passion. I realize you are thinking that could not be all that is happening. Yes, talent plays a huge role in the building of a championship team. But, not unlike the '87 and '89 teams, it took Thorpes to win it all. Yes, I am saying these teams did not go out and pursue other students from other teams. They worked with desire from their own students.

I started high school in 1979, and it was awesome to see the teams play my first year. I fell in love with these teams. Pine Ridge, of course, and Red Cloud were awesome with their players. I would be remiss if I did not mention the Little Wound Mustangs. At that time, Dave A was the coach. He worked tirelessly for their teams to be great. I was part of the building years of Mendoza, and he was one of the greatest influences of my life. He drilled us like the Marines, and then in '87 he won it all. What won it all? Being Indian won it all because Mendoza knew what it meant to be Indian and to be playing for the state Championship. Then of course there was Charley Z; my condolences go out to his family. He was so awesome as he worked with me. He is my hero!

I went to college in Minnesota and played college basketball because of Charlie and Mendoza. They helped me achieve and successfully follow my passion for basketball. 1989 brought the greatest team in Pine Ridge Lady Thorpe history together, and I was away in college. Sue Ann will be remembered forever in Thorpe history. Charley was her coach, and I know he believed in those girls like he believed in me. What a family we have in Thorpe Country! To be a Thorpe makes you family.

Eventually, we will see young women and men want to be state champions. We will watch them in the Big Foot Conference and then as they move on to high school. When it comes to the greatest coaches in South Dakota, Lyle "Dusty" Lebeau is at the top of the list! He is a wonderful ambassador for our Lakota Nation. Notice I did not say Oglala Nation. He is the cream of the top when it comes to coaching. He is magnificent and will go down as the greatest coach in Lakota Country. Add all of this together and what do you have? You have the makings of championship teams.

L Weston is probably one of the best inside, outside players I have seen, and the" Diesel" Tassel controlled the paint. I have watched Weston play all four years of high school and she has a killer instinct that battles to the end. Brewer is young but hopefully will fill the shoes. I know she can do it, but one question needs to be answered is, does she know her abilities? I have nieces on this team and next year too, so I am waiting with anticipation. I hope their parents are telling them I am speaking about them. I know I have questioned my readers this week, because in the end it takes the family to come together for championship teams. We are, we are the Pine Ridge Thorpes! Some people may never understand what it means to be a Thorpe, but we do!

Lakota Warriors...Find Them on the Court
....from 1-29-09

Where are the Lakota Warriors? A few years ago I heard of a person asking this question and then stating the Lakota Warriors were no more. Well, I know the Warriors are alive and well. Over this past weekend I had the opportunity to see these young men in action. They were in Martin. As I waited for our basketball game in the fairly new recreation center, I did not realize we would see one of the best games of the year. There were two Hearts, High Wolf, White Dress, Big Crow, Three Stars, Dreamer, Mav, Cory, Garnier, White, and our friend from the north, Troy.

Tommy White has to be the strongest pound for pound player out there as he goes from the inside to the outside. He dropped eight three pointers and was the high scorer for his team. Wolf, as everyone knows, was great throughout the game.

These are some of my favorite players, and they are great athletes. As the game went on it was apparent this game was going down to the wire. The older Heart started heating up as he hit four or five consecutive three point shots. He eventually led his team down the stretch to the early preliminary game. This was just one game the Regulators were playing. Just when I thought I had seen everything, His Law and Keller were getting ready to beat up on GP. GP is our team; it stands for God's Property. Henry Brown came up with the name and is an original member.

Five years ago we were competing for league championships, and we were playing great. We had a six foot four center named Ata Jack. We would give it to him in the low post and he would score. One time we were playing the cops; the game was close and we were down by two at the end of the game. The Dog, oh, I meant Henry, was bringing the ball up the court with time slipping away. I was open for a pass, and he threw me the ball around half court. Out of the corner of my eye I saw the Librarian; yes, a woman on our team. I threw her the ball. She was on the right side wing where she set up her shot, and it was like slow motion. The ball went up in the air and it swished. Well, that was the game where GP beat the cops, and yes, the Librarian hit the winning shot.

Basketball is a great game because the competition helps motivate you to become better with each game. Our Lakota Warriors are alive and well. Some of them are playing in college, some have played college, but I believe they are strong and can compete at any level. So the next time you want to see some Warriors who have come from names like Red Cloud, Crazy Horse, Spotted Tail, Bull Bear, Gall, Sitting Bull and Young Man Afraid of His Horses, try looking for an independent basketball tournament because these young men are an awesome sight to see. GP is looking for communities to go to in the next few months where we would like an opportunity to play against the locals and bring a positive message.

Use basketball; Don't let basketball use you
....from 3-16-10

Now that the season for high school basketball is almost over, we can begin to rest and watch the March Madness and the upcoming NBA championship. Many people believe it will be Lebron James and his Cavs who dominate. I still believe Kobe will have a few jumpers and slams. I did talk to some experts on the philosophy of basketball, and they are divided. But I am excited as my Blue Devils are on top of the ACC and looking at a number one seed. I like Coach K because I believe he loves his players and the players love him. This helps bring the chemistry for winning teams. Of course, I like the Kansas Jay Hawks, and their impressive basketball program. Whichever team you decide to root for, I wish you luck and a great rest of this basketball season.

I hope most of you were able to catch the State a girls basketball championships. I was able to watch the first game for the Lady Thorpes. I was very impressed with Christian Janis and the rest of the girls. There was one point in the first game when they were up by nine points. The other team scored two quick buckets, and Christian came down the court. She took a ten foot jumper and nailed it with so much poise. You could see her in control of the game, and it was such a great game. Unfortunately the Lady Thorpes had a slow game on Friday night for the semi-championship and lost. But what a run for Christian Janis and the third place finishers as they finish out a great season and a high school career for Christian.

We have had some great athletes come from the Pine Ridge Reservation; to name them all would be impossible. I am thankful that I was able to see Christian Janis play because she is one of the best in the nation. She truly lived basketball throughout her high school career. I like to talk to the family and see her crazy basketball mom. Emma and Charley have been supportive of their children in so many ways, but I believe they are best at the games. Helping to drive the girls to different tournaments and following them around to watch their games. It is really awesome to see parents support their children. I know that we will have some great games as the rest of the Janis girls finish their high school basketball careers in the next few years.

If you want to succeed at anything, do it with passion and love. Basketball is a game of passion for many players, but you have to live it and breathe it every day. One quote says, "Use basketball; don't let basketball use you." I got that from Arlo the DJ who was watching a basketball movie. It also stated that basketball should be a vehicle. You can use basketball to get your education. College is very expensive these days and a full scholarship could mean as much as one hundred thousand dollars. Just ask the people who go on to higher education, and they will tell you how expensive it really is when it comes to paying for all of the books and other fees.

Private colleges can be very expensive, but you can work hard and develop your game to go on to play. I had three goals in my life, play and letter in college basketball, become a pastor, and travel to Australia. Now I have not gone to Australia, but hope to make it there in my lifetime. Dreams are developing on dirt courts all over the Rez. I hope you can encourage our youth to dream dreams and seek visions of a better life. I would like to thank one of the best in the Nation for giving us joy and pride as we watch her play basketball. Thank you, Christian Janis, for living your dream.

Seeing the World Outside of the Rez
....*from 5-11-10*

College is a time of development and change. When I took my young family to Minnesota I never understood the impact it would have on my life. I was intrigued with the television channels because there were about seven using an antenna. Back in South Dakota you could barely get two or three, and the picture was not clear. One day I was laying on the floor in our new living room and decided it was time to go get a job. I had no idea where, but there were lots of businesses in the area. I drove toward Minneapolis and came to a crossroads, Highway 101 and 7.

Cub Foods looked like a good place to start, so I turned into the store. I went to see a manager. I met an assistant manager named Brian;

135

he was very nice and asked me when I could start. I told him I would
be able to start immediately. He gave me a start day and time. I walked
out to my car and headed home. It was easier than I thought it would be,
and I never realized how great the experience would become in my life in
Minnesota. I stopped in another day and went to the break room where
the schedules were posted. Another assistant manager, Mark, asked
me if he could help me? I told him I was checking to see when I was
scheduled to work. He was a tall man, and I later found out his dad was
a great baseball player named Bob Allison; Bob played for the Minnesota
Twins. Sometime later, I heard the assistant managers about me. They
were more or less arguing over who taught me the business. Brian was
saying he hired me and Mark was saying he taught me how to read a
schedule.

I started working at minimum wage, four dollars an hour. I had
no idea about wages because I came from a Christian organization that
paid me four hundred dollars a month. It was really hard living on that
small salary, so the minimum wage did not seem so bad. Of course the
work was pushing carts, cleaning up spills, and emptying garbage cans.
The work seemed fine, and I was just happy to have a job that was not
too far away from school and home. I eventually became a full time
employee and started making more money. Of course the benefits were
better with my full-time status. We eventually made too much money
for food stamps, and we had great health insurance.

My time in Minnesota gave me valuable work experience, but it
also helped me to understand the corporate world. Running a business
is all about the quarterly profits and if you do not do well you are moved,
or worse, let go (fired, but we did not like to use that term). During my
return trips to Minnesota, I have visited with my friends and coworkers.
They seemed to be full of stress. In some ways I miss the action of
working a full-time job, but I would not change any of my life. I have
sought to develop many skills. I have done radio, television, video, and
now a column. I enjoy writing more than anything I have done in the
past fifteen years.

Seeing the world outside of the Reservation has taught me there
many ways we can help our people. My plan this summer is to help our

youth in Pine Ridge Village. I would like to start working with some basketball players and teach them what Jess Mendoza taught me. I was able to fulfill a dream of playing college basketball because of the skills Coach Mendoza taught me. I believe it taught me discipline to keep my job and stay in college. My desire is to give back to our youth and help them to have hope.

We hear so many stories about our youth not having hope. I believe hope begins with goals. When you have goals, it helps you stay driven and focused. We need to use our life lessons in our daily lives and share use them with others. This can help bring our people out of the depression.

Our people need role models. If you sit on the sidelines and don't come out to help, you are only hurting your family's future. We do not need others to come into our homes and clean them up; we can do those things ourselves. My family is going to be planting flowers at our four-way in downtown Pine Ridge. I am going to have free chili feeds this summer in the Billy Mills parking lot. Lots of things can be done practically. So the challenge is to help each other because I believe it is our responsibility to our tiospayes.

Black Indians

Mashantucket Pequot comes to mind when I think of a Black Indian. The year was 1995 and I was helping out with an event at the Indigenous Games where thousands of American and Canadian Indigenous people had come to Blain, Minnesota to compete in Olympic style games. I cannot even begin to tell you how many people there were, but I know there were lots of athletes hanging out and stretching, waiting for their events.

I met a couple of people one day. I was visiting with younger and older people alike. I came across a young lady who was almost blond, but it was obvious she was American Indian. I asked her where she was from, and she told me Pine Ridge. I told her, "No, you are not," because

I would know most of the Pine Ridge athletes, or at the least their relatives. It turned out she was from Martin, South Dakota, a town kind of on the Rez. I welcomed her and wished her the best.

Next, I went on to find the basketball courts where they were playing for the gold and bragging rights. I came to a place where there was a woman's game. I noticed a young lady who was on the sidelines. She had twisted her knee. I felt for her because a year before I tore my ACL and was grounded from basketball. I had my knee scoped and cleaned out and was still in recovery. She was sitting there and I decided to offer a prayer for a speedy recovery. I cautioned her to be careful because she could do more damage if she played before her knee had a chance to fully heal.

As I moved around I came across a young black athlete. She was getting ready for her track events. Actually, there were about a dozen athletes who looked African American. I started to speak to them about their events and where they were from. I was told they were Pequot, but I had never heard of them. I continued to ask about their tribe and found out they were from the Northeast. A man approached who looked to be of medium build and started talking with me. He told me he was the War Chief. I thought it odd because I have not heard of this type of Chief, but then again I was not from the Northeast. I hoped they were not going to war with any other tribe because the Lakota alone must have had at least a thousand. I remember the War Chief walking away. He had the hair of an African American except he had a skinny braid going down his back. He was wearing some decorative clothing, a vest with Indian design. It was a great day to visit other tribes.

I noticed something that was very interesting. The Pequot were sitting alone, and it seemed like no one wanted to talk with them. They were separated by an invisible wall of ignorance. I love to visit people so I had no issues. I just wanted to get to know them. I was ignorant when it came to Black Indians. Well, I remember how the brown-skinned Indians seemed to leave the Black Indians alone and did not really associate with them. I saw how they were treated, but one of the most interesting things about this is the Pequot have now become one of the richest tribes in the nation with their casino. Now you can travel to Mashantucket and see lots of Brown Indians hanging around and helping out. Money seems to be able to buy many things; I guess it can buy friends. I wonder what happened to the War Chief and the young female Pequot I visited with on a warm July day in Blain, Minnesota.

Dealing with Hopelessness

Living with hopelessness is something we need to combat in Native America. You have read my articles about situations throughout Native America. There are young people living daily lives with hopelessness. How can our lives change if our young people do not believe life is not going to get any better? Since I returned home from Minnesota to the Pine Ridge Reservation, this has been the challenge I have experienced. Many Reservations have battled with suicide; it seems to keep coming around. Ron His Horse Is Thunder, chairman of the Standing Rock Sioux Tribe, is talking about public safety issues and taking a stand.

Taking a stand is more important now than at any point in the history of Lakota and other tribes of our Land. I am reminded on the warrior who would stake himself to the ground, willing to risk his own life for others to live. This is more than a call for the warriors; it is call for all of our people to stop and think about what we can do to build hope in our communities. Traveling across Native America you will find a common denominator; it is hopelessness. Hopelessness is growing by leaps and bounds. There are still many people with hope, but when you see nine young people take their own lives and the countless others who have tried, you know there needs to be some intervention.

I once took three young people out to eat Chinese food. The two young ladies were from two very different areas. One was from south Canada above Minnesota; the other was from Arizona on the Navaho Reservation. The young man was from Oklahoma. I realized early in our conversation that we deal with many of the same issues of hopelessness. The young ladies were finishing up dinner and the check came. I immediately saw panic in their face. I asked them if the check made them nervous. They both had their heads down avoiding eye contact and shook their heads, yes. My heart broke because I saw both emotional and physical scars on these two young ladies from Ontario and Arizona. Because they were from similar, and yet very different geographical areas, it made me think about the pain our Indigenous people have had to come through over the past five hundred years.

Skin Tone

We are human, and when you seek to understand our condition, you will know we have the same issues and we need to strive to overcome them. I remember reading a book called The Sacred Romance. It was about our relationship with God. I recall from the book a vision. In living, there are arrows us. We need to keep moving and pulling out the arrows. Maybe getting teased on the playground, being made fun of on the bus, or some boy or girl telling us we are ugly are all arrows shot into us. When I was a boy I had many friends, but most of my friends were Mexican Americans, Chicanos. I use this word because it represented identity. People were searching for civil rights and embracing their identity. The Chicano Movement was pretty powerful. I remember marching with Corky Gonzalas on City Hall.

In my research I found Corky to be a tough guy. Everyone seemed to like the "Macho Guy" when it came to leadership. When there was a block party in the city, it was pretty great to see so many people come together and celebrate life. Thousands of people dancing and having a good time always brought excitement and intrigue. We were having a great time on the east side of Denver, but those days were beginning to change in the late 70s of the 20th century. Why? Because of something called gentrification. Gentrification is the process of people being displaced by revitalization of neighborhoods, usually in the inner-city. I saw young couples move into our neighborhood and start working on homes. The buildings were at least turn of the century homes and in need of work. When you start fixing up homes in a poor neighborhood the property value goes up and eventually people need to leave because they are being pushed out. The housing projects in the 1970s were a bad deal because of the drugs and violence. It kept people in poverty. I always think it is ironic when people in the cities stay in their poverty without upward mobility. After all, we should all have a little George Jefferson from The Jeffersons because of the availability of commerce in the city. Every person is a potential customer and every dollar can bring you out of your poverty.

Growing up in the city, I understood there are people who are racist. People judged others because of the color of their skin all areas of life. The Reservation is full of people who will judge by skin color. You find it the full-blood/half-breed controversy of the Rez. People actually judge you because of the hue of your skin. I have not felt a lot of this because I am a mixed blood, but I have dark skin. I believe we are the people who come from our ancestors. If we took out one of our great-greats, or any of the people we come from, it would change who we are today. I am proud to come from a people who did not see the difference of race but pro-created someone who would eventually have me as a child.

In Pine Ridge there is poverty mentality. Some people do not like white people, and even some do not like half-bloods. I have often stated, I am not a dog with a blood pedigree. I am Lakota and live my life day to day as a Lakota man. I have a different faith than most, but I am Lakota. The thing that makes me Lakota is not me; it is my ancestors and relations.

On the Rez there are people who do not like other people because of their skin color, but I believe we must look at a person's heart to know that person, not their skin color. I know of some light skin people who are strong in a respectful manner and behave more Lakota than many. We need to stop looking at white people like they have money, and we need to start making relatives so they can help our people. Growing up in the city helped me understand there are different cultures but only one race of people. It is called the human race. I like my friends because they are great people. Their lineage makes them who they are.

The Grandma in Green
....*from 2-24-10*

Sometimes people feel all alone. This can even happen when you are living in big cities. This can also happen when you are living with many family members in one home. We by nature are social beings and meant for human contact. We need each other, but we also must be careful to respect each other when we take the journey of life. I believe we are suffering from the loss of our way of life, and we have not recovered from the onslaught of the American Government's policies of destruction. Living on the Pine Ridge is most likely not different from living on the Rosebud or any other Reservation. There are some key issues on each of the mostly isolated Reservations. We have clustered homes that are built with substandard materials. You can see the homes severely in need of siding, paint, and other repairs. Poverty is rampant for most of the population, but there are a few people doing well economically.

This past week as I traveled to Rapid City, I was having a conversation with my wife about the creation of the world, the fall of mankind, and the redemption of mankind. It is known as C.F.R. and it is important to our understanding because it helps us to see the importance of a sacrifice. It was a good conversation because it helps us to put the world in perspective and the way it works. I have followed the teachings of Jesus since I was a boy, and it has been a difficult journey. We suffer loss and change in our everyday lives.

I mentioned in previous writings that I am a person who survived the policies of the United States Government. Relocation was meant at best to our Indigenous people into the mainstream society and at worst to destroy the Indigenous people. Many of our conversations end with the white man trying to take everything from us. In my conversation with my wife, I felt that I was being unfair after hearing her tell me, "You guys always blame the white man." So I quickly told her I will now include white women in my blaming. We both laughed and drove to Hermosa where I was looking to get a cold diet soda (or pop for the people using the latter term).

I went into the truck stop and went for the soda fountain machine. I saw a cup that I wanted and then saw the plastic, reusable cup of my favorite drink. So I filled the cup and went to the counter with my chips and soda pop. The reusable cup cost was three dollars, and the chips were seventy-nine cents. I was ready to give her my four dollars, and she told me the exchange would be nine dollars and some cents. I was taken aback and said, "What?" She quickly recalculated the cost and gave me the correct amount. I just shook my head and said, "It is true." The clerk said, "What is true?" I told her, "It is not just the white man trying to steal from the Indians but it is the white woman as well." I told them the story about my conversation with my wife, and the two clerks just started laughing. It was a pleasant exchange of humor.

I ended my day in the big store in Rapid City. You know, the one where all the Indians end up. If they ever needed a ride back to the "Rez" they can go there and find many people heading home. I sat on a bench and proceeded to ask the elderly lady how that was working out for her? She said, "Excuse me?" I then asked how the green was working out for her. She was dressed in a green hat, green scarf, green shirt, and green pants. I then noticed she had green eyes. She was very nice, and I asked her where she was from originally. I have noticed something in my visits with people. If they are very nice to me in Rapid City, they are usually from some place other than western South Dakota. I saw a friend from Wanblee, and we started talking. He told me he was born in 1969. The elderly lady, who by the way was Irish, told us we were lucky because she was born in 1917. I was blown away because she was ninety-three years old and very interesting. Well, I saw my wife and decided it was time to leave the big store. I said to the elderly Irish woman, "Goodbye Grandma. "

If we take the time to get to know people, we can understand each other. My fear is we have many people living on lands once known as the Great Sioux Nation. What a powerful territory we had for a short time. It is true the white man has broken every promise except for the one; he said he would take our land. I have many stories about being let down by the white man. I believe we can help each other if we understand we are all imperfect. Philosophically we can debate and try to understand each other, but we must come to the understanding that we all belong to one race. It is the human race, and we can know that we are all on a similar journey, life. Life is hard enough without the hate and prejudices. I have man Kolas who are of European descent. We are very close. I often tell people I belong to the tiospaye (extended family) of God, and He takes care of his family.

I am part White, but I cannot prove it
....*from 4-29-09*

The Black Hills are not for sale. I thought of the reasons for an eastern tribe to sue for part of the money that was awarded to the Sioux Nation. It would seem they have lost their way. I heard five thousand people gave a hundred grand for a lawyer to work on the case. I laugh because it is just another lawyer trying to make some money. I would be more impressed if the lawyer did it pro bono. Of course, you rarely see this when it comes to big money. I would ask how much is going to the lawyers. Lawyers aside, it is one of the worst things I have heard about in my adult life. In 1980 I was appalled at the idea of accepting money for the sacred Black Hills. The court ruled the Hills were taken illegally. The ethical treatment of the Great Sioux Nation by the United States is not in question; the Supreme Court said this deed was illegal. So they awarded monetary damages, but there is no amount of money that would settle this in my heart.

Civil rights were not granted to our people until the late seventies. Young men and women joined together to say, "No more!" When our people captured the United States flag, it was a great victory. And since that point we have been involved in every armed conflict the United States has been in around the world. People are really misinformed when it comes to the Great Sioux Nation. West River is not West River; it is the Great Sioux Nation. The quest for gold has driven the wasicu for many centuries. This greed will drive men to do many unethical things. I hope our leadership begins a process to fight for the Sacred Hills.

Racism is alive and well on our borders. We have seen many

incidences in Rapid City over the past few weeks. Our relatives are hurting and trying to survive in a harsh world. Throwing urine at the Lakota and shooting them with pellet guns is very disturbing. I know things are not always this bad. We need some healing between our people and the people of Rapid City. We add to the Rapid City economy because we do not have a strong base on the Pine Ridge. I do not always feel the racism, but I do feel it at times. I get angry because I know our relatives are getting treated badly.

I wear a shirt that proclaims, "I am part white but I cannot prove it". I tell people it is my white gear when I travel to Rapid City. I sometimes get people smiling and laughing at my white gear. I explain to them I am tired of being racially profiled. I tell them, "I am one of you." It is said with humor and meant to show people I am okay with my identity. I tell people my identity is tied to my ancestors and yes, there is a white man in my lineage. I do not let it stop me from living a normal life (this is a joke if you were wondering). I like to have fun with my white gear, and I do not believe it has been offensive to anyone in Rapid City.

Our lives are too short to live with hatred or disdain for another people group. We are all related and if we acted this way, it would be a better world. I have seen too much in my life to let petty differences get in the way of developing friendships. Our Lakota people considered themselves to be friends. Our way of thinking is relational, so when we do not have enough relatives we make more as our Hunkapi, or making of relatives, teaches us. I know our people have a lot to give to the outside world. We need to be involved in all aspects of life. I say be engaged with the world because it will only be through visiting that we will overcome our differences.

Rez Ramblings

WO LAKOTA

Way of Life for the Lakota

Generosity

Oh, it was a very relaxing weekend on the Rez. I had the opportunity to go to Rapid City twice. I saw the movie Wall Street Money Never Sleeps, and it was a great movie! I had a great salad and some pot roast with bread. It was very good. Although I felt full, it was worth the healthy salad. On Saturday I made more bread and was able to have a nice meal with the family. Pasta and bread with family is a great way to spend an evening. I needed some pasta so I decided to go to the store. First I went to Big Bat's and I saw an ex-student of mine. I was sitting in the van. She did not see me, but I was wondering how adult life was treating her. I have not seen her at least eight years. She is all grown up, and I guess I like to believe the students are doing well and adapting to adult life.

I went to the Sioux Nation Shopping Center for some pasta. I found what I needed and proceeded to the checkout line. I was waiting patiently, and the young lady I taught in 2000 was behind me. She was ready to tap me on the back. I saw her, turned around, and gave her a hug. I asked how she was doing. I learned she was in Wanblee, which is about 80 miles from the Village of Pine Ridge. While we were catching up, her sunflower seeds and six pack of Pepsi went through with my pasta. I told the checkout girl to wait, and then I decided to buy the seeds and soda for my ex-student. It was a pleasure to see her. She seemed like she was very happy living with tough circumstance in the community of Wanblee. There is a lot of fighting in the school and not much to do in the furthest community from Pine Ridge. I believe it is great to see your students doing well. We need to be gracious and generous with the people God has put in our lives.

So often we see the pain and suffering in Pine Ridge, but when you see hope in the lives of those you have touched, it is a great gift. Once I was paying for my meal, and I noticed the woman who did a radio show after me with her daughter. I paid their tab as well because I believe it is always great to give rather than receive. I have received

149

much in my life, and I believe we need to be willing to share warmth and goodness with people. Life can be short and after I paid for the lady and her daughter, she passed away. That was the last time I talked to her. I would like to believe it is my being Lakota, but I believe it is my faith as well.

When I was a teenager I was standing in line at Micky D's counting my couple dollars. I was wondering what I could get for a couple of bucks back in the eighties. Not much even then, but out of the blue a lady said to me, "You are Roy's nephew, aren't you?" I said I was and she gave me a ten dollar bill. I was blown away by this generosity and thanked her 20-something years later. Powerful and moving moments are the memories I hope to keep. Let the bad slip away.

Seeking to Understand the Untranslatable

I spent the morning grilling chicken and visiting with some Lakota men about the dream of starting a Lakota soccer and parks project. I visit with many people, but today was a treasure, as I listened to two Lakota men solving the world's problems. I enjoyed it very much because we lost track of time. It is a great thing to find a good human friend who makes you lose track of time. I hope I was able to communicate my words in a respectful manner. One professor and a writer were having a cup of Pine Ridge's finest coffee. I do not know if they were drinking lattes or drip coffees, but they seemed to enjoy the peaceful scenery of a Wednesday morning at the Higher Ground. It is a refuge from all of the bad experiences that comes from living life on the Rez as a Lakota or, for that matter, a human. I believe the writer said the written word is a powerful tool that will make people's souls move in the way they thought it never could. I texted my wife this morning and went back to ask if her soul was moved, and indeed it was stirred. Funny, how we forget the little things after almost 26 years. I used to love writing prose for her in high school.

I was speaking about the Lakota phrase Taku Sku Sku as the unmoved mover. We talked about the spark and Dr. William K.

Powers' book Oglala Religion. Powers says in the book it is better left untranslated because of the meaning in all of its fullness. I am sure the some Lakota elders told him it had a too much meaning and was difficult to translate. I believe it speaks to the mind and heart when you work to move toward a deeper meaning of the Unmoved Mover. I do not believe we can fully understand the perfect being of a creator, and it would seem arrogant to believe you can understand a God who is above everything. In listening to the professor and writer, I understood he was talking about the elders. The prof talked about Black Elk, another bridge between the old and new Oglala. Black Elk, with a helper, wrote the book Black Elk Speaks. It was considered to be the bible of the New Age at one time. It talks of the mending of the sacred hoop which I believe is the whole family society of the Lakota. I have read most of the book but I usually have a red flag because although there is a lot of Black Elk, but I believe there is a lot of the author, John G. Niehardt, in the book as well. The writer was referring to his father, and I could tell he loved his dad. From the stories I believe his dad was great.

One thing the writer quoted is found in Genesis: "By the sweat of your brow you will eat your food until you return to the ground, since from it you were taken; for dust you are and to dust you will return." The idea is if you don't work you don't eat. It is a value of many people and is used in Christian circles to make people accountable. I liked what the professor said about when going to White Clay. He said every time he goes there it is different, but in the end the people always ask him for change. He told me he knew most of them took the money for beer, but in the back of his mind he said they might just get some food. I smiled because both of these are principles of Jesus and the Lakota. Wunsila describes compassion and care, and what I like to say is wrapped in love. When you see a person who is unsika, pitiful or having a hard time, you are to wunsila them. I believe this is the love Jesus talked about. In addition, a Lakota tradition is for the people to work hard and to be able to pull their own weight. When you seek to incorporate these principles which reflect the Lakota traditions and the teachings of Jesus, you can understand they do not contradict. This is where you humble yourself and ask the Creator to teach you.

Throwing of the Ball

Knowing the Lakota have a full culture given by the White Buffalo Calf Woman, it makes me wonder why all of the rites are not being done fully at this time. Today, I mentioned to a couple of Lakota men that I don't hear of anyone performing the Throwing of the Ball Rite. First, it is very physical; and second, it was a great way to teach the young men they need to pursue knowledge and wisdom from the Buffalo Nation. I have seen young Lakota men play games with passion and pursuit. It is great to see the competition and this may be the way our culture has shifted. Okay, back to the Throwing of the Ball. The ball was made from the buffalo. The ball symbolizes the buffalo. This is important because the White Buffalo Calf Woman came as a woman and then left as a white buffalo. The young men stand in the field which represents the Buffalo Nation. They wait for the throwing of the ball. Then a young lady, representing the White Buffalo Calf Woman, turns her back away from the boys and throws the ball backwards. The young men scramble for the ball, symbolic of going after wisdom and knowledge.

Today, Lakota people today do not practice this rite, or I have not seen or heard of the obscure place it is done. Lakota men have turned to the basketball courts and pursue the competition on the hardwood. Not all Lakota play ball but there are many and you see it across the Reservations.

While visiting Asia I understood Confucian culture. The main theme is to set study as a main pursuit. You have probably heard of how smart Asian students are and how they study hard. I believe Confucianism has influenced Asia; many seek knowledge and this is highly valued. Seek it like you would a newfound lover; do it with your heart, soul, and mind. It must be at the top of your list and the way you live your life.

I had a Korean mentor for a bit and he was teaching me new things. When some white missionaries moved in he stopped. Maybe he felt his job was complete or that there was no more room for him. Perhaps this was due to the insecurities or the brash ways of the American missionaries. I do not fully know, but he taught me many things and as a follower of Christ. I must continue to study and seek wisdom and knowledge. So my thought is that we as a people need to implement the pursuit of wisdom and knowledge as a basis for our future. This is not to say we must worship the Great American Bison, but we must seek to understand what our ancestors did in previous centuries. The Throwing of the Ball is symbolic of seeking knowledge and wisdom. School is a great tool to gain knowledge, the foundation of wisdom. As we seek to build the New Lakota Nation, our physical activities need to continue also. I like that name, "NLN". We need to incorporate all activities that make us who we are. Our ancestors valued wisdom and knowledge.

The Plastic Medicine Man
....*from 10-27-09*

There are two pressing issues that have come to mind. When I was sitting with my mom sharing a cup of coffee, she mentioned seeing her dad and uncles come home from the fields. They were taking care of the cattle, and it seemed that my mom was happy to see the men in her family come home for dinner. My grandma Francis made supper for the men after a long day of work. They ate supper and as they finished they got up from the table and were leaving. My mother asked the question, "Where are they going?" Grandma Francis hushed my mother and told her to wait. When they left the house my grandma told my mother they were going out to have an inipi. Of course that brought many questions to my mother, but she was left with the idea it was just something they did without great accolades, but did it with humility.

This brings to mind the deaths of three people in Sedona. I have seen many people write about this issue. Of course many of you remember the "Plastic Medicine Man" writings in the 90s. How they were about people taking our Lakota rituals and making money from people who desired a spiritual experience. Sometimes I would run into someone in Minneapolis and wonder if they were part of the Plastic Medicine Man series. I really do not have a strong opinion of someone paying lots of money for something that should be free, but when people make lots of money (like nine thousand dollars) to take part in a weekend retreat I have to say something. You see, someone taught the Guru of Sedona how to put up a lodge.

I was once told you should not sing Amazing Grace in the sweat lodge and you should not sing sundance songs in the church. It is clear from this statement that we have come to a place in our history where we have both traditionalists and Christians among our people . There are guidelines which will help us in our walks. As a Christian I believe the Bible guides me with my spiritual life and it continues to shape my life. I use the life of Jesus as my guide because he lived a life of humility and eventually gave up his life for the people. No one says anything bad about Jesus because he truly lived to help people. Of course he turned over the tables when there were money changers and people making a profit from the offering and sacrifice in the temple. This should help you to know Jesus saw this as a wrong thing and then he turned over the tables.

There was a controversy over making a curriculum for Lakota Culture a few months back. This has some pros and cons when it comes to keeping our culture alive. Making money is not a bad thing, but how it is accomplished and what the money is used for can become negative. We have many issues in Christendom, and I saw them first hand. I was traveling in Florida and came across a place for a youth ministry. It looked like the white house with a circular drive. It was huge. I shook my head and drove away from the building when I saw the pillars. These pillars looked to be about a hundred feet high. I thought to myself, how much did these cost, and why do they lead to nowhere? These pillars were in an empty field and were purely for aesthetic purposes, a waste of money. I know there are people hungry and starving all the while there are pillars in an empty field for beauty.

We are involved with many changes in the world. I was listening to Neil Cavuto who is a financial expert. He said it was not a question of if we move to a global dollar, but when we are going to move to a global dollar. I do not know how this will affect Indian Country, but we do know we have an eighty percent unemployment rate. This is shocking as the national level is around nine percent unemployment. We need to begin to look at new ways of putting our people to work. We need to realize we have problems, and we need to work on these issues.

We have people around the country performing ceremonies and calling them Indian because there are many people in search of meaning. I find my meaning in my Lord Jesus. He takes away my sin and allows me to live a guilt-free life. I choose to live for the Truth. My experience of Jesus Christ is not unique because there have been many before me and more will come.

Inipi

Jesus told the religious leader no one could see the kingdom of God unless he was born again. Nicodemas asked Jesus, "How can a man be born when he is old? Surely he cannot enter a second time into his mother's womb to be born!" To be born again, what does this mean? If a religious leader could not understand, what hope do we have as untrained people? Of course, Jesus was speaking of a spiritual rebirth, and the religious leader was thinking literally of a physical rebirth. I see that Nicodemas wanted to see the Kingdom of God and wanted to have an eternal life with the Creator. Jesus' exchange was great. It can be found in John chapter three. I have often thought about what would happen if Jesus came across a Lakota man and the same questions were pondered.

For the Lakota, the Inipi is the womb and a rebirth of sorts occurs as one enters and oftentimes is brought to the earth because of the heat. I have heard there are people who end up in the fetal position hugging the earth. Lakota have known for centuries that the first man was made from the red dirt of the earth. I believe Lakota have understood where we have come from in the Creator's hand. But the sweatlodge is powerful when you understand it is a place of prayer and cleansing. Why would anyone want to be cleansed in such a climate? I believe Lakota understood there must be a cleansing as we often become unbalanced. Without going into too much detail, I would interject the inipi comes with spirit calling songs. This is where the Christian and Lakota rebirths differ.

155

When I was learning the Lakota ways and trying to understand more of where I came from, I was given a mentor. He was very gracious. We would talk for hours about the ways. He was my uncle's best friend when they were growing up. He took a lot of time teaching me the ways and trying to help me understand the contradictions of today's society on the Pine Ridge. He is well known, and after years of instruction a question was posed to me. He asked me if I would participate in a ceremony. I remember bowing my head and praying for wisdom. I told him I had complete freedom to enter the inipi, but because of who I am in regard to Native Christianity, I could not. If I did find myself in a lodge, it would be with my brother Terry Mills. I believed it would be a safe place for me to experience the inipi with a brother. Well, that changed my relationship with my mentor. I believe it was for the best as they were trying to convert me from Christian to Lakota. I do not apologize for my decision, and as I have often stated, I will never apologize for my faith in Jesus.

The rebirth is vital to have a relationship with the Creator. "You must be born again," means the Spirit of God must come and bring transformation into your life. The Spirit comes into your life and lives in your heart. I know many people ask how this can be. I do not need a spirit guide to watch over me as I believe I have the Holy Spirit of God in my heart. It is what makes me born again and it is what has kept me intact. I know the Lakota have been under great oppression by Christians and the Government, but I do not bring either of these to the table. I believe I bring the message of the cross and Jesus crucified. He died so I could live, and his blood has purified my sins and washed them. I am no longer unclean because of the precious ceremony Jesus performed to make me clean.

I am aware of the struggles of our people, the way we were forced to become Christian. It is not my way. I made a decision to believe in what Jesus did and taught. The United States Government wanted to destroy a People and their culture. When I was visiting my mother one day on my front porch, she was reminiscing about being a young girl. She lived pretty far off the main road on the north side of Slim Buttes. She was helping her mom with supper, and her father and uncles came in to eat supper after working with the cattle. Once in a while my grandfather would come home with meat and tell my grandmother a cow was hurt so they had meat. My mother thought for sure my grandpa butchered a cow on purpose. After dinner the men got up and left to go somewhere. My mother was hushed when she asked where they were going. After they left, my grandma told my mom they were going out to sweat. They were doing what our ancestors did for years. My great uncles and grandfather lived their Lakota ways.

My grandfather was an Episcopalian and my grandmother was Catholic. So my mom was Episcopalian from my father's side of the family. Of course, I heard his parents were Presbyterian. When my mother and father were married, all of their children were Catholic, five sons and a daughter. I made the decision to leave that religion because I felt it was not sufficient. I fully understand the way our people were made to be Christian. It is up to the individual to decide and now the Lakota people have chosen to move toward the old ways. I have been approached by great Lakota men to join them, but I do not have the freedom because of my views and who I am in regard to the Native Christian Church of America.

There are other Lakota Ministers who agree and some who disagree with my method. The ones who try to mix the Lakota ways are most like people who are not comfortable with the idea of them truly being Lakota. I know of a Lakota man who grew up off the Reservation and uses a hippy method to blend his being a cultural Lakota. His mother is from Rosebud and his father is from Pine Ridge. He came to his roots after Dances with Wolves. He grew his hair, learned some songs and dances, and even started a Christian Pow Wow, which doesn't make sense to me because a Wacipi or Dance is a dance; a dance cannot be anything but a dance. There are some interesting ideas about the Inipi, but it is truly a great ceremony as it speaks to the mind. It has the belief that you must have a rebirth and you must purify. Of course, I believe it is in Jesus.

A wise man once said, you should not sing Amazing Grace in a sweat lodge, and you should not sing Sundance songs in a church. They are different ways and should be kept separated. To lessen the ways is disrespectful.

Hunkapi, the Making of Relatives

Networking is not a new concept to the Lakota. In the 1700s, the Lakota lost a lot of babies. The Oyate (people) decided it was time to come together and figure out why the babies were dying. The leaders met in the middle of the village for some time. When they came out, they decided it was because of the Hunkapi; they were doing it wrong and needed to rethink the ways of performing this vital ceremony. The Hunkapi was given by the White Buffalo Calf Maiden, along with six other rites of the Lakota. These are sacred ceremonies and the people were reverently driven to ensure it was done correctly. They decided a horse's tail should be used and only a Wicasa Wankan, or Holy Man, would perform the ceremony. When they reached a consensus, they came outside. They looked to the north and saw the Spirits; their consensus was confirmed.

When you understand the Hunka and its role in Lakota society, you will better understand the Lakota were inclusive rather than exclusive. A person's skin color or tribe never made the Hunkapi void. Lakota people have innate ability to see the hearts of people. When they took a Hunka, or relative, it was like blood, and the Hunka was considered family. I like the movie Next of Kin because to the country boys, "kin" means a lot more than just family. La familia means the family. If you were a part of the family in Mexican American culture you were protected. I am sure we can go through many different cultures and see how other cultures deal with family. But to the Lakota, Hunka gives a person the same privileges as a biological relative.

I am writing about Hunka because we have a great deal to offer the world as Lakota people. We need to begin to understand who we are and how it affects the world around us. I have many friends in the world. When I think about the Lakota way of life, I understand we need to teach the world how to treat others. Today, some Lakota have lost their way and do not follow the old ways; this is due to the systematic destruction of our beautiful culture. A ghetto has developed in much of our social and economic systems. The United States decided it was in their best interest to destroy who we were, the Warriors of the Plains. But our history and culture is powerful and has a message for the world.

My good friend Mark is Caucasian, but he is truly a Lakota because he has a family. When you see him, ask him who his relatives are. He can probably even reply in Lakota. His family accepts him like a blood relative. It is powerful when you think of Lakota people and know we have a culture the United States could not destroy.

My belief system does not contradict my culture. Some may be frustrated because I believe in Jesus. Jesus has a message that wraps up the whole revelation of the Holy Book. I seek to love Creator with my heart, soul, and mind. The other thing I do, and fail just as much as loving God, is to love my neighbor as myself. Jesus understood as humans we can be consumed by ourselves. Every appetite we have is focused on ourselves. By nature we are selfish, but Jesus told us to be selfless and serve each other. He even went on to wash the feet of his disciples. Our Lakota leaders or Itanca were people who served the people, not themselves. If you find a true Lakota, he or she would be a very humble person. I like to interact and listen to them because they have a unique worldview; most would say they were brought up by their grandparents. John Blunt Horn was my grandfather. I believe he has left important lessons for me to explore. I seek to write about Lakota life in his honor.

Making of Relatives

I have witnessed this ceremony or rite of the Lakota and it is an honorable event. I was a teenager the first time I saw this conducted. My girlfriend's mother wanted to give her a name. I would have loved to say the name but it is difficult for an English speaker. The name given means dependable, or one you can count on for help. I like the idea of the name because it embraces the being of the person being named. I know you may be thinking, you thought this was a Making of Relatives rite. It is, as the woman who named Belle became her mother. My understanding of the Hunka is the woman or man who named you becomes your relative, and her family is to treat you as a relative as well. I believe every time the woman saw my girlfriend turned wife, she greeted her as a daughter. It was a beautiful ceremony, and I more or less stood off to the side. It was very Lakota with a campfire, people waiting to be fed, and there was a giveaway. When the meal was being served, I looked over at a place. I thought it looked surreal. I found out they were passing around the puppy soup. I know it makes you become a bit squeamish, but Lakota usually did this at very important events. When the meal was complete there was a giveaway with beautiful star quilts, and everything you could imagine could be saved for about a year. Socks and handkerchiefs were given to the men. Towels and dishware were often given to the women. It seemed as though everyone received a gift. An eagle plume was given to Belle, and she was made to be this woman's daughter.

Lakota understand the meaning behind relationship, and as culture changes I believe people adapt and develop the ceremony. I have no doubt in my mind that because culture was illegal on the Reservation the people changed some of their ways. As a Lakota family I believe it is vital we develop and realize who we are in our heritage. My daughter Tamara was also given a name which means Strong Willed. I believe it was from her toughness as a young girl, but she is a wonderful young woman. She still has a strong personality; I saw her stand up to injustice even when most other people would not. When she graduated, we had a dinner and small gathering. It was a beautiful day as we also chose another mother for our daughter.

Life brings many hardships. You will be able to read about our eldest daughter; her name is Wankiya Ohitika Wi or Brave Lightning Woman. She lived a short but very powerful life. She loved the Wankiya or lighting and thunder. Ohitika, meaning brave, is the way she lived her life as she walked into the hands of Jesus. The night before she went home there was a powerful storm in Minneapolis. It was the greatest light show I have ever seen. She will greet us when we go home to heaven, and there will be a celebration!

Making relatives is a great ceremony, and I believe it is vital to our survival as a people. I realize the Creator has given us the opportunity to become his relatives. In Lakota society it does not matter how much money you have; what really matters is how much family you have. I smile when I think of the way God provided a way for us to become his children. Someday I will greet my father in heaven and it will be a great day. I believe in the end the gates of heaven will open up to the relatives of the Father God. It is more than my way; it is my purpose to help people understand the gift of life comes from the acceptance of becoming one of God's children. I walk with the Spirit of God, and my journey ends when I am with my relatives... Hetetuwelo. That's the way it is.

The Sundance

Gazing at the Sun is a ceremony performed during the summer months. At one time the Oglala had only one Sundance each summer, but things have changed since those days. I am sure there are at least 60 sundances each summer throughout the Oglala Sioux Tribe alone. In addition, the other sundances performed by other Lakota tribes and places where they have adapted the sacred ceremony of the Lakota. When I was around 18 years old I was not always the best decision maker. I wanted to help out my then girlfriend's family at the Sundance. Fools Crow was a respected elder and medicine man. He could very well be one of the last great leaders of the Sundance. I told my girlfriend yes when her family asked if I could watch over the camp. Of course I wanted to be close to her, and her family was involved in the dance. They told me they would drop me off at the camp and then return with food and supplies. I was happy to be there, but what I did not realize was that I would be without food for what seemed like days. They were serving taniga or guts in a soup with crackers. I do not do guts so I was left with crackers during the evening meal with water. I have been known to be a soda pop drinker for some time, and I was feeling the sacrifice of the dancers who did not partake of nourishment.

I sat there all day in the hot summer sun watching the people and but not really interacting. While I was walking around I came to a little cabin with an old man sitting on the porch in front of the house. I did not know then but later found out that he was Frank Fools Crow. Wow, what a name and an honor to have earned this name. The Crow were our great enemies, and one would assume with the name "Fools Crow" this family was good at tricking the enemy. Initially, I saw an old man but I later learned that I saw a great Lakota Wicasa Wankan. He would help me to understand the way of life for the Lakota. He never spoke to me, or I to him. But in a way words could never express, I learned lessons from this Holy Man of the Lakota. Humility came to life in this man. He could have so much more in the contemporary life of the Lakota, but he lived for the people and not himself. I use Fools Crow to gauge the life of shamanism.

Well, the family returned a few days later, and I was glad to be around people again. Funny thing is I was around people while they were gone, but I did not know anyone so felt alone. I saw the sacrifice of the young men and old alike. I witnessed the songs and can still hear them in my head decades later. I saw the dance and the gazing at the sun. I saw skulls dragging from the piercings in the dancers' backs. One particular dancer was dragging around seven or eight skulls. The skin would not break, so little children were placed on the skulls to add weight. I saw eagles circling and the day was hot with the sun beating down on our brown skin. I walked with my girlfriend to where the women were offering flesh, but my girlfriend would not participate. She was a follower of Jesus and did not feel free to give flesh. These are very sacred ways of our people and I truly respect them. I believe Jesus paid the price for me. I wanted to share my experience with others because I believe it is important to understand the Lakota.

Lakota consider the tree in the middle of the grounds to be the tree of life. Contextualization of the Lakota way of life can be done as there are many correlations and terminology used within Christianity and Lakota way of life. The dancers wear a crown of sage and there is a strong sense of sacrifice throughout the ceremony. I am sure there are a few varied ways of doing things, but I am glad I saw what I did in the early eighties at the sundance. I have great respect the Lakota ways.

Keeping of the Ghost and Others

Keeping of the Ghost is a ceremony that seeks to help the grief of our people. I have seen this practiced in many different ways. It is done with "Wasna" or sacred food, which is a mix of dried meat and berries and also cornmeal by itself. People keep the spirit of a loved one for a set time and offer "spirit plates" of food. The plates are placed outside. It was great when I overheard a Christian question why the food is offered. This person told a Lakota man the dead could not eat the food so what is the purpose of doing this act. The Lakota man said when the Christian stops taking flowers to graves because the dead cannot smell them, he will stop offering food. After the time of mourning there is a wiping away of tears ceremony, and it is a time of letting go.

Puberty Rites of the Lakota are something that is not done as widely across Lakota country. I have heard of times when the older women take the young ladies and teach them about womanhood. I believe it is vital to our community. As Lakota people we have seen the ways of our ancestors attacked through Hollywood and America. It is vital we have a renaissance in the 21st century. The teachings of our elders are important to our young people. The females had the puberty rights and the young men had the throwing of the ball. These are vital if we are going to sustain the life of the Lakota people, two of the rites help the passing on of wisdom and knowledge.

Someday I will seek to be a part of the "Inipi" or the cleansing rite of the Lakota people. I was asked to be a part of this ceremony but at the time I felt I could not do this because who I am as a follower of Christ. The ceremony is beautiful as it takes us back to the womb and helps us to rely on the earth for comfort. The fire is hot and the steam cleanses our bodies, and for Lakota people it cleanses our spirits. Someday I will do this as my grandfathers did in the past and I will honor them as my ancestors, not to be mistaken for ancestor worship.

Lakota people have been inclusive rather than exclusive. People were made relatives via the Making of Relatives Ceremony or the "Hunkapi". I have seen this done in Lakota society and today they usually give the person a Lakota name. Culture is always changing and we can see this through the combining of the naming and making of relatives. Lakota people were often seen as generous because if they saw someone in need and liked that person they would give everything away and make that person a relative. But it was a powerful sight when you saw others who liked the person's generosity and then gave to that person many more gifts. Today we see this ceremony being completed at graduation events and it is done throughout the Pine Ridge. I appreciate the way our Lakota culture continues today. There have been many case studies about the culture, but the one thing that makes us Lakota is being related. It is at the core of our identity and the making of relatives is important because it is the highest value in Lakota thought and understanding who we are as people.

Crying for a Vision

My mom and my Uncle Skooter, who I understand was a bit mischievous, followed a man who would go to the Slim Buttes every year and cry for a vision. I believe in the old days this must have been a sacred moment in a person's life. I was taught in my young years that you did not speak about the Hanbleceyapi. I now know it was not talked about because for many, many years the white government made it illegal for Lakota to practice their religion. That too will be talked about another time. My mother said they were lying in the grass and watching this man go through this rite of the Lakota. They were spotted by the man. He got his belongings together and told my grandparents what the children were doing. They, of course, were in trouble and the man never came back to Slim Buttes.

Crying for a vision, seeking wisdom was usually done with a Holy Man. A blanket and pipe were needed to seek the vision. Only water was to be taken; no food. It took between one and four days. I believe when Jesus went to the desert for forty days he was preparing himself. The devil came to tempt and Jesus told him off. The angels came and cared for him. I see Jesus as preparing himself for life. Many Lakota men have gone up to the hill and sought out wisdom. The vision Jesus had, was to empty himself and deny his HUMANNESS. That may be the hardest test we can go through in this life. "Deny yourself, take up your cross and follow me." Jesus, please make a way for me. Help me to be a seeker of knowledge and wisdom as I seek to not hurt one man.

Help me to deny my feelings, attitudes, wants, and desires. Allow me to walk as a Lakota follower of your teachings. Hecetowelo, or "That's the way it is."

More Reflections on the Spirituality of Lakota Rites

I had the opportunity to go to White Clay. I drove up to six men and yelled out the window. I told them the fastest way to kill yourself is to stop eating and just drink. When I got back to the Higher Ground Coffee House, the Kid (as I call Katrina) put up a saying on the door. "If you want to kill something, stop feeding it". I was blown away by this; I think there are messages in the messages. When I came in the door I saw a Lakota professor from the college. I will not call him an elder, but he would surely work for the experiment of sitting around a table and discussing creation. I shared a few of my ideas. Then I told him about sitting around the table with some Lakota leaders and asking them if they believed there were different or more than one creation with a first man. He thoughtfully shared what he thought about the matter, and I was blown away because it made perfect sense. He told me he believed there was only one, and yet it was like the Sundance and different ways of doing the rites. It meant the same in the end, but there were different ways of going about it. I was not clear on the understanding of the Lakota belief in the first humans coming from the Black Hills of South Dakota, but I like the way the conversation went. I believe the message was important because a Lakota worldview is important to understand if you wish to serve among the people.

He spoke about the Sundance and the fact that everyone had the same goal in mind. What people do in the Sundance is up to them because if you do not prepare for the four days and you dance in the sun for four days, you may end up just wasting four days. Finding the meaning behind the rite is important. The way we do things is secondary to the meaning or goal of the rite. The means are for the people to decide.

165

We discussed the Hanbleca or Crying for a Vision. I told him about the eighties when no one talked about it. It was too sacred to speak of and so it was "hush-hush". Because of the historical suppression of religion of the Lakota, people did not openly talk about the rites of the Lakota. But today everyone talks about spirituality. The Professor told me he sought a vision 20 years ago called "The Hill". He said it was very spiritual with anger, tears, euphoria and peace. I believe the experience he shared was not supernatural, but was a result of his looking inwardly. We must look inwardly to who we are in order to understand truly who we are. That understanding is profound and full of truth.

This brings me back to the beginning of time, when the Creator created the heavens and earth. It should make us humble. We are tempted to see ourselves as separate from the Creator. We believe we can make our own decisions and not be concerned with a Creator. The Creator breathed life into our bodies. Taku Sku Sku is the unmoved mover, the one above nothing. The Creator is the "Great I am". The "Great I am" sent Moses into Egypt to set the people of Israel free. I believe it is a powerful message when you realize Jesus says he is the Great I Am. The Creator wants to have a relationship with us. He does not want us to worship the creation, but the One who made it all.

Thoughts on Creation

I have often thought about creation and how the world sees the beginnings of the human being. Lakota believe we come from the Black Hills of South Dakota. Wind Cave is located in the southern hills and is a good size cave. It is thought the Lakota came from here and were tricked by Iktomni. I thought about this and wondered what a group of Lakota leaders would do if they were sitting around my kitchen table and we were discussing the beginnings of mankind. I thought about this for a long time because I believe it is important to try to understand where we come.

So I talked to a couple people, and out of convenience they thought the Lakota Leaders would say there are different creations or more than one. So following this canku, or road, would lead me to believe there are different species of humans. But that would not explain how we are the essentially the same. So I believe it is illogical to believe we have different beginnings.

I have referred to Taku Sku Sku, the Sacred Mover, before. I believe this is the unmoved mover. It is thought Taku Sku Sku should not be approached because there is too much for a human to understand. I fully believe the Sacred Mover is too vast for our finite minds. When I use my theology and understanding of the Alpha and Omega, I get a glimpse of what my forefathers thought. The vastness of an infinite being is beyond my understanding. Jesus stated he was the beginning and the end and this may help us to understand Jesus as the Creator. The Deity must be characterized by omnipresence, omnipotence, and omniscience which are everywhere at once and not bound by time or space. The Deity must also be all powerful and all knowing. These attributes help us to understand a Being worthy of worship.

To think about creation with the understanding of one creation and one creator helps us to understand we are all human and no different in our ethnic identity. In my quest to find truth, I have found great beauty in creation. I can imagine when Taku Sku Sku (The Mover) created the universe. It must have been breathtaking, especially when the first man walked and his first words were spoken.

Lakota World View

- Came from the Earth: a Cave enclosed
- A Lie= Good Life on Earth
- Trickster: Iktomni also spider
- A Temptation or enticement of the plentiful Tatanka or Bison giving false hope to the First People

Biblical World View

- Formed from the Earth: Garden enclosed
- A Lie=Being like God

- The Earth Was found to be Harsh and not Plentiful

- Serpent or Trickster: Satan the evil one

- After the Fall of trying to be like God and make their own decisions. Childbirth hard/Work the land for food

Re-culturaliztion Holds the Key to the Future

Culture is how we complete our day to day lives; all aspects of a human being are considered his culture. When you look at life on the Pine Ridge and Rosebud, you can see characteristics that make us distinct in the world. We come from a powerful group of ancestors who not only survived on the plains of America, but thrived until the westward expansionism. The greatest threat to the Lakota way of life was the culture of consumption. Appetite is more than a desire for food; it is people try filling a void and struggling because nothing satisfies this need. Our new leaders need to find ways of overcoming the Americanization of the Lakota way of life. The number of our people who are imprisoned is outrageous, and I believe it is because of the Americanization. It is not about having a particular skin color. It is the culture of greed. Lakota understood the ways of the newcomers to the plains and saw this as the takers of the fat.

In the current situation, we Lakota need to fight off the acculturation of the United States. I believe we need to start having more cultural events across our reservation. Pine Ridge Village is in severe need of pow wows and hand game tournaments. Naming ceremonies and the making of relatives need to be done in every community. These are just a few practical ways we can begin to live as the Great Plains Warrior People. We need to begin a new transition from the onslaught of the American Culture. I have studied theology and learned the understanding of culture from many great professors who brought the Bible to life. I do not believe Jesus contradicts my life as a Lakota man. Jesus does contradict the American way of life. As a follower of the teachings of Jesus, I have come to a point in my life where I believe the words of Jesus are the way to freedom. Love God with all my heart, mind, and soul and love my neighbor as myself; this does not contradict my life as a Lakota Man. So, when are the leaders of our whole tribe going to rise up and begin the re-culturation of our Lakota way of life? I will be glad to help in any way I can.

Heart of the Lakota
....from 11-03-09

We have a beautiful people. I was watching an independent basketball game, just to cool off after my game. It featured Tommy White and Wallace White Dress, two young men I am very impressed with because of our common love, basketball. I watched Wallace do a no look pass to Tommy and thought to myself, how did he see Tommy? These guys are such great players. I hope for them because they are truly gold and all that the white man searched for in the 19th century. I was asking about Jess Heart, one of my all-time favorite ballers. A woman in the crowd said she saw him in Kyle. I asked her what the conversation was when she saw him. She told me her aunt asked if Jess was going to Minnesota. My question exactly! Jess Heart is only a step away from the International game of basketball. He is going to be living the dream of every Lakota basketball player! Now that is a great feat for our Lakota Oyate!

I was told by an onlooker of the game being played in Martin, South Dakota, that Jess was participating in the ceremonies of our Oglala Lakota. I was impressed that Jess was now interested in exploring the belief systems of our universe. How powerful is this idea of searching for what our ancestors lived for in the pre-historic years of our own oral history? I was once told to not write anything down because we are from an oral history. We need to record our history because we have moved into a written culture. Jess Heart is amazing and should be celebrated because he is only a step away from the NBA. I believe he can make it to the NBA because I have seen and played against some of the best in the nation.

It has been almost been thirty years since my uncle Manuel

Martin talked to me about the 2012 year. I love my uncle and am amazed he had so much knowledge about the Mayan years. Recently I asked my uncle if he thought it was amazing that, now we sit at the eve of 2012 after his speaking to me about it 28 years ago. I believe the Creator has given me some amazing people to guide me through this journey. Uncle Manuel is one of these men I hold dear to my heart. He explained to me, "We each have a spark in our hearts and this spark is God." I truly believe the Creator has breathed into our beings. Taku Wanka Sku Sku has moved in our hearts and this is the Creator trying to breathe life into our beings.

Throughout the world there are many belief systems. One is animism, which believes there is a spirit in everything. New Agers believe this, as do many tribal peoples around the world. It was said the Sun God was all powerful until the clouds took away the power. The King decided not to tell the masses in fear of an uprising that the power of the Sun could be taken away by mere clouds. My belief is based on a monotheism which simply states there is one God and Creator. I do not believe in a dual creation but believe the True Creator created this world and seeks to know you! How powerful is that statement, when you consider the Creator wants to know your being!

There are some who would have you take a pill rather than have you not know the truth. They are fighting to keep the reality from you. I hope to bring an understanding of the Creator and the relationship the Creator desires with you and your family. It is time for our people to begin to seek truth and not illusion. Illusion can be a deep trail. It is our duty to help people to know the truth. The Creator, who our ancestors sought, is seeking to find you. If you desire to know more about my words or you have been offended, I would hope you would seek me out so we can have a conversation. Dialogue is vital for change. Our Lakota people have lived this way in dialogue and visiting. It is part of our culture to offer food and drink as a way of bringing people together.

Let the Wisdom of the Cangleska Guide our Health
....from 5-25-10

Summer nights bring out the mosquitoes. I do not mind them as much as in Minnesota, as I have seen swarms of the bloodsucking bugs. It is because there is more standing water in the land of ten thousand lakes. Still, I believe it is terrible when you are fighting these bugs and you have to put repellent on; that is not always fun either. Schools are ending and more children will be around and walking so we have to be careful. It is always nice to see young people walking down to the parks and playing ball and hanging out. I remember when I was growing up in the city of Denver; summers seemed to last forever. Every day there was swimming, playing ball, and going downtown to watch all of the people. Summer should be a time of memories that will last a lifetime. Unfortunately, there are happenings around the Reservation. Fighting, alcohol abuse, killings, and a list of other sordid events happen during the warm months of the year and do not help our progress.

Good parenting can make the difference in many of the issues we face as Lakota people. Boundaries are a key to developing a healthy young adult. Making good choices is a great start in child development. Giving in to children is not always helpful and can be detrimental to their maturity because the child learns to manipulate for what he or she wants and pouts when they don't get it. As a parent, no one can be perfect, but you can learn some healthy tips by doing your research. The greatest gift you can give to a child is a book. Books can open the universe to a child that they would not normally see on television or movies. Limiting cell and internet use is a good idea as they need the exercise from outdoor activities. I remember rolling around a used tire and acting like it was my car. I hated when my car was filled with water because rubber and stale water do not smell good.

Our Lakota people have the Cangleska to help us develop as healthy tribal members. When I researched some of the issues we face as a people I can see our ways are important for our survival. We need four aspects in our life to live healthy. Spiritual, mental, emotional, and physical parts of who we are will help us in every part of our lives.

171

We can talk about our social lives and if these four components are healthy we can see our communities growing healthy. Our tiospayes, or communities, will be able to develop and grow stronger if we can work on our health.

Spirituality is important because it helps people to begin the understanding of the Creator. Since the seventies we had an oppressive religion placed on our people. If you were Lakota you had to be a "Christian" which led to some negative effects in our spiritual lives. Since the Freedom of Religion Act in the seventies, we have seen many people turn away from the Government-induced Christianity. Enculturation is where one group places its beliefs and values on another group. It happens over time; it has failed in Lakota Country. Our freedom to believe whatever we want is healthy, and we can begin to search the truth and develop as our Creator wanted for our lives.

Mental health is important because it helps us to make rational decisions. It helps us to understand right from wrong. I believe we need to develop our mental capacities so we can begin to grow our communities. The World Health Organization defines mental health as "a state of well-being in which the individual realizes his or her own abilities, can cope with the normal stresses of life, can work productively and fruitfully, and is able to make a contribution to his or her community." How many of our tribal members do not handle their stress in positive ways?

Emotional health helps us get through our days by dealing with all of the everyday stresses. We can be seen as a people who have had arrows shot at us. They stay in our back and around our bodies because when people say things about us it affects our lives and our state of mind. Maybe we have abandonment issues due to some of the boarding school tactics of the government. Abuse is rampant in our communities and we need to begin to find our health by talking with counselors. Our lives can be more productive and positive if we begin to find our emotional well-being.

Physical health is something we need to tie all of these things together. I believe we can release stress that builds up and can help fight off stress related disease. Our ancestors were in shape. They did things that kept them strong. I once read a book called The Red Man's Gospel. It spoke about our ancestors. It presented the point the United States Government was killing off a more superior race, the American Indian, because of the physical shape and strength our ancestors had two hundred years ago.

Addressing these four aspects of life will be life changing across Indian Country. I truly believe all aspects of our lives can change if we can look into our own ways and develop practical ways of life for our people. I believe suicide would be conquered and our members would become stronger in dealing with poverty. Poverty, imposed or naturally developed, can be changed by finding health. I have had to go through counseling to begin the process of health. It is not going to be easy, but I believe we can begin by humbling ourselves before the Creator and know we can change by His power.

Cosmology

Wow, can you believe I was asked a question whether or not the Lakota were more spiritual than others? Here is my opinion about the spirituality of Lakota. Our ancestors lived in a world they wanted to understand, and they developed their cosmology. They looked around and sought to understand the earth and stars. They developed a complex understanding of who they were with regard to the world around them. They had star knowledge and used the stars as a guide. They knew there were spirits around them and used them in their worship. Taku Sku Sku is more than the English language can handle in translation. I like to use the term because it means movement and it is the beginning of the cosmological reasoning. I believe it Taku Sku Sku has the understanding of cause without cause. The actual beginning or first movement is the belief in the Creator. The teleological argument was most likely used by the Lakota in developing their spirituality to explain their existence as well as all other beings in the universe. Their spirituality indicates they viewed a designer behind the creation of the universe.

Lakota are intelligent just like the rest of the world. There are people who are intellectuals and those who are not. We have different gifts we can bring to a community. I believe one of the areas that we Lakota need to develop is better business sense. When a Lakota succeeds in business many people look at them as no longer Lakota in their thought. Lakota people would often gauge their leaders as providers because they were able to feed their people. Crazy Horse is the greatest example because of his will for his people. He loved them, and they loved him. He led them in battle, and even more, he led them by providing. This is the cultural understanding of the Lakota way of leadership, and it translates into the Lakota way of life. Big Bats is a prime example of providing for people. We need Lakota entrepreneurs to provide and stop the crab mentality of pulling people down. Let's lift up the few leaders we have.

ITANCA

Leadership

A New Year and New Hope
....from 1-05-10

A New Year should bring new commitments and goals. I was watching Escape from Alcatraz with Clint Eastwood and I noticed something in the film. There was an African American man who would deliver books to the other inmates. I thought the movie was interesting when the African American stated, "Here, maybe this will help you," and he handed Clint a book.

When I drive to Rapid City and I go by the Rapid City Library it is great to see people waiting for the library to open. When I sit at Borders drinking coffee and visiting people, I am amazed at the books in the store. If you can attain some of the knowledge in the books on display you will be able to change your future. On the road to Hermosa, South Dakota from Red Shirt Table you will find a newly built library on the right side of the road. Here is a little village on the edge of the Black Hills with a LIBRARY.

My point is that education is important. It will change your future and help you to earn a living for your family. If our elected leaders would undertake the library issue of Pine Ridge we could actually begin to change our future. I know there are programs worldwide to help with literacy, because being able to read is important for future generations. We had one rule in our family that I really appreciated when our children were growing up. It was if our children wanted books we would buy those books. We would visit libraries in Minnesota and South Dakota for our children. It is very important for students to read as much as possible. Of course it takes a little effort, but it is just that, a little effort. Our children are now young adults and hopefully they will do well to stay in college and finish their education.

2010 is an exciting time because I believe we will be able change from poverty to growth on our reservation. Shannon and Todd Counties are two of the poorest counties in America. Ziebach is the western part of the Cheyenne River Sioux Tribe, and the poorest county,

Buffalo, is home to the Crow Creek Sioux Tribe. Can you believe the IRS took land and auctioned the property to the highest bidder? That is absolutely ridiculous with an economy like Buffalo County. I realize the tribe should have put the land in trust, but they did not, which gave an opening for the IRS to call the tribe on debt. These are the issues we need to guard against to prevent further shrinking of tribal lands. I am shocked when I see these types of issues because at one time the Great Sioux Nation occupied all of western South Dakota and beyond. Our understanding of land needs to be updated because of the issues we face as Lakota and Dakota people.

We need to begin to build our reservations like cities. The most basic understanding of city building is to bring people to your city so they can spend their money. Rapid City just stated they were going to receive 1.9 million into their local economy because of the Lakota Nation Invitational. Now, I like the LNI in Rapid City because they have the facilities. It is great to play on the big floors like the professionals. They have the shopping and motels to house all the people. I like going into the mall where you see lots of Natives shopping for Christmas. During the LNI you can see all of the restaurants filled with Lakota people. My point is we need to begin to build our reservations like Rapid City and other cities of that size. I heard President Theresa Two Bulls speak at the faith-based conference. She talked about serving forty-four thousand Oglalas. Now that is powerful because we have a fairly large membership. That does not include the Oglalas who are not enrolled.

Being one of the poorest counties should not be a badge of honor. We need to change our mentalities in 2010. We need to understand self-determination and stop looking to the United States government to take care of us like children. We determine our own fate and we need to build our own future. This future has libraries and tourism. Make these the goals and you will be able to have a foundation of city building. The future will change as our children reach for the stars and the tourism will help develop our economy. We can change our future with this understanding. I look forward to seeing 2010 because a New Year brings new HOPE.

Which way is Crazy Horse pointing?
....from 4-22-09

When I think of April, I remember the saying, "April showers bring May flowers." I cannot wait for May to come because that is when everything is green, and the land does not look so bare and cold.

April is a good month, but always brings to mind tax day. Now, I know most people do their taxes early, but some procrastinators, like me, wait. As in the movie Meet Joe Black, our friend Brad Pitt says, "Death and taxes? What an odd pairing."

It is funny, because Joe Black, played by Mr. Pitt, is "Death" and is pretending to be an IRS agent. The certainties of life are you will pay the IRS and you will die. I know many people who do their taxes the same week their paperwork is received. Get it over with as soon as possible. I wonder if anyone still uses paper and the post office. "Save a tree and e-file" should be the motto of the conservationists.

Death is a necessity of life. If we never saw death, there would not be enough world for all of the citizens. Sadly, too many of our people leave us prematurely. Then we are left with people who do not want to feel the pain of their loss. Often this leads them to medicating themselves to death. It is a sad, hard cycle. I had a conversation with a few people last week about the idea of changing White Clay, Nebraska. The only way you can change it is by changing the "Rez", and that is going to take many people.

I know our relatives who stand in White Clay are not making the four businessmen who sell alcohol millionaires. It is the car traffic that buys the cases and cases of beer. I am saddened, because I know the people are full of pain. So we need to change. When we change, there will be no more White Clays.

Change is difficult, but I was thinking through why alcohol is not sold on the Reservation. I talk to many people, and we all have our views and opinions. But, the bottom line is we have a lot of alcohol on our Reservation. Pine Ridge is legally considered to be a "Dry Reservation," but it is not dry. The Kennedys became rich by bringing whiskey from Canada. When I was a high school student, I did a paper on prohibition. Guess what? It does not work. We have bootleggers all over the Reservation, and people are still drinking. I know we also have people who are sober and living a more healthy life, but all the while, we still have businessmen making money off the pain of our relatives.

My goals are to make our home a better place to live. Having people get rich on the other side of our border is wrong. How many of us go to restaurants where alcohol is served? How many of us go shopping in towns where it is sold? Every one of us that leaves knows there are tons of places where alcohol is served.

I ran into a young guy in Hermosa. He was of European descent, and he told me a joke about Native Americans. He said, "Which way is Crazy Horse pointing?" I said that I did not know. He said, "Toward the beer." Even the young people have a warped sense of humor, or perhaps it is simply a racist view of another people. Many of my favorite Indian people do not drink alcohol; many of my favorite Indian people do drink. It does not change my opinion of any of them.

I thought of a few other things, but they will have to wait. Actually, let's talk about them... I talked to Alltel, and they said they have the equipment for the cell tower in Pine Ridge. So, why don't we have a great signal in Pine Ridge? These are things we need to debate. We need answers.

Why the Tribe does not work on the easy things seems to be a difficult question to answer. I will have to work on some more thoughts today, but know that death and taxes are here to stay. As for taxes, governments need money to run their operations. When you think of more program money, someone is being taxed for it. Rest assured, taxes will come and so will death. These are just points to ponder.

Decriminalize Alcohol
....from 1-19-10

This week we will celebrate the life of Martin Luther King Jr. He was a great man with a dream of a better America. I once marched with the civil rights movement when I was a child living in Denver, Colorado. It was a powerful movement because it brought many people together. I now live in a part of America that does not seem like the United States. We cannot buy a pair of pants or a jacket on the Pine Ridge Reservation. We have very little development, and it is hard to find housing for the homeless. If this were part of the rest of the United States things would change. I have lived in lived in other parts of America and have seen great growth in some areas. But, the one place I see very little change is on the Pine Ridge.

I was listening to KILI radio the other day. They were asking the question, "Why do people start college and leave during or after the first semester?" That is an excellent question. I do not wish to offend anyone, but it is because we as Lakota love our family. That is not to say the ones who stay do not love their families. We are tied to our relatives by our tiospaye (extended families) and tiwahe (immediate family). Being a relative is what makes us Lakota, and when you pull apart the layers of our societies you will find kinship. Oglala Lakota College is a great resource because it allows our students to stay home and work on their education. I went away for college and was gone for seven years, but I would return as often as I could. I worked full time and went to school full time; when it was time to come home I left a job where I could have retired with a good pension. The most important thing to me was coming back to family. To be among my relatives is the place I want to be as I live out my life.

We need to build hope into our communities. This past week, and I hope in the weeks to come, we will see more suicide prevention activities. It is time we start looking at our own problems and face them like we did our enemies centuries ago. We cannot believe the lie that we are less because we are "Indian". We are a beautiful people. Our people have a unique understanding of the earth and the ways of our grandfathers and grandmothers. We have survived on this land for centuries without the convenience of the new technologies. The United States Government agreed to pay for the land in good conscience, and I believe we need to hold them to their word. Not only was it their word, but they signed binding contracts that will hold up in court. I do not listen to the ignorant people that live on our borders because they believe they have a right to our land.

The reservation system is not working the way it is supposed to because we have too much of an entitlement mentality. We need to take control of our homelands. This includes encouraging businesses and other entities that will make us a stronger people. In the little village of Whiteclay, Nebraska there are four businessmen making millions off of the sale of alcohol. The only way to stop them is to stop the flow of alcohol across the border; this, of course, will never happen. People will find ways to bring it to Pine Ridge. I believe we need to decriminalize alcohol on the Reservation and start policing all of the other crimes committed like assault, burglary, and rape. Some would have you believe it will only get worse if we start selling alcohol ourselves, but most of us realize it can't get any worse. We need to fight for the survival of our people, and this problem will never go away. The people who do not drink will not start drinking because it is now for sale and legal on the Reservation. And for those who do, they will continue to make their choices daily.

The State of Nebraska wants to beautify Whiteclay and start a recycling business center. This will never help the situation because people are going to drink. I hope someone builds local businesses on the Pine Ridge because I do not want to buy my clothing or go to the movies in the border towns anymore. We need to establish our own economic development and housing. It is vital to help our young people to thrive with hope that tomorrow will be a better day. If we lose the hope we will lose our young people who, by the way, are the seventh generation.

Little Big Man and the Real Savages

Chief Dan George is one of my all-time favorite actors. Last night I watched him in Little Big Man. If you have not seen this movie you need to because it is awesome. Chief Dan plays Old Lodge Skin. Here is the sage observation, "There is an endless supply of white men, but there have always been a limited number of human beings (Cheyenne People)". It is a depiction of the uncivilized white man, and it gives a great account of the Cheyenne or human beings in how the west was won. Custer's character is brought out with the idea he is a lunatic and thinks if he can get just one more victory he would become the President. In the movie a preacher's wife becomes a prostitute, Louise Pendrake. She says, "Well, Jack. Now you know. This is a house of ill fame. And I'm a fallen flower. This life is not only wicked and sinful. It isn't even any fun". There are great moments in the movie but it has to do with the idea of it is better to be a human being.

When you watch the movie it will help you to understand who the savages really are. It is a great movie made when movies were all about acting and not visual effects. I enjoyed it so much I am going to buy the movie so I can show it to my friends. It is a sad fact that our Lakota people struggle so much today because of the civilization that was imposed on the Indigenous people. We have the keys within our own ways but it will be interesting to see if we can overcome the American influence.

A few years ago I talked about revolution. We need to come together for change, and we need leaders to rise up out of the ashes. I think we need a cause we can agree will be for the betterment of our Indigenous people. There has been talk over the years but it has not touched the masses. One thing I remember brought a lot of people together was the death of two Lakota men in or near Whiteclay, Nebraska. Hundreds and even a thousand came against the treatment and murder of the two men. That was a great movement but it slowly ended after a few marches to the border village.

Dick Wilson brought a lot of people together with jobs and was a force back in the seventies. Of course the civil rights movement brought the American Indian Movement, which was a great cause to fight for because it was needed among the minorities of America. Poverty is such a strong power on many of our Reservations and the ones who are picking themselves up are inundated with the same influences across Native America.

Self-determination
....from 3-9-10

When friends come from all over the country, I am bombarded with questions about the Pine Ridge Reservation. I appreciate the strength and courage of the Civil Rights Activists who put their lives on the line for the benefit of our American Indian people. I was thinking about 1973 when I was eight years old and walking down a street in the city of Denver, Colorado. I remember seeing this church steeple and wondering to myself if I knew God. I know it sounds strange that a little boy would be asking the questions that plagued the greatest minds in the universe. Philosophers have sought to understand the meaning of life, and the role mankind plays in our world for centuries. In 1973 the American Indians were still being eradicated by the policies of the United States Government. Our children were being shipped east and other places to be raised in Non-Indian homes. And last but not least, we did not have the right to freely worship through our religion.

Look, our own leaders need to begin to hold the United States Government to what our Grandfathers fought for in the early history of our people. We are to be a sovereign nation of people, but since the 1970's we have seen very little change on our reservations. We do not have clothing stores, and it is difficult to get good produce. I was talking with a friend of mine and we were discussing the issue that twelve packs of soda pop hardly ever are discounted in our one grocery store here in the Rez. Yet when you go to Rapid City or even Chadron, you can find cheaper prices. Many of our people do not have the means to travel to distant towns to buy proper clothes and food. It is time for us to demand more from our life on the Reservation.

Self-determination is a right that we should have had since the beginning of the Reservation. The Great Sioux Nation was one of the greatest accomplishments of our Grandfathers. We need to understand that we were at one time the richest people groups on the planet earth with all of the resources we could need for multiple lifetimes. I believe this is the key to our understanding when people say we get government checks or we are welfare recipients. Land that was paid with the blood of ancestors was taken, and we were placed in detention centers. The self-determination act was a great movement of the Congress for our Lakota people. I want to say it is ridiculous for the government to say we can now determine our own fate. The reason is because the rest of the country was seeking to get rich in any way they could through the American Dream. We need to grow up and seek the betterment of our people. Stop the crab in the bucket mentality and instead instill hope for the members of our tribe.

I sometimes run into people who were adopted out. They really do need our help. I believe we need to seek to help our children find good homes if they need a place. When the adopted ones find out they are members of the Oglala or Rosebud they often times go into an identity crises. My personal belief is that we need to bring back all of the ones who have been sent off to live with other people groups. The Indian Child Welfare Act is important because the government tried to eradicate our people with policies that did not take care of the children. Losing our tribal identity makes us brown Americans, and that is not good for our tribe.

Finally, the Freedom of Religion Act is important to us. Forced Christianity was wrong, and I am ashamed of any entity that took part in Christianizing the American Indian. Of course, it will never change the fact that I am a follower of Jesus Christ. If people understood Jesus was not a white man, they could begin to understand he stood against the injustices of the world. He came from an oppressed people group and was being pushed into the Hellenization of Greek Culture. He changed the world by telling his followers to pray for their enemies and seek to do good to others. He sought to become a servant of the people rather than be served by the people. He fed people when he knew people just wanted to eat.

I believe it is my right to worship the Messiah. I also believe every man, woman, and child in Lakota Country should have the same right. It is important to note that everyone has a right to believe in whatever they would like. I think these are the paths to true freedom. It is time to start building up our people and thinking about the coming generations. It is time for more conversations so we can plan.

Reconciliation, a Worthy Gamble
....from 2-2-10

I am not a great advocate of gambling. When I was around the age of thirteen I went to my friend's house, and we were sent to go the movies. He was a little older than me, and I liked hanging out with him. We did many things in the inner city of Denver. One of the things we liked doing was playing billiards. Back in the seventies there were many pool halls and pool sharks just waiting for a mark. I was never a mark because I never really had any money. My friend Rick had about three hundred dollars. We were going to go to the movies and to eat some burgers. We walked a few blocks from his house to a nearby pool hall. There were about thirty tables in the room. This guy walked up to us after we started playing and wanted to play a few games. They played for two dollars a game. Rick won a few games in the beginning, but in the end, later that night, we walked out completely broke. My dad, Doug Matthews, told me, "Son the house always wins." Of course he was saying when you gamble, the chances of winning versus losing tip toward the owners of the gambling business.

Gambling is a huge deal in South Dakota due to the video lottery and the town of Deadwood. The Indian casinos are limited in their machines because of the state not wanting their revenue to go down. The way the State does business should be a lesson to tribes. South Dakota lives for tourism, and there are some great things here in South Dakota. The tribes need to find ways of bringing tourists to their homelands. Our casino on the Pine Ridge is the biggest source of nonfederal monies coming to the Oglala. I believe we need to have a destination point to build the source. Here is an idea: maybe we should have a fuel station that sells other items the people would like to buy from us.

Next month, Governor Mike Rounds will be holding a meeting in the Rotunda in Pierre to mark the 20th year of Reconciliation between American Indians and the white Americans. I think it is a great day that the Governor and the Tribes would seek to reconcile their differences in the state. I realize we need to have reconciliation in South Dakota, but we need to build trust in order to have true reconciliation. I met the governor a couple of years ago at the National Day of Prayer at Mount Rushmore. Of course, it was humiliating for me because I was asked to say a prayer at the shrine of democracy. Just before the event was going to start a coordinator came up to me and said I was not needed to pray. Instead I was to come up front, and I was going to have my name announced. I thought that was ridiculous that they would not allow me to pray. This was when I met Governor Mike Rounds. I thought it was nice to meet him. We talked about our philosophical beliefs, and it was a great pleasure. The church needs to be reconciled as well.

It would be a great show of true reconciliation if the State and tribes renegotiated the gaming contracts. It would show the tribes the State would like to sit down and take a serious look into our gaming interests. I would also like the tribes to begin to take a stronger stand on self-determination and what it looks like in the next decade. It is pure and simple when it comes to taxes and revenue. Every time a dollar is spent, the tribe gets four percent. So, if we there is more business, the tribe would collect more money. It is time for us to grow up and become our own leaders. We can work as partners because we are coming to maturity. Our people need money to feed their children. It is time again for us to hear from our leaders. Remember, our votes do matter, and we can vote our elected leaders in or out.

All Roads Lead to the Pine Ridge Reservation
....*from 08-11-09*

We need to change our attitude when it comes to economic development and opportunity. Chadron, Nebraska wants the Heartland Express to be a four lane highway instead of what the Governor is talking about, a super two lane roadway. Due to a lack of funding for the

187

Heartland Express, they would like to scale back. Of course, towns that want more commerce want the expressway to stay as planned because it will bring money into their local economies. When you build a city, or a reservation in our case, you need people to bring their dollars to your community. This will help with our tax base, which is really non-existent in our homeland. Because we do not have a property tax, it is going to be more difficult to develop our Reservation economy.

When I traveled in Asia, I saw people selling everything they could find that people would buy. I like to see people selling in the market place because it shows drive and initiative. But like many years before, the traders in the marketplace are outsiders. It is great to see our people selling food and having yard sales at the first of the month. These are not very well controlled, but it is always good for our people when they do not have to travel to off-reservation towns.

We just finished up the Oglala Nation Fair and Rodeo. It was reported in the Lakota Country Times newspaper that we become one of the most populated towns in South Dakota over the first weekend of August. It was a pleasure to walk down to the pow wow grounds and see so many people walking and pushing baby carriages. How many places in the country will you see horsemen riding bare back around town? It was truly a beautiful picture. The police and security did a great job and were seen everywhere throughout town. Of course, the committee did a great job with the dance and new facilities. It is a wonderful sound when you can hear the heartbeat of the drum into the night.

We have proven we can host a great event with the people we have among us. My point is that we need to start building up our own home. We have many programs that are going to Rapid City to have workshops and retreats, spending dollars that should be kept on our Reservations. It is said we put out about $4-5 million dollars every year during the Lakota Nation Invitational. If you think about those numbers in a realistic manner, you will hopefully conclude we can build up our economy. Those numbers are very small if you took the whole year and saw how much money the Reservation puts into the surrounding towns.

If we do not change our ways of doing business, we will never be able to develop our village. We have millions of dollars going out and very little to show for our spending. It is time to bring people to our place of business and to stop travelling and spending money elsewhere that can help our people thrive here. We have a hotel and conference center at the Casino. We have a motel in Medicine Root District. We have many local shop owners ready to sell their goods and services. Think about the businesses we do not have and begin to dream of a better way of life for the Great Lakota Nation. We have intelligent and professional people who are tribal members and want to step up. It is time to develop our Lakota Nation. Next week I will write my ramblings with the thought if I were the President.

Being President
....from 08-18-09

Being President is one of the most difficult positions you can hold. It requires you to deal with lots of people. A balancing act is probably the best way to describe what an acting president must go through in their daily schedules. I do not believe the job of a President is easy, because a President needs to set priorities and seek to complete his or her goals. People are demanding because we have so many issues plaguing our contemporary culture. We have had many men and two women who desire to lead the Oglala Nation. It is a high calling to lead a tribe in the 20th and 21st Centuries. We have many obstacles to overcome, but if we work together I believe we can be successful in this new century.

Our lives have changed dramatically since being forced onto the Reservation. Some would have us believe we lost the wars of our grandfathers. 1868 marked a year when we as a people defeated the United States. Our ancestors defeated the Americans and were able to force them into a treaty. Most people do not want to admit we have treaty rights. They do not understand the history of the Great Sioux Nation. We were able to bring the United States to its knees, and we won the war. Unfortunately, we were fooled into this new way of life because of the dirty tricks, for the lack of a better description. By 1900 there were only 800 buffalo left on the prairie. At one time there were millions of buffalo. The bison herds were killed off to destroy our food source.

Once our food source was destroyed, which made it easier to force us into concentration camps called Reservations. We became dependent on the rations from the U.S. Government. We were forced to live on land barely inhabitable and this is where we are today. Our lives have changed so much that it has put our whole way of life in shock. We were guaranteed health care and education and the right to live abundantly. But we are battling for our lives every day. It is time we took our rightful place at the table. The Americans have treated us as children or less, and it is time to go back to the treaty obligations. Dependency is a silent killer.

We need more men's groups to help the emotional and mental stability of our fathers. Our men have struggled for many years due to the systematic destruction of our Lakota society and communities. Dignity has been stripped away from our men and this has caused a snowball effect in our everyday lives. Young women are seeking out the father figure in all of the wrong places. Young men do not have enough strong role models to follow and to show them how to be men. We need the men of our tribe to be strong and healthy. When we see our men strong and healthy we will have our communities caring for themselves.

My personal commitment is to strive to build up our people through self-determination. We as Lakota need to take a hold of our own destiny and walk as our forefathers and mothers walked. To hold the United States Government accountable for their treaty obligations is the first and foremost act we should concentrate on in our tribal government. If we succeed at this, we will help our economic structure and social structure at the same time. Moving away from dependent attitudes will be difficult, but I assure you when you experience true sovereignty, it will be the greatest success we will have for our Lakota Nation. Nation to nation status needs to be developed between the Lakota Nation and the United States.

Of course this would be great if I was able to become President, but I have said before I believe I am not smart enough to be President. So I will sit in my arm chair and do the work God has intended for my life. I will continue to pray for our leaders.

Can't Repair a Dam with a Piece of Gum
....*from 5-04-10*

Jesus lived in a brutal world. I thought I would begin with a Jesus statement. I have a friend on the east side of Pine Ridge Rez who told me he reads my columns up until I start writing about Jesus. So I thought I would begin with a brief statement about Jesus. Another friend almost dared me to write a Jesus statement and see if the other friend would actually read the article. We live in a diverse Reservation, and there are many people who choose not to believe in anything. Of course we know there are people hurting because of pain and loss.

This past week we heard about six white students who made some t-shirts and wore them to school. I believe it was a Celtic cross and peace symbol with "Cracker" on the back. The front read, "White Pride World Wide." It was said the community was divided over the issue. Apparently they wore the homemade t-shirts to protest the Native Pride t-shirts and to protest the absurd allegations of white students and teachers being racist. Here we are in the twenty-first century, and this type of behavior exits. We live in western South Dakota and the largest minority group is the American Indian. Let us try to be clear - Governor Rounds, your Year of Unity needs teeth.

Some people thought the 7th Cavalry returned; well I was in meetings in the tribal building so I was not a witness. I have to believe if they have a Native Liaison it must be a Crow or some other longtime enemy of the Lakota. They actually had the audacity to try to land on ground where they killed over three hundred people. Somebody made a bad decision. That would be like trying to make a destination, or I mean an amusement park, at Wounded Knee. We as a Lakota people need to fend off these types of approaches because of what was done in 1890. I have to just shake my head at such a bold move and cannot believe

191

there was no earlier warning about this act. I usually try to keep up with regional news via the Rapid City paper; of course, I did not read anything except for Facebook about the attempted landings.

We are gearing up for the summer when we will see many people come to Lakota Country. Many of our relatives will make the journey to visit and celebrate at many Wacipis (dance or Pow Wows) across the state. We will see three on three basketball tournaments as well as softball and baseball games going on all summer. The rainmaking carnivals will travel through both Pine Ridge and Rosebud. I often wonder why it rains on their weekend, but it could be just a coincidence. When I was young I used to like to walk around and try to win the stuffed animals. Ah, summer is a great time of the year on the Rez. When I see the extreme sports on television, I wonder about those athletes. If they had the challenge of trying to walk through neighborhoods on the Rez and fight off the dogs, they might not be jumping off buildings and perfectly good airplanes. If you think those things will give you an adrenalin rush, try the Wild Horse Race in Manderson.

I ran into my long-time friend Mike, and he told me he was able to get a pair of pants at the trading post in White Clay, Nebraska. We need to build commerce and stop taking our business off the Reservation. It was great to see some dignitaries from the Education Department come to Pine Ridge. I know it is strangely ironic that they were coming to see the new dorm and talk about education. I do not know the current drop-out rate, but we need to encourage all of our students to stay in school. My dream is to one day see our people moving in industry and commerce. Corporations are not the end, but they can surely be part of the vehicle to get us to the destination.

Speaking of corporations, I watched Avatar over the weekend. I was fascinated by the depiction of the corporation because it was in line with what the Euro-Americans did to every tribe on the North American continent. They basically did not care to understand the ways of our people because they were seeking after their god, gold. Or maybe it was just the idea of MORE. We live in a world we do not understand because greed is held higher than generosity.

192

We have the opportunity to make major changes, but it must come from within the people. My message to our people is we need to seek to bring hope to all Lakota. We need to bring hope to our people because they are dying. It is like the commercial where the inspectors are at the dam, and there is a water leak. The inspector takes out his gum and puts it on the hole. We need to bring hope to our people through social change. We need to help raise our children because we have known for centuries it takes a whole village. Something practical for all of the council people, bring the people from D.C. here so they can experience what we do on a daily basis. I will not support going to Rapid City or any other city for meetings unless it directly benefits our people. We need to stop spending tribal dollars off the Reservations. Change starts by making the effort. Buy Local should mean we buy local.

Buy Local....Empower the People

I seek to speak and write from the heart with the desire for people to judge my heart and not my misspoken or misunderstood words. I write for the Lakota Country Times and they want to stay positive. I do not want to put them in jeopardy, and I seek to stay positive. Still, some may complain about my words. When I did radio I would sometimes say something a tribal official would not like. One time I must have offended a chief because when he saw me, he started in on the words I spoke. My only reply was, Itanca (or Chief for a lack of a better word), I would hope you would judge my heart because sometimes my words do not always come out the way I meant for them to be heard. I watched him walk away, so my friends and readers I hope you would judge my heart and understand I want more life for our Oyate or People.

Someone asked me if I was happy with the election, and I guess I do not know how to answer this question. I have not seen a change in the coming General Election. We need people who can govern and stay focused on what is at hand. We have a poverty level that is outrageous and if any other place outside of an Indian Reservation had the same situation, you would see revolution. We have people starving for nutritional food yet we have people traveling to Rapid City and beyond spending thousands of dollars on workshops that do not help. Okay, we understand there must be some travel, but we have people who are not healthy because they lack a good diet. In America it would be normal for a Euro-American family to sit down for a meal and hear the parents say, "Eat your vegetables because there are people in Pine Ridge starving for nutritional food." Yet we have millions of dollars leaving the Reservation every couple of weeks because we have no proper supermarkets. We have a store in Pine Ridge Village where the prices are sometimes three times higher than other stores in the surrounding communities. We see people from Nebraska driving to work on the Pine Ridge where we have an 80-90% unemployment rate. Food is essential to our survival; yet we see our elected officials traveling all over the country and not doing anything to meet the basic life necessities of our Oglala People. I would love to make this a project of change and start to make people accountable. I worked as an assistant manager in a grocery store. I know the amount of money that is made by grocery stores. We have enough people on the Reservation to rival Rapid City in the coming years with regard to population.

Last year the Chamber of Commerce was awarded a buy local grant. At the end of the year dinner in Spearfish Canyon, the Chamber celebrated "buy local" and patted themselves on the back. Maybe it is just me, but I believe we have the casino and Kyle with motel/hotel rooms on the local Reservation. Why Spearfish Canyon? We need to build for the 21st century. We could have a soft drink or potato chip warehouse, and it would provide jobs. We have an overabundance of land not working for our people, and we need to change our future. On January 4, 1975 the Self-determination Act was passed by Congress. No longer would we see the government looking to terminate treaty obligation. Now it would be up to the tribes to work with the BIA to contract services and to have a say in the future, giving us the right to become human beings. We have been in captivity for too long and now many of the old people are gone; we have been born into this way of life. We need to start developing strategies of change, and local should mean local.

Policing is vital, but people are upset because they have been caught speeding. We need to make our roads safe for all people. We need to slow down. Unfortunately, we do not have the resources to police the roads effectively. We need to allow the Chief of Police to do his job without repercussions from the tribal council. Stay out of the way or do not call because someone you know goes to jail. We need to legalize the sale of alcohol, but we do not need the tribe to own the stores. People would take advantage or steal from the stores if the tribe owned the business. We as a people need to have the opportunity to go into business for ourselves. If the Council wants to shut down Whiteclay, Nebraska, we need to open up the sales. Look, we have four million dollars going into Whiteclay yearly, and that is not counting the other communities around the Reservation. We need to own our problem, and stop the drinking of hair spray in the alley behind Sacred Heart Church in Pine Ridge. I wonder if any of our leaders ever walked through the alley. It is a bad area for chronic alcoholics. This needs to stop and we as a people should have the right to police and legislate against of the sale of harmful products to our citizens.

Stop interfering in the everyday activities of program directors! Allow every tribal worker to show they are doing their jobs and have the directors review the performance of each worker. Qualified workers are hard to keep because we have people governing who have little education. Legislate a higher standard. Do not let someone without an education direct or oversee million dollar programs. We most likely have people in place that do not know what they are doing in their positions. Performance is important because you will be able to track what is being done on a day to day basis. It is time we put our minds together and develop the Oglala Nation.

We need jobs. It is difficult because we do not have a good track record, but I know there are people who would like to take a chance on the Oglala Lakota Nation. We had around 60 people go to jail for the sale of cocaine in the past couple of years. They made millions and this is the reality of our people. We can run business and we can run our own lives. We need empowerment not a hand out. It is time to change and develop as the great people we are. We are the Oglala Lakota.

Political Monster or Machine

I am getting excited because we are on the threshold of a new tribal council. I do not know if anything will change in the next administration, but it is always fun to listen and take in the promises of change during the election.

A few years ago, I was involved in an election. We talked about honesty and integrity, which I thought was important at the time because of the council in power at that point. I do not know why I was thinking about running for office; maybe it was my ego. I have not done a lot of study on ego because it is from Freud. I do not follow the psychology based on wanting to have sex with a parent and all of the other crazy ideas this man had. I am sure some of the information can be used, but you really have to glean the information. I follow a different way, and it begins with the nature of man. I have gotten into arguments with some great people because we disagreed on a key point in life. You could talk about id, ego, and superego all you want, but what you believe in the development of humanity is important.

Total depravity or total corruption is an understanding that helps people to know we need a savior. People across the globe are imperfect. They naturally are selfish; you do not need to teach people to seek after their own interests. Instead of serving the Creator they serve themselves and place themselves as lords of their own destiny. All men need a savior, and as I have grown older I understand we are desperate for a change. Jesus has been the change in my life.

What does all of this mean? It means political leaders are naturally for themselves and their interests, which destroys morality and integrity. This is not to say people cannot do good, but their inclination is to do for themselves. As a follower of Jesus for thirty-three years, I have understood that there is a battle between the old nature and the new nature when it comes to people making good choices. It begins with understanding you have to have a new life. The Lakota at one time celebrated spring as a new life because of the blooming of the plants and the fields coming back to life. I suppose it is good the elections are in the fall because of the change that comes every year in the spring. I like the concept of the Inipi, or sweat lodge, because it too promotes an understanding that you must be born again. If the Inipi, our purification ceremony of the Lakota, was properly contextualized or looking for opportunities to share the message of Jesus we might have had a different environment within American Indian societies.

Eternity in the Hearts is a great book about looking for ways the Creator has imprinted himself in cultures around the world. Lakota people have understood the concept of being born again as you enter the Inipi, and the water is poured on the hot rocks the steam begins to cleanse the body. It is said some drop to the earth in a fetal position because of the heat. When the rite is over and people leave the lodge, it is like being born again because of the fresh air hitting the skin like when a baby is born. The Lakota rite of purification is a powerful rite of understanding there must be a rebirth.

So when you see people running for office you need to ask yourself if these people are seeking to be selfish or if they have the People in mind. We are people who have had leaders with the interests of people in our history. When you begin to understand the nature of man and the development of society you can understand the saying, "A little power totally corrupts." I do not believe I am smart enough to make positive changes in Tribal Government. Many people ask me why I am not running. The main reason is that I do not believe I can make positive changes in this world of corruption. So instead, I share my faith and focus on freedom and peace. Plus my wife won't let me, but actually I am very busy with my own life and hope to help where I can.

What Changes a Man

I have heard it is women who carry the most influence over men. I have also only heard in my sociological studies there is only one obscure culture in the world where women make all of the important decisions. The way the country is at this moment, some people believe women should be in charge! We now have had two Lakota women at the highest level of our tribal government. I am not a strong advocate of who should be in power. I believe there are people in both sexes who can make good decisions for the Oyate or People. I know both of the women that have held the highest level in the Oglala Sioux Tribal Government.

Cecelia Fire Thunder is most likely one of the strongest women I know. She speaks around Indian Country. I know she is an avid book reader; maybe she will read my book. When I first met her I was doing a radio show called Pine Ridge Ministries on KILI Radio. Cecelia would come on after me because I started a job working at the High School in Pine Ridge. I had the eight o'clock time slot on Fridays and when I moved, Cangleska moved to my old slot time. We had many good visits and still are very respectful of each other. I loved listening to her because I knew she was a fighter for what she believed. I believe she was a bit more toward the liberal side than me, but it did not stop us from warm handshakes. I respect her to this day; I just don't believe in what she does. Because we are both Oglala and American, we have the right to have opposing views. I know we will visit again somewhere down the road. I believe it will be when we least expect it.

One day, I was coming home from a trip went outside of the Rapid City Airport 1 for some fresh air. I traveled down the escalator and went right outside. There was Cecelia. She gave me a hug and said, "We need to make sure Theresa gets into office." She was campaigning for who she thought should be in office. I was on the opposite side of this election than her, but I just smiled and went on my way.

Theresa Two Bulls commands a lot of respect from being in and around the tribe for a very long time. She went through the ranks of tribal government and is a great lady. I appreciate her ability to get things done in a very difficult place. Both of these elected Presidents of the Oglala Sioux Tribe should be praised for the work they did for the Oglala Lakota people. Strong women are in leadership and in directing our journey.

Alex, Harold, and John are great men in their own respects. I have tried to help when I could and I have developed friendships. I believe it is important to help your sitting Presidents. I walked with Harold Dean Salway to White Clay, Nebraska when it was over 100 degrees. I have tried to be available for John, and, of course, I went to work for a day with Alex. I did not feel the freedom to work for Alex White Plume but I respect him very much. John F. Kennedy said, "Ask not what your country can do for you - ask what you can do for your country." I hope I can serve my tribe and country if God allows me to have the freedom.

Women have a close connection to all people because they have natural love for people. It is uncommon for a mother to leaves her children. My view is we can have both men and women as leaders. We have to seek out the best candidate in each election. Our lives on the Reservation have been radically changed due to the tearing down of the family and extended family. I understand what was done to the American Indian family. It is truly one of the worst acts of humanity. They thought they were saving us, but in the end they were killing us. Of course, as a follower of the teachings of Jesus, I must live understanding of the destruction the white Christian brought upon the Lakota and other tribes. I know this may offend, but it is what has taken place in our last 150 years. And now I seek to help people through this pain. I believe when both men and women actually perform their roles lives can be changed.

Sacred Ones

You hear empty promises every election year, and people just keep getting away with it. I know there are some people who actually do work for the betterment of our future and work with youth in many capacities, but come on; we need solutions to the problem of youth suicide. One young man told me he would be willing to give a lot of money to a prevention plan, but there is not a plan of attack. A one night or week long concert will not affect change in a youth's life unless there is a change of direction. I see youth and children who have no boundaries; they are running all over the Reservation. Some are as young as four or five, and if life does not change, they will lose hope in a better life.

I remember having to be in bed by ten o'clock in the evening when I was in high school. I do not know if that was because my mom wanted peace and quiet or if she was teaching us the value of boundaries and bedtimes. I thank God for my mother, and her raising ten children to the best of her ability. I have been thankful for many years for her guidance and willingness to let me leave home at the age of fifteen. I could not see myself finishing up my high schooling in the big city and am grateful for the opportunity to finish as a Pine Ridge Thorpe. I like the fact that we have a strong tradition of Thorpe Pride even though many people love to hate us. You will never understand because it is a Thorpe Thing. Sorry, I got off track with my Thorpeness.

Okay, back to when politicians use the wankeja, or sacred ones. I believe they know it touches our souls, and they use it to get votes. It has become a way people have tried to manipulate votes out of the people. I believe you will know when people have the interest of people because it will be seen in what they do now. It is not just a future promise. Our desire to see hope built in the children is real, but do not let people fool you by saying they have the answers. If they did, they would have already implemented the ideas, and our youth would be on a good road. We need people who are willing to work with children and youth to put feet to their words. Empty promises of solving issues should not be a norm. Instead, the people fixing the problems should ask how to come together to build a future of hope instead of despair.

It was funny. Last week we heard the woman who is running for U.S. Congress say in a commercial that she was going to balance the budget. One woman from South Dakota is going to fix the United States of America's budget. We laughed because that is absolutely outlandish. Maybe she could fix the budget for her town, but to take on such a task is ridiculous! Don't let people make false promises. Give me one issue you can fix, and let's start with that idea.

True Leadership for the People
....*from 10-16-08*

Now that we are finished with the primary election of the Oglala

Sioux Tribe we need to turn our attention to the General Election. The list of candidates is smaller and now ready for the scrutiny of our people. We have talked a little about leadership and how it affects our lives. We must now seek to identify our voting choice.

The top two choices for President and Vice President have their voting blocs set, and now it is up to the people who did not vote and the ones who cast their votes for other candidates to make the decisions. My hope is we can find the best possible candidates to lead our tribal government in a meaningful manner. I want to give my appreciation to each candidate because it is very difficult to run a tribal government in the new century.

Many people have commented on my new column, and I would like to thank everyone for reading my words. We have many difficult days ahead of us. The Department of Public Safety is still making front page news in Rapid City. We have water, unemployment, commerce, treaty, and a gamut of other issues that will not go away in the next term. I have stated time and time again these issues did not happen overnight; it took decades to bring us to this point. I was talking to a few people at the coffee house; we discussed the past, present and future of our Reservation. We had a public swimming pool, a start of a golf course, a drive in, soda shop, arcade, movies at the high school and I am sure this is a small list of the things we had before. So where does this leave us?

In the near future we could most likely predict an economic breakdown that will destroy our people. Although we have seen gas prices go down significantly this week, this will not last, the experts say. When oil prices go up, food prices will rise. World hunger and famine will increase once again. We saw a huge price increase in milk this year, and if you were keeping tabs of your grocery receipts, you too know that we are all paying a lot more for food. The problem with the rising price of oil is that we pay for it in all areas of our economy. Transportation costs are very high and this leads to higher prices in goods and services.

In light of all this, what are we looking for in our tribal candidates? I have already spoken about the need for change. We all know this! And, we know that only we as a people can bring good for us and our children. I would like to see more networkers, people who can relate with others and build success for common goals. For example, our housing problem is a major issue. Our leaders need to be able to connect with people who would like to help us with this problem. I will explain myself. Banks are uneasy about lending money to our Reservation. We need to have increased ability for businesses to collect debts. It is already difficult for banks to collect a mortgage with the shortcomings of the economic woes of the world. Here is another example. If two people come to you for a loan and you know one guy always pays you back and the other never does, who will receive your money? Exactly! If you cannot get your money back, eventually, you will stop loaning to this individual. The court system needs to be strong enough to make someone pay what they owe to the banks and the businesses. Our next leaders need to be reformers of our judicial system - allow it to run without interference. A tribal council person should not call the police to tell them to let someone go. Accountability at all levels needs to be instituted as a means to a successful courthouse and community.

We are our own worst enemy in this area. We have a strong cultural conflict. We want to take care of our tiospaye. We say this at all our meetings. This is also taught in our schools. And yet, when we allow them to get away with wrongdoings, we are not helping them! We are actually destroying our families when we prevent the law from seeking to correct actions that are destroying themselves and our reservation. Other places call what we have seen in the past corruption, leaders interfering with the law. Do we not see the difference? Loving our tiospaye does not mean letting them get away with things. True love for our people helps them to be held accountable for wrongs. Long, long ago, our leaders understood this well. Young and old were often cast out for a time or for good, to pay for crimes. Shame was also a vital part of our way of disciplining.

Our leaders need to be people who can get things done. We need to move away from micro-managing and begin establishing stronger laws. If we had stronger leadership things would fall into place. I feel that we are building a house of cards, and we need to strengthen our foundations. We need leaders who will accept the help of people in America in the hope that it will begin to change our whole system.

It is time for our people to take a stand for a stronger government. Our leaders need to think of others before they think of themselves. They need to humble themselves and allow people to be held accountable. We need to have meetings in each district for sharing our hopes and dreams of a better tomorrow. If our leaders cannot project hope maybe they should not be running for office. Look at each candidate and ask yourself if they will be able to help the whole tribe. Each candidate is a representation of their families. Transparency is needed so that we can see what our council is doing. We need a Revolution. This will be my topic next week.

Wanted: A Revolution

The American Revolution changed the course of the world. A newly formed government would emerge, and just over two hundred years later the United States of America would become the strongest nation in the world. Of course, it is not a perfect place as we have many struggles and different views. But with many of the imperfections we have freedom of press, which I thank God for, because it gives me the ability to write without concern of being jailed for my views. We enjoy voting privileges and the opportunity to change our communities. We may be at the most important political race of our lives. Russell Means and Theresa "Huck" Two Bulls will face off in our tribal election and Barack Obama and John McCain will contend for President of the United States. The times are dire and it will be vital for the next leaders, both in the National and tribal elections, to be able to get us through these troubling times. Remember leadership is all about influence.

My desire is to see our people thrive in the next decade. As a spiritual people we should be seeking the strongest candidate who exemplifies change. We need leaders who will make the changes to the system, which are needed. Revolution as defined in a common dictionary is, "An overthrow or repudiation and the thorough replacement of an established government or political system by the people governed." A couple of years ago I told a person who served on the tribal council we needed a revolution. Reconstructing the whole system would help our people to begin to see change in their everyday lives. I believe this is what is best for our whole people, not just a few people. I have been around long enough to see the politicians act like the mainstream; what I desire is a group of people who would like to see change in the everyday lives of our Lakota people. This means we will see our leaders act on behalf of the people. And this is why we need to speak and write about a revolution of ideas and acts that will change the makeup of our Lakota Nation.

It will be our people who will overturn the system that has held our local people in bondage. You see, it is not the United States Government. It has been the local candidates who have held the power to change, kept us from building a stronger Reservation. We have shot ourselves in the foot, when our educated people run for council positions, and we have not voted for them. This stops the progress we need to change our system. I know I may be preaching to the choir, but it is vital that we seek to find change that will feed our people. I realize we have some Lakota leaders who are seeking the good of our Oglala Lakota people, and they should be praised; but, until we see change they will always be suspect.

Revolution is what we need! We need people who will work for change and see it though till the end. Change is the desired affect we the people want and it must come from the People. I desire a place for our college students to work. When they finish college they need a home where they can provide for their children. Sitting Bull stated, we need to take the best of the Americans and this will help us. In talking to a lawyer he said that we have the power to draw from the American and the Lakota values to make something new and better for our people. How powerful is this, as we seek to change the world. We can change the world if we work together. Lakota people have been around for a long time and a change of the old needs to be implemented.

Now I realize people are thinking to themselves, how can we change? We can change ourselves and when this is done we can begin to influence people around us. The power of the pen is powerful and we can write about a better life. People need to rise up from the tribal districts and demand change. If the Council and President ignore the voters, we the voters need to oust them. Get involved in what decisions are being made at council meetings. Demand time with the Council and President and the rest of the executive board. I hope we can begin to have meetings in all of our communities. In the end it will be our responsibility. It is time to stand for change. Revolutions have begun because people get tired of the way they are living. I hope you are tired of living in poor conditions. I know I am tired of the poverty. We need to change ourselves, our communities, our districts, and our tribe. Our children will thank us.

Personal Finance for Elected Leaders

I was shopping for dinner one evening and I had a friend stop me. He started talking to me about some issues he had with the election code. He informed me that some people were actually upset because it cost eighty dollars to have your name put on the ballot. You also have to have a background check and get a hair follicle drug test. This test costs more money than the urinalysis that was required before. I told him I was not comfortable with people who could not come up with the money to get on the ballot. I would be more comfortable with people who could manage their money. Of course it is important, and if you do not have eighty dollars, how would you expect to manage millions of dollars?

During our Pine Ridge Village forum in 2010, there were a number of people who did not show up for the forum/fund raiser for KILI Radio and The Walk youth group. I heard one of the candidates talk about the class issues of people with money versus the ones who did not have money for a hair follicle test. Again, I stated that I am not comfortable with people who do not have money and then would expect to get into office and be responsible for millions of dollars. I am not rich, nor do I have even have tens of thousands of dollars in my bank account, but I do have a couple hundred dollars. My point is, people who cannot manage their own money and want to handle the people's money should not try to get into political office.

I am shocked that candidates do not use radio, which is on the

205

World Wide Web and broadcasted across the Reservation. We had two council people come back from meetings hundreds of miles away because they know the importance of being on the radio. Local access to the radio can be a powerful tool if you want people to hear your platform. You may reach people who may not be able to attend a rally. We have many problems, and I believe it is important to be able to manage your personal finances. I know sometimes people get into trouble, but it is vital to have people in office who are equipped to make good decisions for our people.

If We Build It They Will Come
....from 12-04-08

When I went to college I did not fully understand how it was going to change my life. Although I feel like the same person, I know I have been changed by the education I received.

My favorite classes were with a Dr. Caston because he challenged us with the culture of the Bible. Understanding the culture would help us to see the meaning behind the scriptures. I also took a class called Hermeneutics, a process of biblical interpretations. I actually got a good grade in this class and felt like I left the class with a stronger understanding of scriptures. Classes were great. I enjoyed sitting and listening to some professors. Philosophy stretched my mind with what seemed like endless possibilities.

I feel better about myself because of education. I believe it has helped me to break down information and understand it in a more profound manner. My point is, we have many students and graduates here and we need to build a strong society for them.

Our lives on the Reservation are complicated. There is a struggle because of a lack of direction. Dreams are vital to any people group because they set the path needed to accomplish goal. I would not say we should pursue the capitalistic way of life, but we need to accomplish goals so that our young people can build a life on the Homeland. My vision for our people is to adapt to the ways of a global economy where we can be a part of a better life. This means we will have jobs for our young graduates.

One simple way to help the economy for Pine Ridge Village is to slow traffic down. Highway safety is a must if we are going to bring dollars to the Reservation system. Have parking on Highway 18 to slow the non- Pine Ridge drivers and allow them to see businesses. More stop lights are needed so people will not be driving fifty miles per hour in the business districts across the reservation.

People live for the Lakota Nation Invitational basketball and wrestling tournament. This event alone brings $5 million to the economy of Rapid City. This $5 million eventually goes around the Rapid City area seven times, making the LNI a $35 million business. The hotels raise their prices, and we pay it to watch our student athletes play for bragging rights. Now do not get me wrong, I love to attend the event. The grand entry is a powerful view of the magnitude of our Lakota culture. But, we spend millions of dollars on a weekend that strengthens the Rapid City economy. I like Rapid City, and believe we should use their model of how to build a strong economy. They have basketball games, rodeos, pow wows, and now hockey games bringing dollars into their thriving economy. I know of a builder who continues to build houses, and it does not look like the market will slow. They are continuing to build houses and growing their economy.

We need to be like the Rapid City Chamber and bring dollars to our reservation; after all, we are the Oglala Lakota Nation. People have a heart for Pine Ridge, and we can build on this as we are a great Nation. If we build it they will come.

As the new Tribal Council comes into office, they should know many are praying for them. We desire a stronger nation, and the Council holds the power. President Two Bulls has a difficult road as well and many will pray for her. Prayer can change the lives of our people. Rev. Cecil Weston stopped by the Higher Ground Coffee House last week and shook my hand. I was moved by this great elder. He has carried the torch of Christ for many years. I pray we can use his prayers as a beginning to help our Oglala Lakota people.

I would like to publically thank Rev. Weston for his support of me and my family. Thank you. It is great to see the elders with all of their influence. I have many great memories of elders speaking to me. I would like to thank all of the elders for their wisdom and graciousness.

A Library for Pine Ridge

Okay, I thought I would write a few things about my library experiences since everyone went to bed and won't talk with me. When I was growing up in Denver I remember my sister brought back some tapes from the Denver Public library. I tell you this story because I was framed. Someone taped their voice over the story, and I was the only one in the lineup. It sounded like me, and I thought it was me, but of course I did not destroy the property. My mom drilled me, and my sister was there. She was very upset because she had checked out the tapes. The truth had to come out, and we found out it was my brother Wally. Man, I thought it was me, but I guess that is because we are brothers. I still have issues about that event, but I am better now. I really did get in trouble because I was falsely accused.

I have another story. I had a little pickup truck when we lived in Minnesota. My wife would take the girls, and they would check out tons of books. They had a crate they would take to the library, and they would come back with all these books. My oldest daughter Kay was a great reader, and she loved books. Well, they went to the library and came back. We forgot the books in the truck. Well, it rained and we ended up having to pay for the damaged books. Would I do it again? Of course! I would buy my girls any book they wanted. Reading is vitally important to any society. Here in Pine Ridge people get upset because Red Cloud High School requires their ninth graders and transfer students to read at a sixth grade level. I believe the bar is too low, but it is what they set so they can have a standard.

I love libraries and built my own library of books. I continue to

208

refer to my library when I have some questions. I read a few books when I am not writing, and I have a few favorites. I have a big philosophy book I like to read to keep my mind sharp.

I was thinking about this idea because I was in a conversation that ended abruptly due to misunderstandings, but I am sure things will work out. I believe God puts people together to accomplish his goals. Do I believe God wants a library for Pine Ridge? Absolutely. I believe it is important because it is one way he chooses to communicate with us. If people cannot read or comprehend what is being said, then we are in trouble.

So, I was thinking tonight about MORE and what that would look like. I know people will misunderstand more. It would be an adventure and if people would come together it could get done. I think it is a worthwhile project. We have to have trust. I believe the best place for the Pine Ridge Village Library would be by the Episcopalian property. The property has not been used, but I believe they might be influenced by some important people. We could have meetings, and I know the church would meet with us at a local level. A level of trust would need to be developed. I am willing to work on this project and need help. I believe reading is one of the most important things we can give to our children. Ah, the possibilities are endless adventures. But first we need commitment and people not falling asleep on the project.

Pro-business and Pro-Lakota
....from 10-06-10

At the time of this writing I have no idea who won the Oglala Sioux Tribal Primary election. I have been speaking to many people about the changes that need to happen in the next two years. We have heard the promises of some of the candidates and how they are going to have certain goals for the two year term if they are elected. Suicide has been talked about because of the high rate we have seen grow among our people. Also the gang issues are a talking point. I see the issues we face have become epidemic because of what has happened over the last century.

We have seen our people pushed on the Reservation system, which is really a concentration camp from the nineteenth century. I understand what people mean when they make promises, but the problems persist because it is difficult to make change in place that was never developed to succeed. This has been the problem with politicians, and their wish to make our homeland better. I know people have good hearts when it comes to promises, but usually we see people fail because they do not know how to get things done. Two years will pass, and people will continue to work in a system that is broken and not meant to succeed. We need to work outside of the government, and also work to change the everyday life on the Reservation. This means we need outsiders to help with the changes.

I have been home since 1995 from college and very little has changed. Yes, we have a great casino and hotel, but we have yet to see it thrive with outside dollars. I have known for some time we need to get people to Pine Ridge to spend their dollars because it builds economy. I believe we should work on issues we can solve and develop our communities to a place where we can make people feel safe. I believe there should be more policing of our roads to make them safe for everyone. That includes our relatives and people who visit the Pine Ridge. We have so much to offer the people of America; we need to make sure our homeland is safe for people. No more speeding and driving while intoxicated should be the first issue the tribe council deals with. Public safety is vital to any community, and we need a strong police force which actually polices our communities. We need our officers to be able to do their job without repercussions if they arrest the "wrong" person. If people do the crime they need to be willing to do the time. People need to be responsible for their actions and not be let go because they are related to a certain person.

Another goal we can have for our leaders is to bring libraries to our people. We need to learn as much as we can from books. We need our children to read. We had a rule in our family; if our children wanted a book we would buy the book because books give us knowledge and help us to change our future. Education is vital, and we need libraries to build our communities. We may have forty-some thousand people, or even if we have less numbers do not matter, because we still need libraries to grow our people. I believe people would help from all over the country, and I have written about this before. It is still important. We as the Oglala Sioux people need to understand there are things we can change but until we meet certain goals, things like gangs and suicides and unemployment will always be with us.

Job creation is difficult, but you must understand there are people coming from Nebraska and working here full-time. This takes jobs away from our people. We need more grocery stores and other businesses our people use in the surrounding communities. Clothing stores would be great as we have to travel many miles just to get clothes for our families. There are other businesses such as banks that need to be built on the Reservation. There must be a willingness to have two, five, ten, and twenty year plans to build our home.

One of the aspects I would like to get away from is a county system of government because we have the Oglala Sioux Tribe which is a sovereign Nation. The county system is the interest of the outside entities that would like us to give up our treaty rights. This is not a good move for our Lakota people. We need innovators of industry to bring jobs, not more state regulations. I believe our people can run their own government, but it must be with the idea that we control our destiny. Better yet, God should control our destiny. I told Jason "Jake" Little the other day that I am glad I try to live by the standard of Jesus. Without such a standard I would be a terrible person. Jake is working on his education, and it is a good thing to do. Keep up the good work Jake!

Here is the Hot Topic of our day. Legalizing the sale of alcohol has come up in some of the talk across the Reservation and here is my take. I believe the tribe should issue licenses and have businesses buy them yearly to control who is able to sell alcohol on the Pine Ridge. I do not believe the government should get into the sales because it should be owned by a person who will control the stock. The government should be the ones who regulate and make laws governing the practice. The taxes should go to our tribal government not states. I am tired of seeing non-Indian people becoming millionaires because we refuse to get our heads

211

out of the sand. It is documented.... prohibition does not work! When alcohol is legalized, crime goes down.

Tribal Government is expensive and we do not have a money tree. We do have the ability to make our own laws and destiny. Pro-business and Pro-Lakota should be the rally cry of our people. Networking is vital because there are people who want to help, but do not be fooled by the Snake Oil Salesmen. If deals seem to be too good they are probably not good for us. Do your homework!

The World is at Our Fingertips
....*from 9-29-10*

I had to make a stop at Big Bat's Convenient Store to fuel up for our trip to Rapid City on Saturday when I met some friends from Nebraska. They were on their way to an art show in Custer, and the daughter said they were going to pan for gold. The father said he did not bring the pan or equipment so they would not be looking for gold. The father said, "They say most of the gold is still in the Black Hills," but I laughed. It is said 10% of the world's gold came from the Sacred Black Hills. In the history of the Black Hills the gold was first discovered around the Custer area and later near Lead where Homestake Mining would eventually take most of the gold. Ten percent is a huge percentage of the world's gold. Throughout history, many people have sought the lost cities of gold around the world. The gold rush of the Black Hills started after George Custer took one thousand soldiers into the hills in 1874, and it peaked between 1876 and 1877 when numerous people came to seek their fortune.

America has been known as the place of dreams and vision when it comes to making a more abundant life for you and your family. Many people come to America from all parts of the world. You hear young people telling dreams of coming to America and striking it big with music careers or education. I have met many people who want to go to Hollywood and do pictures. I have met people who want to perform on Broadway in the Big Apple. How many dreams and visions make it to those levels? Not everyone can see their dream come true, but it is sure fun to dream. I almost forgot the dream of becoming a star athlete in the professional ranks. There is still a lot of hope in America, and people can still get a piece of the pie.

On Tuesday people will get the opportunity to vote for the Council Vice President and President of the Oglala Sioux Tribe in the primaries. I am mostly undecided at this point, but I want to make a point to use my vote by being informed. I would like to see change in the way we do things on the Pine Ridge. We need to have more people come to Pine Ridge so they can spend their money and build the economy. I guess what I am saying is do not let the politicians use the same old rhetoric about the sacredness of the children when they do very little to help the children. This past week I heard a basketball bouncing at ten fifteen at night so I went out to see who was shooting around on our basketball court. They were mostly pre-teenagers and maybe two thirteen or fourteen year old girls. I told them curfew was 9 p.m., and they should go home and get ready for school the next day. The youngest boy threw up his hands like a gang banger and was saying, "What?". I told him that did not mean anything to me. We need fathers and uncles to step up and teach the children boundaries.

I have enjoyed watching young people grow up on the Pine Ridge. I know many of the youth, and the one thing I believe every teenager needs is direction. I share with youth all the time; they need to seek the truth and believe God cares for them and loves them. But, when they look around, it is difficult to imagine a better life. Look we live in the land of opportunity, and the world is at our fingertips. When the corporations are dealing with corporate wages we seem to waste our votes. We need people who will deal with millions not hundreds of dollars. The world works on a bigger scale here. We need mid-level managers and higher to start making better lives for the future. We also need better education. We need to stop thinking a six grade reading level is too difficult for our high school students. The Reservation has not changed in forty years. We need people who are progressive and can offer hope in place of hopelessness. We have homeless people living in one family dwellings, and we have the same unemployment we had in 1970. Something needs to change.

Every elected leader needs to do an inventory of what they can actually get done, and then, get it done. Don't tell me you are going to bring jobs if you do not know how to accomplish the goal. Promises of change when broken, crush the spirit of the people. You want to cure suicide? Bring hope into the lives of young people and you will be able to dramatically reduce suicide. The Oglala People are powerful and beautiful.

One of the greatest gifts we have is friendship. I know who my friends are because they can finish my thoughts when I forget. Relatives are special and my Uncle Mike Her Many Horses is an uncle all should have in their lives. Uncle Mike came into the coffee house after reading my article last week and brought me a hand towel from the Denver Broncos Orange Crush Defense of the 1970s. The Broncos went to the Super Bowl and lost to the Cowboys in 1977. I was downtown when they came home to Denver for the parade. It was snowing and such a beautiful day in the Rocky Mountains. So I would like to thank Uncle Mike for being a great uncle and teaching us our family history. Thank You!

Feed the People

We have work to do on the Pine Ridge Reservation in every detail of our lives. I have often heard we need people who can see the details, and we also need visionaries. I hope to be a visionary who sees both the big picture and the details of what needs to be done. My understanding is we have many issues facing our people, but we have yet to see a great movement of change. While I was at a meeting in Rapid City to discuss some issues on the Reservations, we wrapped up the meeting with little hope of the Senator's staff being able to help us. Everyone decided to have supper, and we chose to go to Chile's where they serve Mexican food. They have large tables so it was good to sit and hear the different conversations going on around the table. I was sitting and just listening to what was being said, but it is rather difficult to hear so many ideas from the people around the table. We had some good people there, and I realized I was in the midst of some great minds.

As I was sitting there, an idea came to mind; if you want to be king, feed the people. I enjoy movies where there is a king, and I especially like the nice kings. One of my all-time favorite movies with a king Robin Hood Prince of Thieves. The king was not really in the movie but Sean Connery did an amazing kingly performance. He was off fighting a war and came back to his kingdom to find things calming after the storm. My point being, people will follow you to the ends of the earth if you provide for them and protect the people.

Our council and executive officers need to grasp this idea of providing a new hope for the coming years and decades. I can see we have many people running for office once again, and it is vital we develop new strategies for the coming years. We need to ask ourselves what has changed over the past few years in order for us to develop as a Nation. I am calling on the New Lakota Nation or the NLN because we need each other. I do not believe we can continue with the conditions we are faced with today. How long do you think you would be in office with an 80% unemployment rate if you were anywhere else in America? What does 80% mean; it means 8 out of 10 people do not work in the Pine Ridge. These numbers are outrageous, and it should be noted it has not changed much since the 1970s. We have a system created to fail. I do not believe we should continue in the same system if it is failing. I would call on the New Lakota Nation with the idea that we can decide our own fate. We live in a system of handouts and these ways are killing the spirit of our people. I believe we need to help where we can, but in the end we need to rise up and take our place in the world. Truthfully, we have been to the place of annihilation and have come out of the extermination polices of the United States. Now we need to pick up the pieces and start to evolve into a great Nation.

What does the New Lakota Nation look like? It would have jobs, jobs, and more jobs so people would want to come here and provide for their families. If our leaders developed a plan to lure industry here to Pine Ridge, we would start to see growth. I do not want to hear that no one wants to work; people will relearn that it is vital to provide for your family. I see many women who have taken the burden of providing for their families and this is a good thing. Of course the men have struggled because most of the jobs on the Reservation are geared for women. The

United States has stripped the dignity of the Lakota man because they wanted to destroy the spirit of one of the greatest warriors who walked this earth. What is at stake is not just a few jobs, but with the man not working, the children are also taught this way of life. It is our whole way of life must change. It must be understood that women are the strength of any society, but when the men do not support their roles as women, it is difficult to grow as a community.

So in the end, we need to have our leaders lure business and generate growth in our entrepreneurial endeavors. Our leaders need to be able to understand who they represent; they represent the Oglala Lakota people and that is a high honor. I know the leaders are constantly being bombarded with requests, but we should also understand we need our leaders to support policy that would welcome more business on the Reservation.

It is time for the young people of the Pine Ridge to rise up and ask for change. I hope we can get more young people to the polls to support change in a system that has proven it does not work. It is time we elect people to office who want to work for the people and want to change the way the status quo. It is time we start to look at the best for the Oglala and not the best for our own family. That has created a lot of dysfunction on our homeland. If you are running because you think you have a big family and could possibly be elected because of this fact, I would question your motive. We need to understand we are all related! When a Lakota stands, he addresses his people, and it must be with the idea to help all of the people. If you want to be Itanca or king, feed the people, give them jobs!

CONTEMPORARY
LAKOTA

Everyday Life Today

Not Socialist, Not Capitalist.....Lakota
....from 9-29-09

I grew up watching my mother take a drink of soda during the hottest days of summer. Imagine no air conditioning and people using water hydrants to cool off. I grew up during the seventies when people were marching on city hall and civil rights were beginning to come to a reality. Wages were low for many of the Mexican Americans, but it was always more than just the wage. It was the banking and employment practices of the so called "Man". The "Man" was the cop trying to get you jailed or the guy in D.C. running the country. Establishment was what the people were fighting against in the days of the civil rights movements. We were allowing ourselves to become part of the melting pot of America. There was really nothing you could actually do to combat this because of the "Machine". It took some people who were willing to risk everything to get the United States Government to take a look at how minorities were being mistreated.

Some may wonder why I started out with my mom drinking a cold soda. It was a Coca-Cola, and just the memory of my mom drinking a cold soda is refreshing. When I began researching the topic of colonization, I came across some interesting facts about Coca-Cola. It is a fact that Coca-colonization is an actual term. It was once said Coke wanted to give the whole world the refreshing drink. Coca Cola boasts consumption of 1.7 billion servings a day, from their 2010 statistics. I do not know what the average sales of a serving of their soft drinks come to but that is a whole lot of money in a year. There are 365 days in the year. Their mission is, "To refresh the world, to inspire moments of optimism and happiness, to create value and make a difference." It is truly a globalized effort and an attempt to control the market. Coca-Cola is capitalistic at its core and a powerful weapon for the efforts to globalize the economic systems of the world.

When I started researching colonization it became clear to me, we are not very colonized in Lakota country. I realize we have many people in our homeland that are more capitalistic than most. I believe we are both Americanized and Lakotanized (new word). We have the crab syndrome of pulling each other down because of our attempt to stay in the past. We have mechanisms in our society that would have worked in our tribal/socialism lifestyles but will not work in a capitalistic society. I am honored to live on the land our grandfathers fought for, and we need to recognize the true enemy.

The enemy is no longer the United States government; it is the poverty we are dying from in our everyday lives. Long ago we lived as a body. If one part of the body was not doing its share it was dealt with swiftly. But today we can see our people are hurting. We can talk about decolonization, but at the end of day we still have dysfunction. I fight these feelings almost every day. I am not a very good socialist or capitalist, and truly do not want to be either. But, I know we must seek to feed our families. I am not an expert of colonization, but I know imperialism is alive and thriving through capitalism. We need to continue looking for balance.

Our future can be bright if we seek to understand our past and our future together. I like the idea of getting back on the horse and picking ourselves up after a fall. We are a beautiful people, full of intelligence. Lakota people have lived through acculturation and have still held onto the traditions and language. Acculturation is a change in the cultural behavior and thinking of a person or group of people through contact with another culture. We have been profoundly affected by American culture, but we are distinctive in our daily lives. Culture is how we get things done throughout the day. This is the point we need to build on to help our people survive.

A person asked me if I felt Pine Ridge has changed over the last forty years. He said it looked like things were better because there were more businesses and many are Indian owned. I thought about this question and did not agree. We have a larger population, and there is still an 80 to 90 percent unemployment rate. Many of you know we once had factories here and now we do not. President Clinton designated our reservation an empowerment zone, and I hope we can continue to build on these ideas of empowerment. Our people deserve the right to be empowered after the full onslaught of a government set out to take away our identity. When you think of who you are, remember, we are our relatives and our relatives are us.

Culture of Culture Shock
....from 1-22-09

Twenty years ago I was going to college in Minnesota. If you had asked me if I knew what I was doing, I would have said, no! I was in a mostly all white Bible College. Being the only Lakota, or maybe even the only American Indian at the time, I stood out like a raisin in a bowl of rice. Yes there were a couple of African Americans and some Mong from Southeast Asia, and I had my beautiful wife and young daughters to stabilize me during the culture shock. After all, we had just come from the Pine Ridge Reservation. Making the transition from being in a predominantly Lakota community to a predominantly white community was difficult.

It was during my sophomore year of high school when I felt the calling on my life to become a minister and knew this was the canku (road) I needed to travel. Many American Indians believe the Jesus Road is a white road. We as Lakota have been introduced to Jesus way by the white man, but I assure you, Jesus is more Lakota than wasicu. He cared for the poor and destitute as well as people who needed him. He was socially minded when it came to people. The company he kept was constantly questioned. His first miracle was turning water into wine. He fed thousands of people. After the people had eaten, the wateca (leftovers) was gathered so that no part of the meal was wasted. The correlation between the life of Jesus and the life of the Lakota is great. As I have studied the ways of Jesus, I appreciate him more and more. I enjoy learning about Jesus because he speaks to the way of Lakota life.

During my second year of college I found myself in a speech class. Now, those of you who know me will testify that it is sometimes difficult to get me to stop talking. It was my second year of college, and I was to give a historical speech. I chose Martin Luther King, Jr. and his "I Have a Dream" speech. I grew up during the civil rights era of America, and I have been intrigued with this preacher. He chose to walk among his people in civil disobedience and did it without violence. The time was difficult as racism was a daily struggle. Before 1970 the minorities of the United States had very few rights. Lakota people were struggling as they did not have freedom of religion. Of course, I believe our Lakota people still worshiped as our ancestors did centuries before.

We all needed to question the attitudes and policies of United States Government; but now we are in a different time. This week we will see the first African American inaugurated as the President of the United States of America. This week we celebrate two great men, Barack Obama and Martin Luther King Jr. Hope is here and we need to remember North America is a place of dreams.

My hope is we can work to make our reservation a better place to live. I believe it is true; any child can dream of becoming anything they would like to be. I chose to be a minister of the Gospel of Jesus Christ, Barack Obama believed he could be President, and MLK believed we could have a better world. Dreams can be fulfilled; we need to listen to the dreams of our people.

When our people say our children are sacred, I hope they want the best for our children. This means we need to seek a better home for our people. We need to be involved with our community just like many great people have done over the years. My hope is that we can begin to change our reservation from within. This will be accomplished by outsiders. The people, or Oyate, will be the ones to guide and encourage the dreams and visions of our young people. You are the change! When you understand this idea, you will understand the Canku (road) of the people. Our children are the legacy we leave in the world, and the way they live their lives will reflect the choices we make today.

Building Up our People Begins with our Youth
....from 1-26-10

We are in the tax season when we either get money back or we have to pay. I have only had to pay in a few times. We usually get tax credit because of dependents. There has been a lot of money around the Rez these past few months, and we even have a new tax business in Pine Ridge Village. As I drove across the border into Nebraska, I noticed two used car dealers had their cars parked by the road. Lots of people have been around White Clay. I read some of what the politicians said about the border village. One said they could not shut down businesses as that would be illegal. They thought if they cleaned it up they could add more business because we have around thirty thousand people who are potential customers.

I like the end of January because I know we are moving toward spring and summer. It is awesome because we get to see the flowers and the beautiful fields change colors. We are well into the basketball seasons for both girls and boys. Life is good on the Pine Ridge, and I know we have many students in college seeking to get their degrees. I love to encourage the students because we need to see greatness in them. Our children are beautiful, and I like to hear the stories when they go to colleges and universities around the country. When I went to college in Minnesota it was great but I did not like the weather. It was too hot in the summer and too cold in the winter. I gave the best years of my life to Minnesota physically. Some people wanted to hate on me because of the fishing rights of the tribes in the upper Midwest. But of course I do not even eat fish. Maybe just a little sushi, which is raw fish made in Japanese restaurants and some Chinese places as well.

I learned many things in Minnesota, but what I really enjoyed was a class on Biblical Interpretation. It is important that we look at scripture and apply it to our lives. When believers look at the Bible there is a need to understand it has the power to change lives. It is a book of power because it is authored by the Creator. When I was leaving college and coming home, a minister asked me what I would like for my going away gift. I told her I wanted a Bible with extra-large print so I could read it when I got older. Last week a woman asked me if I have bifocals yet. I told her no, but I also realize I have not been to the doctor for a couple years. I am passionate about many things, and the Bible is a great tool to empower a better life.

I worked at Pine Ridge High School for a year or so. I loved being with the freshmen because they were excited to be in the big school. Now, I like to ask them how they like adulthood; it has been a few years since 2000. I have enjoyed watching them grow into adults and now many have children of their own. It is great to know some of them even read this column and enjoy it. We need to lift up the young people, and see them develop hope to make their dreams come true. Our hope needs to be about a better day. I remember when I was in the depths of sorrow. I did not know if my life would ever change, but it did. This is the message we need to have because we can overcome our emotions.

One time I was playing ball in Sisseton and I ran into Floyd "Red Crow" Westerman. His son was a basketball player too. This was just after Dances with Wolves came out, and I knew he was working on some other things. I talked to him about Denver and the seventies. He remembered my mother from those old days. We have some great people to look up to. I like Custer Died for Your Sins that Floyd sang. It made me smile when I heard it. Life is short, and we need to live life to its fullest. It is time to build our people instead of trying to destroy them.

We Have Each Other
....from 7-15-09

The driving force behind suicide is hopelessness. In these past weeks Senator John Thune spoke about the devastation of hopelessness in Standing Rock. Chairman Ron His Horse Is Thunder is talking about policing in regards to suicide prevention. I have seen the devastation in my own family as two close cousins took their own lives. Our families have been shattered by hopelessness. My vision of a better life comes from my faith. Faith, in itself, is hoping for a better way of life. The hope of more abundant and fuller lives is what keeps me going. We all deal with depression as our bodies have lows and highs because of the chemical makeup of our systems. We live our lives believing no one can be struggling or going through difficulties like our own, but this type of thinking is untrue. Most people have issues that affect them in a negative manner. We need hope and a movement to bring our people back from hopelessness.

This past week I traveled to Denver to be with my family. My brother lost his daughter. Twenty-two years old is very young, and she seemed to be healthy. I do not have the answers to why we lose young ones. My own daughter was taken at seventeen. Illness is hard to explain, but we must seek to help our relatives deal with the losses we endure during our lifetimes. I struggle with feelings of aloneness because of my mother's passing; she was the strength of our family. And when I look at my cousins, two of them I visited with in Denver, Gerald and Ted Red Shirt, I realize they have become the uncles. The Martins are special men to me. I saw them treat my mother with so much love. Uncle Roy and Frank were my mother's brothers, and I remember them the most. These men were great role models. I realize I fail because of my own grief and the struggle to overcome loss. How do we get to a healthy way of living when we are burying young people?

Hoping for a better way of life breeds life and this hope will lead to a stronger community. In counseling they teach us that we need to grieve. If we do not work through the process fully, it will affect us emotionally, physically, and in all aspects of our lives. This is why we as a people need to strive to take care of ourselves and our families. Our daughters and sons need us to be healthy so they stop reliving our mistakes. I know I struggle and fail, but it is the people around me that give me the strength to go forward. During the darkest times in my life I found my own weakness became strength. This happens when you realize you cannot change the future, and you are at the mercy of life or death. At this point it is crucial you reach out to the Creator of life and seek to have Him guide you as you rest in His care.

Last week I saw the devastation in Standing Rock and heard of many other incidents across the country involving our Native people. We need to revolutionize the way we do things because of the issues we have among our people. Our greatest leaders wanted more for us. We as a people have a great way of life. Yet when you see so much pain and hurt, there must be some conclusions about our current situations. Before I moved home from college I had the opportunity to meet some really awesome Native youth. Two young ladies and a young man were with me eating Chinese food. The young man was from Oklahoma, one girl was from Arizona, and the other girl was from Canada. We were finishing up our meal and the waitress brought the check; it was around fifty dollars. I looked at the girls, and they looked very nervous. These two young ladies were divided by a whole country and yet they were similar in their worldviews. There was a lot of pain in the ladies. I wondered about this for years and have come to my own conclusions. Grieving needs to be done throughout Indian Country. Overcoming our past will lead to great success for our future in Native America.

When you see hurting people, and they look like they want to give up, encourage them. Life will get better, and we can live for our relatives as role models. We need our emotional health, and it begins when you see you are powerless. God wants us to rely on Him to find completeness. I often find myself pondering life's issues, and I realize I was put here on earth for a reason, to live a life that will build a legacy of faith and hope in the God I serve. I encourage people to talk with me, and let me share in your struggles because, after all, we have each other.

Emotional Health Brings Hope and Change
....*from 9-08-09*

Hope for a better way of life is healthy. We learn about upward mobility from sociology; moving up and down a system of social hierarchy in a lifetime happens naturally. Growing up in one of America's ghettos taught me how to be street smart; going to college has taught me how to break down information. Education is valuable to anyone who would like to change their social stature. We have many obstacles in our path; we must strive to build a better life for our children. Native America is encountering the effects of being imprisoned. There really is a better way of life for our Lakota people. Suicide is not the answer, and that choice correlates with feeling hopeless.

My search is for emotional health. I believe it is a journey we all need to be working on in our lives. In my research, I found that about 23% of Americans are affected by unhealthy emotions. My personal belief is that on the Pine Ridge Indian Reservation, 77% of the population is dealing with dysfunctional emotions. It is seeking to know the truth and not believing a lie; illusion is a part of our everyday lives. I battle my insecurities on a daily basis. Our insecurities come from within and believing they are true is devastating. I thought I could know what are people are dealing with on a daily basis and I really couldn't until I dealt with myself. We are living in one of the most devastated areas in America. Our children are struggling because it is difficult to see a better way of life.

My own struggles have seen addictions that have become uncontrollable. I was addicted to basketball for fourteen years until I blew out my knee. I became addicted to the internet back in the nineties. I became addicted to Chinese food and the list goes on. Some would believe that I am addicted to religion, but my belief system came before I started on the road to addiction. Having issues is what makes us human. Our way to health and maturity starts from within. We need to take a close look at ourselves and begin the process of change. Of course we need God to help us to become all that he wants us to be.

My commitment is to have a men's group to help with any kind of issues we have as men. I believe when our men our emotionally healthy, we will be able to give our children a brighter future. I know some would say Cangleska is in place, but I am not talking about de-colonization or trying to change what the Christians did to us. I am talking about men helping men to come to the realization that we need to be better grandfathers, fathers, husbands, uncles, and brothers. Can you imagine a place where fathers know where their children are at times? Protecting, providing and caring for their children is the place we need to come to in Native America.

A few years ago I promised to start a vocational school. We started the school and continue to strive to make a difference in the lives our young people. In the coming year we will be offering classes in auto mechanics. Leadership development is important to our people and it all begins with emotional health. I became bitter and unforgiving in my life and I did not like myself. I am trying to become a better person. My model is Jesus and I believe I am not the man I will be someday, and I thank God I am not the man I used to be. Look for emotionally healthy groups to start at the Gospel Fellowship in Pine Ridge.

I look forward to seeing healthy men and women in our community. Let's make a better life for our children. They need us more than ever and there is hope. I would like to thank everyone for reading my articles over the past year. My family has been great! The ones in North Dakota and Colorado are very special to me, as well as the ones here in Pine Ridge. I have not always been the best relative and for that I am sorry. I hope to find forgiveness and offer it as well. Forgiveness is one of the first steps we need to take. Pilamiya(thank you).

City Racism

It is quite amusing when I say "city," because Rapid City is a big town and not really a city at all. Some believe the gangs are getting worse, but the police keep it under wraps because of the heavy reliance on tourism. Rapid City is the gateway to Mt. Rushmore and Crazy Horse. There are many people who also come to Pine Ridge via Rapid City. When I ask them about their visit, they often tell me they first visited when they were children and have returned to share with their own children.

I was on a mission today as I sought for New York Pizza by the slice. I am a passionate believer that if pizza is great, it should come by the slice. I drove to the place where I saw slices being advertised. I pulled up close to the doors and walked in with six others. I wanted a pizza slice and was hoping they had a few good slices under warming lamps like they do in the Big Apple. Yes, I went to the Mecca of Pizza and found a phenomenal slice. I enjoyed it very much. Well, I went in and asked if they had slices and the woman said, "No, we don't have slices." I asked her how long a pizza would take. She then yelled at me, "We don't have slices." I immediately asked her in a loud voice, "How long do the Pizzas take?" And she said in a calmer voice, "Thirty minutes." Well, that was too long, and I decided it was not worth my time. That got my racism radar going, and I was ready to make sure I would not be mistreated.

As the day moved forward I found myself at the Big Store with a new planter for my indoor basil deluxe. I hope to make sauce for pasta and pizza throughout the winter and into spring. As we got through the lines and made it to the parking lot, I grabbed my jacket. I found some products we had forgotten to pay for while checking out. I went back into the Big Store and found myself in line with four people in front of me. Then, while I was patiently waiting, I must have been a little close to this guy's cart. I was pretty burned by the look of disgust he gave me as I was standing there. I told him, "That was a disturbing look," and he said, "What?" I explained to him about the way he looked at me and then he told me he did not like the long lines. I excused him because I was in a good mood, but without great pizza my good mood was running on empty. The rest of the day I found myself watching out for racism, but there was little activity. Now I am home making my slice of pizza!

Ramblings about Rapid City

My first stop after leaving the Rez was Hermosa. I got out of the van, and some Indian men were there waiting for someone to come out of the truck stop. I greeted them with a wave, and someone in the back waved me over. I went up to the truck. There was a man talking to me in beautiful Lakota. I asked him what he was doing because he was a little buzzed up, and it was just now noon. He told me he wanted to get a horse, but they told him it was going to storm. I shook his hand and walked into the truck stop. I got my Diet Pepsi and headed for the counter. The lady behind the counter was wearing green eye shadow; the last time I saw her she was wearing purple like they did in the 80s. I asked her before if she was trying to bring back the eighties and she told me, "Yes!" She continued by telling me she was going to bring back leg warmers, too. I laughed then and walked out of the store. Today she told me she was going to bring back the hair styles of the 80's, too. We laughed and I was on my way to "Fast Town". Rapid City, South Dakota is home to about eighty thousand people, but it is a city where the whole region shops and comes for entertainment.

We went to the mall which was the first official stop on this shopping day. Belle told me she was going to get coffee, and I told her I was going to have some Chinese food. I stood in line for about five minutes. I got my lunch to go because as I looked around there were no empty tables. I saw a family from the Rez. I sat down and got my food prepared to eat. A little chit-chat and I was ready to stand and eat my food. I walked to a table where I saw a lady was ready to get up and leave. When she stood up I asked if I could sit. She told me I could and so I did, but just then her friends came over. They asked if I minded them joining me. I told them it would be fine. They sat with their slices of pizza, and I had my Chinese food. I struck up a conversation because it seemed a little weird sharing my table with some grandmas. One young man came by and told me to slow down as I was eating. Great to see other Lakota walking around, but I was sitting with some white women. I asked them if they were from the country club because they were all dolled up and had on some strong perfume. They told me they were on a bus tour from Canada. We talked a bit more, and I offended them by telling them they do not really have a REAL Country.

Belle called to say she was ready. As I was talking to her on the phone, she saw me and started walking toward me. I told the women, "I'd better leave 'cause my wife is mean and she might get mad at me." They laughed as Belle and the kids came by. I walked away with them and Belle was smiling at the women. I told Belle they were grandmas, and she told me they were not. It was a funny moment in a shopping day. Off to more errands and enjoying the day.

We made it to the big store otherwise known as Sam's Club; a great place to shop for lots of stuff. I was walking in after checking my accounts when I ran into a lady I knew from a school on the Rez. We were catching up, and I told her I needed to find Belle and see what was going on. I found my four blend of cheese, put it in the cart and then went to the office chairs to sit and hang out. I sat there for a while and decided I needed a new chair. I bought the one I thought was most comfortable. I went to get an empty cart and saw a couple looking at Windows 7. I told them they would love it; I always like to help out when I can. Then I took the cart and put my office chair in the cart. I went to the cashier and noticed she was very fair skinned. I commented because that is the way I am; I tend to share what I am thinking. She was so fair she was literally almost glowing and translucent. She said, "Goodbye, have a nice day." I smiled and walked away. I waited for Belle as she was checking out too. I was standing there and a Chinese lady saw me. She smiled and very happily said, "Hello." She told me she was well, and I should come see her. The only problem is I recognized her, but I do not for the life of me know where she works. I am not going to eat that much Chinese to find out either.

Well, I was prepared for a great day and ended it with a Philly cheesesteak. Makes for fond memories, have a nice day!

Looking for Knuckleheads in Rapid City
....from 7-28-09

A knucklehead is a person who just doesn't get it. Whatever is put there, they will never get it and it is a terrible thing for any people group. I have seen many people across the country and have seen some knuckleheads in my travels. So with regard to this type of person, I can assure you we have knuckleheads in our region. Surprisingly, I have not found any of them in Rapid City today. I went to Combat Alley and found an Indian couple trying to get a ride across town. I do not know where "across town" was in relation to where I was in the downtown area. I met numerous people downtown and everybody treated me very well. I was surprised to say the least; when I treated people well they treated me well. I met some young people who went to Central High School, Red Cloud High School and a homeschooled student. All of these students treated me like a human being, with honor and respect.

There have been times when I have been treated like an Indian. I get very upset when this happens because I know they must treat other Lakota people badly as well. One of the things people in the region will do is look at me funny. This is the first sign; it might be simply because they are having a bad day, but it puts me on alert.

One time I was standing in line waiting to pay for my items, and a guy was grunting and trying to look at me. I was trying to mind my own business, but he was getting me upset. I looked him with the AIM look, and I think I scared him. He tried to back down, but before he did I asked him a question. I said, "Have you ever had an Indian look into your face?" He said, no. I asked if he knew why. Again he said, no. I told him it wasn't because we are weak; it is because we are respectful. We do not even need to teach our children not to look at people because it is modeled and learned through our actions. If we are looking at you it is because we are upset and ready for a fight. Cultural issues are important to learn, and we must strive to learn the differences.

Other times I sense that some people do not trust me because I am an Indian. I have people follow me around a store and this upsets me. I do not like being referred to as, "You People". One time I had my potatoes thrown into my shopping basket at what I refer to as the big store in Chadron. My sister-in-law shared her experience from shopping in the old grocery store. She took all of the hamburger meat available to purchase. The meat department guy comes out and says, "Damn Indians." Now I would think he would be happy someone took all the meat. He was very upset and made my sister-in-law upset as well. One time I went into the big store and the customer service woman was giving me a hard time. She was thinking I stole an item and wanted to see my receipt; of course I never showed it to her. Instead, I showed it to her boss and went on my merry way.

I can share many recollections from my experiences in the border towns. I am sure you have some memories as well. My main point is that I want to be treated like a human being, not like a "damn Indian". I visited a few businesses in downtown Rapid City last week and everyone treated me well. I guess next time I will leave my computer bag in the car. It is all leather and very expensive. Actually, I believe when we treat people with respect and honor, in most cases we will receive honor and respect. I know there are people out there that just do not like us because they are racist. They just do not like Indians. I am cool with that because those people usually just stay away from our people.

We are human beings with good and bad within our people group, similar to any other people group. I grew up with many different types of people and I assure you, the people you want to be around are the good people. Sure, I was called a dirty Indian but that never bothered me because I know our stories. Our people broke the ice in the winter to bathe. Because of the western movies, everyone knows the cowboys bathed once a month. We are all human, and I appreciate the nice people. In closing I would have to thank God because he loves us all the same. It is powerful to be a child of God. And yes, the knuckleheads will never get it.

Mall of Rushmore in the Morning

It was a blistering day in the land of the Lakota. Lakota have enjoyed the Black Hills for centuries. Today, we seem to enjoy the Rushmore Mall in Rapid City, hunting and gathering in the American way known as Mall Shopping. Finding a parking spot was rather easy on a Tuesday morning here at the Rushmore Mall. I took out my backpack and started for the doors. As I was walking in, I saw a Lakota man sitting outside in the cold wind. He got my attention and asked for a cup of coffee. I told Belle what he said, and she said I should buy him a cup of coffee. So I took a right, and she kept walking toward the shopping area. I, of course, am not a shopper but a blogger. I went into to Starbucks and ordered a couple shots of espresso and a 16oz cup of Joe for the man. I like espresso because it makes you feel like you are drinking something other than tea. Sure, I enjoy a cup of dark roasted coffee, but when you are looking for a pick me up, order the espresso and see the clarity of life.

I took the coffee out to the Lakota man. He was still sitting outside in the cold wind on the bench designed for smokers. He tried to get my attention again, but I told him I needed to get moving on some thoughts. I was in blogging mode and wanted to get the feeling of the food court at the Rushmore Mall. I sat down and an older couple was sitting on the other side of the load bearing pillar. She was eating Chinese, and he was having some Mexican food. I told her I gained the most weight in my life eating Chinese. Of course, I ate a lot of other things as well, but we talked about Chinese food. She assured me she did not eat it much because her husband did not like it. She reserved her food preference for the Rushmore Mall. I saw an Indian couple get their Chinese too. They sat close to me and finished off their food. Mall food should have a variety, and I think people like to grab a quick bite of choice.

I saw two non-Indian women walking around the mall for exercise, and yup, one just looked at me writing the blog. It is very interesting how people get through their day here at the Mall of Rushmore.

Over the weekend I was talking to my daughter's boyfriend, and he made a remark about Native Americans. I told him it is better to use the term Indian because the United States did not make treaties with the Native Americans. Instead, the United States agreed to treaties with the American Indian tribes or American Indian Nations. I believe this is important. There is talk of the Great Sioux Nation coming together to ask for the Black Hills back. The Black Hills were illegally taken by the United States. I should really get some views from others as the meetings are taking place in South Dakota this year. In 1980 the Supreme Court ruled the Hills were illegally taken and awarded a monetary judgment against the US Government. We must keep the fight for the people. Lakota people should band together and start to make their own life in what is known as the Great Sioux Nation.

Being progressive in the 70s was difficult because we did not have the rights of full United States citizens. Now we have the ability to contract with the US Government for our treaty rights. Robert Grey Eagle once told me a Republican Congress was responsible for the Self Determination Act of Congress. Many people believe American Indians are in a welfare state but in actuality most American Indian Tribes have treaty rights. We are Nations of people with a contract with the Government. We need to help people pull their heads out of the sand. Educating the people around the country is vital as we move forward in the 21st Century. In my life I would like to see the Great Sioux Nation grow up and take their rightful place in regard to their obligations.

As a follower of Christ I find it absurd that people cannot

234

feed themselves properly. We may not have starvation but we have malnutrition across the Great Sioux Nation. We have children who are not getting the proper diet, and this leads to illness. So we have a high rate of diabetes and cancer along with many other illnesses contributing to the continued destruction of the American Indian Nations. It is difficult for people to give attention and interest to faith when they are in survival mode. This is not the way our ancestors wanted us to live. Usually people are self-centered. We almost always seek self, but we need to start living in selfless ways in order for us to survive. I talked to a guy about leaving the Rez one day and he said, "Are you giving up on our Lakota people?" I told him maybe I could help in other ways from the outside, because I believe I have had enough time to work from within. People have been caught up in a dependency with no relief in sight. I believe we need to rise up and take our relationship with the Creator. Our people have been affected in unbelievable ways. They are now the ones destroying themselves. The destruction was started by outside forces and over time it has become an inside job.

Bikers in the Church

Apparently, I have not been shocked as I need to be in my life. This afternoon I was waiting for a wedding party and thought it was going to be a private gathering. I was waiting and sure enough they arrived with flowers, dresses and biker gang members. I was surprised by the national gang members who were in their vests and riding their Harleys. I joked a little with the members but was very cautious as well because, after all, they are gang members. One told me the last time he went to church to pick up his daughter the steeple was hit with lightning. I assured them because I was the Pastor they would be fine. I am a sinner which makes it clear that we do not keep people out of church. It was a pretty nice wedding with about 60 people in the church. The coolest part of the experience was that they gave me a vest to wear. I will most likely wear it and tell the story about the day a motorcycle gang came to the Gospel Fellowship. They were glad the cops went by with their sirens and did not stop. They were very nice, but I could tell they were gang members with attitude. I asked only a few questions but made sure I was not too forward. Yes, I guess life on the Rez can be very interesting when you live life to its fullest. I have met a few bikers, and I believe they are people just like the rest of us. I do not like to think about everything associated with the biker gangs.

One day I was greeting people at the coffee house and in walks a man. He was of medium stature, and I could tell he was a guy who could take care of himself. I asked him where he was from, and he told me California. He was passing through Pine Ridge, most likely on his way to Sturgis for the annual rally held in early August. I asked him what he did with his life. He was a writer. I asked him what he wrote. He wrote about his experience being a founder of a chapter of the Hell's Angels. I am not always the smartest guy around and asked a personal question. He just looked at me. I put my head down and told him never mind. Well, he went out to his car and brought in a book. He autographed it for me, and I said thank you. Funny thing is, I could never really read the book because it was too powerful. I thought to myself if a guy was willing to write about his experience of all the things he and the gang did, he must be really brave. Well, there are many people passing through the Rez. I am sure we as a people are closer to the outlaw gangs of bikers than we are to the millionaire business men who happen by once in a while.

Our lives are full of surprises. I believe God has our lives intersect with people who you would never expect to come in contact with and often we become lifetime friends. I believe we must be obedient in our lives and press on to see what the Creator of the Universe has in store. Moving forward in a battle for the Kingdom of Heaven and being a vessel He chooses to use for the advancement of that Kingdom is where we will have peace. I want to be a person who will be remembered for my faithful service. When people remember my walk it will be a journey of the Kingdom of Heaven. Salvation is not the end but the beginning of a journey walking with Jesus seeking to set people free of their chains. I do not want a religion but a relationship with the God of this Universe. I know him as Jesus. I thank God for the person praying for me as I seek to help people understand Truth. I told a good friend over the weekend the Creator has left his imprint on man and seeks to draw us closer to him.

Setting some things straight, I am an Indian

It seems I am a critic of sorts, but I have had some great people help me to overcome some angry posts on the blog. I was walking in an alley a few weeks ago and came across this hole filled with hairspray bottles and Listerine. Of course they were empty. But this was only one place and when I looked around I saw hundreds of bottles lying around the area. It seems these products have alcohol in them, and the people who consume them are watering them down and drinking them. Why? I do not have all the answers, but I am sure it is an addiction at this level. I would like to speak to some decision makers and see if we can do something about the consumption of hairspray.

On another note, I have decided to not use the term white guy, white woman, or white man due to the bitterness it creates. I will use Wasicu because, after all, it was our ancestors who gave the Euro-American people a name. Not all of the white people are Wasicu, but I feel it is a better term and less derogatory than white. I have a shirt that says I am part white but I cannot prove it. I am gonna burn that shirt as soon as I can start a fire in the pit. I will do it the proper non-Wasicu way.

Apparently I have been using Tea Bagger in the wrong manner, and the Tea Party does not want me to use the term. So I decided to figure out what they believe, but that is difficult too. So if there are any Tea Party Supporters reading this blog, and I cannot for the life of me understand why. I want you to know it is your right to bring all your anger and frustration, but please sign your name. Do not expect me to just let you say negative things about me without telling the world who you are. I know many of my friends have stated I just need to let it go, and I will. But, I want to assure this blog remains a place for my personal RAMBLINGS. Even though you may not understand why, some people actually like to read the posts.

I believe I try to be open and honest with people. I fail at being a human being on most days. I struggle to live up to any standard. I am not a Wasicu pastor and never even acted like one. I have been me. I question my position and role in life, but you must understand it is from an Indian view. Why? Because I am Indian. Do not read the blog if you cannot stand me or if you personally attack me. Okay, that is my rant and I am done. I am gonna ignore the Tea Party.

White Man, White Guilt

A guy on Facebook asked me if I hated white guys. I gave him the LOL because it is the day of texting and Facebooking. Funny thing is I tried to explain to him that my closest friends are white. He did not buy it and continued to engage in what I believe is white guilt. They want me to support the Tea Party and right wing politics. I truly believe the context is about the White Americanism they fully pledge to in regard to being American. I support the troops, and I voted in every election I could since I turned 18 years old. But in the end, not wanting to pay taxes and being worried about the spending budget does not interest me.

So I wrote about some guy attempting to use some humor and it failed. I was having a bad day. Some, or most probably, understood when Indians talk they usually want to know if you are referring to a white guy or Indian guy. I get tired of people equating Christianity with American. So to be a good American you must be Christian, and to be a good Christian you must be an American. This is not true, and I had some Facebook drama. I told the guy he should have called me and heard the inflection in my voice because he would understand the culture. But of course he believed I should behave as a good Christian and a good American. I do not like people telling me I must abide by their cultural norms when I do not live in the culture. I live in a place where the White American Government set out to destroy my ancestors and their descendants. So, am I a little leery about what the White Man has done in the name of Christ? Absolutely! Life is too short, so I defriended the guy. I have to deal with what my white Christian brothers have done and continue to do among my people. Yes, all in the name of Jesus.

Well, I hope if you are white you are not offended deeply by my post. Ramblings is about the everyday life of a this contemporary Indian.

I have so many white American friends, and some are closer than my own siblings. I was mentored by one of the greatest men in the world. I believe he is as white as they come. He will turn 90 in a few days, and he is a GREAT man. I am secure with the white men in my life. I believe they understand the history, or at least trust me to deal with the issues effectively.

Okay, this is Facebook drama caused of white guilt, or maybe just another white guy trying to make me drink Tea. Here it is…..I am a social conservative, and that is the only box I will fit into.

The above is a statement I left on the blog because some people believe the Tea Party is Christian. I have learned to just delete angry people. I am ok with people speaking their views as I like to share my views with the world, but I will not tolerate people trying to force me into their box.

Perspective on an Indian Way of Life

People need to understand that as a blogger we only have our perspective. If you want to give yours, start blogging. I believe we need to be able to hear things from others, and I hope we can settle our issues in a good way. I had one person tell me I was a racist, immature, and then the ultimate slam, they questioned my faith. It was all done in a nice way. I have had people talk down to me and try to put me in my place before so I was well aware of the tactics. They were not able to deal with the history of America in a professional manner so they used a personal attack. I was okay because when you are on Facebook you can just defriend them and life continues.

There was another guy who was upset because I spoke about an incident. He told I did not have the facts. I said, "Well I could talk to everyone involved and write everyone's eye witness testimony. I bet we will still have a different picture than his." It was funny because I mentioned that the blog has gone worldwide. But when I said I have reached six continents, he basically said that I was doing it for my ego.

239

Of course I laughed, and still today I believe a blog is meant to be read. I thought his response on the blog was shown as spam. I was glad to read his response. I believe we are still friends. What I write and blog about is my perspective of my world.

We decided I would write about the issue of the Lakota acculturation into white culture. So I hope you look forward to hearing a Lakota perspective on Lakota Acculturation of a Wasicu or White Guy.

It's all about perspective
....from 8-25-09

Last week we were driving in the country and my wife asked, "Is that a bird of prey?" I said, "I don't know." We kept driving and she spotted a porcupine by the side of the road. She told me I should have stopped, so I backed up and by the time we returned to the place the porcupine was sitting, it was gone and moving up the side of the hill. My wife said to me, "It is like a little scruffy bush." Well, on the way home we saw a tan kitty. We were almost home, and I thought I saw a raccoon, but of course my wife thought it was a big fluffy cat, because it was not round and pudgy. Two different perspectives and two different conclusions left us in one of those areas where we disagreed. I totally believe I saw a raccoon but I might be wrong. Some people would have us believe we were both correct. But the truth is the truth, and either it was a cat, a raccoon, or something else. The reality is we were able to see more wildlife on a nice country drive and that makes the whole evening wonderful.

This past week we traveled to Lawrence, Kansas and watched our daughter start her senior year of college at Haskell Indian University. It is a beautiful campus and my favorite part of the campus is to see so many different Indians. I even met some nice Crow this time. Overall I believe they like to keep the unity of the campus, and people seemed to get along well. I even met some of the same people I met last year. Henry Crow, the leading rebounder for Red Cloud Basketball, was there, and he had a couple of friends with him. We had Mongolian barbecue, and I had sushi with my meal. One thing I noticed is that I do not have the same appetite.

It was a great trip, and I hope more people from Lakota country will go to the Indian University. Knowledge is power, and if you gain enough knowledge you can change your future.

We were just a couple of miles from Leavenworth where the famous federal prison is located. I thought of Leonard Peltier who has been in prison for 32 years and is serving two life sentences for the death of two FBI agents. I wanted to drive by the prison and see the magnitude of a federal prison. The high walls, wire, and guard towers are a sight to see. I wondered how many prisoners escaped from the federal prison. I do not have enough knowledge about the 70s as I was a young boy for most of those years. I did not even know we did not have civil rights. Some people argue about what happened, but I do not have a clue. The only guy that was prosecuted for the Pan Am flight was let out of prison, and he was responsible for over 200 lives. Makes you wonder about the world and its perspectives. Last week Leonard was denied parole.

Last week we were in a cabin on a small pond in northwest Missouri. I awoke early and went out to the deck because I wanted to pray with my wife. I realized that I had feelings of death on me while being home in Pine Ridge. There was so much oppression, and I wanted to let her know about what was happening with me. As we were sitting in a little paradise with no cable television, and time to be alone with our little family, I came to an understanding. We are living with too much stress and that alone is a killer. I want to make some changes in my life. When we came home I talked with Arlo from KILI radio and asked him if he felt emotionally healthy. He said, "Is anyone?" I thought there must be some people, but many of our people on the Pine Ridge are not healthy. I told him I wanted to start a group for men. Let's get healthy. He agreed with me, which made me feel great as my favorite DJ is willing to come to the group.

Truth is not relative. We may have different perspectives, but when everything is said and done we will still have truth. My belief is we as a Lakota people struggle with many issues and we need to start moving forward. I am committed to making some changes and battling the lack of hope. In a couple of weeks we will begin to deal with our issues. Remember to respect others and their perspectives because you just might be wrong.

Finally, the Indians beat the Christians
....*from 2-12-09*

I had a great week listening to the "Voices of Haskell." There were over two hundred people in attendance at the open microphone event. I listened to most of the people who participated, but I had to go out and find a diet cola at one point.

I believe there were three bands and numerous poets who shared their talents. So what am I doing on Friday night listening to more poets and guitarists at the Bean Broker in Chadron, NE? I am wondering how we can develop more of the arts on the Pine Ridge Reservation. Establishing the arts of our people is vital to bring hope and life into our Nation. We should maybe begin a "Voices of Pine Ridge" open mic, so that we can hear what is on the hearts of our artists.

A couple of years ago, I was invited to Porcupine to take part in a music festival. Father Bill Paulie, a Jesuit priest, invited me to come out and pray. It was a powerful event. We saw some Crow come down from Montana, Native Era from the Pine Ridge, and Deb Iron Cloud, who by the way is one of my favorite singers. I talked with Deb after she sang and asked her when she was going to get a CD made. She told me they didn't know how to get it done. We decided to help with a music studio. After a few years, I have found a friend who would like to come to Pine Ridge and record one of my favorite artists. I am hoping Deb reads this column, as I believe she should know we are going to record her music. We have many people who need to be recorded. Deb is an artist who should have been recorded a long time ago. I used to play the four track recording of Deb on my show on KILI. I am by no means an expert, but I am a person who enjoys music. I would buy her CD, because she

242

has talent and I like her as a person. I believe many people, given the opportunity, would love to see another local artist making it big.

Speaking of poetry and music, I found some of the content to be rather disturbing at the open microphone nights in Chadron, NE and in Lawrence, KN. There were professors from three different colleges in attendance taking part in these events. They were from Chadron State College, Kansas University, and Haskell Indian Nations University. I can tell you with honesty that the "Voices of Haskell" was not nearly as crude as the open-mic night at the Bean Broker. It says a lot for the different tribes represented in Lawrence. There are some great minds writing and performing in Kansas.

It is nice to see some of our students down in Kansas studying for their future. Haskell has a rich history when it comes to our people and a great campus as well. Everything is close and the huge stadium is a sight to see. It reminded me of the movie Rudy, when he played for Notre Dame and was able to play in the last game.

I had the opportunity to watch a men's basketball game where Haskell took on a Christian college. I was excited throughout the game as Haskell was up for a few minutes, but the Christian college took over around half time. I had the opportunity to get into Big Nation's face and tell him it was his house. Big Nation is a very large Lakota man who played center for the Haskell Indians. He is a very nice giant. Well, I had to have my popcorn, so I went out from the game and ended up having to wait for my popcorn while they were making a new batch. By the time I got back to the game, the Haskell men's team was winning again. I thought of Smoke Signals where the dad says, "Finally, the Indians beat the Christians!"

I enjoyed visiting my daughter, and it gave me a chance to see Haskell in different manner. I hope to see more Lakota go to Haskell and consequently see a brighter future as we become a more educated people. I like the diversity of the tribes at Haskell. It is powerful when you have different tribes come together who share similar life experiences. So, if you are looking for a place to go to college, Haskell Indian Nations University is a great place to learn and grow.

Fast Times

I was just thinking about my youth. It seems like I just turned around, and now I am like in my forties. Don't get me wrong, I am happy to be here. But man, the time passed by so quickly. It seems that time doesn't stand still for much of anything. We are moving fast toward the teens of the new century. Wow! We are going to have teenagers telling us they were born in 01 or 05, and before you know it we will be in the roaring 20s! Just a thought, but do you think time is moving fast or are we watching the end come? What if you had a year left, or maybe five years, what would you do differently?

I do not want to sound like a dooms-dayer, but I believe we are in some turbulent times. The next few years will bring us to new times. I was watching a show about China and how they were seeking to build their economy. One worker was employed in a sewing factory, and she was making 250 dollars a month. Makes me wonder how the world will change in just a few years. Global, or a one world system, is on deck. We have already seen a globalized system come into play. We have witnessed how our economy and stock market affects the world. The phrase, "New World Order" was made famous by the first George Bush. I remember hearing about it, but now we see a movement to one world religion. I am wondering how long we can watch the world move toward one world systems. Maybe it will force people to pay attention to world events.

To be honest, I am not a prophet, nor am I an expert in the end times of the world. But I fear for the American Indian. We live in remote areas and are barely making. It could mean hard times for the tribes. I was talking to a good friend, and I mentioned I love being American. Why? Because we have all of the opportunities the American system has to offer. We have the Lakota Funds working with people to help secure loans for small business opportunities. We have counseling and family programs with many organizations trying to help the people. But we have one area that is not being helped or served. We have a spiritual problem. I was talking with have a friend today. She mentioned she came home on Sunday, and when she arrived home she felt the heaviness of the oppression over the Reservation.

I believe the oppression comes from the severe ungodliness our people are faced with every day. I have known of the oppression, or the dark cloud, for some time, but I have not talked about it before this time. Maybe I have talked about it, but I did not write about this issue. I hope to find resolution because we have our children at stake here. I had a great day today but I sensed the spiritual oppression growing. When you travel as I have, you can sense the change in the location and how it feels. The only other place I have felt this kind of oppression was in India. There were many conditions in India that resembled the Pine Ridge Reservation. I believe there are spiritual dark forces that want to keep the Oglala Lakota people in bondage. Lakota have a wealth to offer the world, but we see people lost in hopelessness. My personal opinion is the Lakota would be the greatest warriors for Jesus. It is time the Lakota rise up and take their stand in the Spiritual warfare that is attacking their world and the world around us.

I have thought of this many times over the past couple years. I believe it is because I seek to be in the Creator's will for my life. I live in the poorest place in America and hope to make changes in our everyday lives. I started talking about a dark cloud above the Reservation, and I have mentioned before we live in a "Culture of Death". With the number of people dying young, it is no wonder people are caught in a grieving cycle that holds them in darkness. I like the analogy of moving through a storm. It is very hard to believe you will move the other side of the storm when you are in the midst of its power and fury. The darkness does fade and the sun does come up in the morning. The darkness is the darkest just before the dawn. We have been in the storm for some time, and we need to break the cycles of poverty.

I was talking to a friend named Danny today. We were talking about social communities and raising taxes for the richest 2%. We debated on whether President Obama would leave the Bush tax cuts in place. If the tax cuts are ended it is being said the middle class will have their taxes raised as well. I am not an expert in taxes or whether they should be raised, left as is, or lowered, but I do believe we need to work together to build our tribal economies. Danny thought it would be good to keep the programs for the poor as a safety net. I liked his idea because it shows a depth of compassion. He has traveled to Africa and other places of poverty and knows the conditions faced in poor economies. I shared with him that people in social communities 200 years ago pulled their own weight. Ah, so you see, we do have a boot strap mentality of pulling them up and getting to work.

I have debated poverty with the "haves" and the "have notes". I really believe when you live in community from a tribal perspective, you should have everyone working together. So we need to empower each other and help each other up. Instead, there is a "crab mentality" that is a destructive force. Our life on the Rez has great opportunity, but we need to get moving with a greater understanding. We as a people have great friends who want to empower the Lakota people, but we are too busy fighting over crumbs. I heard a great idea today about building office space for the purpose of renting that space for programs and businesses. Lakota Funds showed you could rent space for a fair market value. If the building was here in Pine Ridge Village, it would pay for itself in a few years.

So the question is, why are we involved and living in the poorest place in the greatest country in the world? It is because we are willing to sacrifice. We are not all called to sacrifice, but we can pray and help empower a better tomorrow for the Oglala Lakota Nation. Thanks for reading and influencing change in the mirror.

The Global Dollar, End of the Mayan Calendar, and Armageddon
....from 9-01-09

A new age is becoming clearer every day. The Prime Minister of Russia, Vladimir Putin in recent months talked about a global dollar. That statement sent many people into shock, including this writer. When I was growing up, we talked about the future and seeing a future without cash. While traveling, I love to see the different types of money. This summer I was able to find Yen, Rubbles, and French Euro from some passing tourists. I find the paper money fascinating because it is distinctive and has special meaning printed on each bill. So, I try to collect paper money when I can find people who are willing to help me or who will exchange with me for our American Dollars.

The winter solstice of 2012 is coming closer, and I have pondered what is in store for the world as the end of the Mayan calendar seizes to exist. I do not want to scare people, but it is worth taking a look into prophesy and future events. Growing up in a Christian environment has taught me some of the things the Bible talks about. Armageddon, the war that will end all wars is in the future. Magog and Gog seeking to destroy the state of Israel is a prediction. A cashless society is also talked about. When I was a child, it made me feel unsafe. The prophesies speak of a mark on the forehead or wrist; without it, you will not be permitted to trade goods and services. I am no expert in the predictions of the world, but I will share with you what I have learned.

2012 is the mark of change; some people believe it is the end of the world and others believe it is a time of enlightenment. I am not a scholar of the Mayan Calendar, and I do not put my trust in this system of thought. My system of thought is placed in the Bible. As I have studied with some of our people, I have found the Biblical prophecy to be trustworthy. We are now coming to a point where a cashless society or global dollar can be put into place overnight. As I stated before, when I was a child, I was sometimes overwhelmed with anxiety; but I now feel confident in my belief system and trust in Jesus. He is ultimately in control of the future of the world.

In our little business in the Village of Pine Ridge, we struggled to bring a credit card machine for payments. It seems like a scam because the company gets a certain percentage of each transaction plus nineteen cents. If you added all of the fees for each of the transactions for every business across the globe, it is a huge amount of money. Many people no longer write paper checks. Everything is paid over the web or through automatic deductions. I seriously wonder why I have long distance on my phone because the cell phones call long distance for free. But, we are constantly allowing ourselves to go without cash. When you realize how much time we spend thinking about the future, I have come to the conclusion we need more people working on our future. We need to dream and envision a brighter future. Our young people need hope! I met a guy last week who basically told me we need to forget about this generation growing up and work with the children. I plan to work closer to this generation. They hold the keys to our future, and they understand technology. We are moving at faster speeds. It will be the young people who will make the difference. I believe our ancestors worshipped the creator, and they want for us so much more than we can understand.

When all of the dust settles, we must know we only have ourselves to change. My hope is people will begin to understand true change and transformation of our being. I do not want to behave like a human or act like a good guy. I want to be emotionally healthy. I sense among our Indigenous people across North America, we are really unhealthy. My purpose in rambling this week is to encourage health, not worrying. A great majority of people struggle with their emotions. We need to take a hold of our emotions and know the difference between illusion and truth. Jesus says he is the Canku(Road), Wowicake(truth), and Wiconi (Life); because of this I give my worries to him.

A Bucket List
....*from 11-10-10*

While I have been on the Pine Ridge Reservation since 1979, I have found great hope in our people. I have been struggling with many issues because as humans we go through difficulties, and most people understand the struggles. I have met some people who have no idea what it means to have faith. They work their whole lives and find out in the end, it is empty. I have sat with millionaires and know they wished for more. We have been dealt a blow because of what is known as Manifest Destiny, the 1840s expansionism from coast to coast by the Anglo-Saxons. Unfortunately, the negotiations our Lakota forefathers fought for in the nineteenth century and resulting treaties have been broken numerous times. We know what was done, and now we as a people need to come to grips with the aftermath.

When dealing with the family it is important to understand we all have the same issues. These issues come from the destruction of our culture. Now in my mid-forties, I hope get some things accomplished in the second part of my life. I know of one friend who has a bucket list, or a list of things they would like to accomplish before they die. I still want to go to Australia to see the land, but I am a bit concerned about the wildlife. I have accomplished most all of the goals I set in my teen years, and I have decided to make a new list.

I would like to author a book. I am really close to this goal so it will be my first on the list. Another goal is to see an Indigenous Church in Pine Ridge Village. This is difficult because Indigenous Church would mean we need to develop our doctrine, pay our own bills, and propagate our faith; it is a bit simplistic but good for these ramblings. I would also like to overcome my own issues of pain in my life. I hope I do not have to walk around with bitterness and unforgiveness the rest of my days. The last goal in my life is to see my grandchildren grow up understanding who they are in the 21st century. I want to teach them where they come from and for them to know they are Lakota.

Four goals is a good start. I hope I can accomplish many other things in my life. I would like to grow old, but not too old. We live very short lives, and I have failed many times in my life. I am ready to start learning from these mistakes. I know we are dealing with supernatural beings that want to affect our lives. The Bible teaches us there are two forces, good and evil. I have often not lived up to the standard God has given me. I hope in my short life and after I am gone, that my grandchildren will understand their grandfather lived through difficulties and survived a destructive way of life on this earth.

Being survivors of the American holocaust as an American Indians we need to rise up in these years to let the world know we have withstood all that has been done to us. We can make a better life for our future, our children. We have all made mistakes; this makes us human and in need of a savior. I have lived as a follower of Jesus since I was twelve years old. I know it is not always easy to live as a follower of Jesus when rest of the world seeks to go its own way. I remember being a boy and listening to sermons. I heard about the old man verses the new man. I have struggled in my life to fight off my old selfish nature and to embrace the new giving nature of Jesus. Jesus helps to transform me into new being.

Zuya Mani is a warrior's journey, a place of hardship. I am not sure I can give this concept justice, but I will try. I imagine a Lakota warrior traveling to scout out an area before his people. I have often thought of my life and what I am here to share with the people. I was told that when I am done with the Journey I have traveled, I will have something to share with the people. In my early life I failed more than I succeeded. Ultimately, my life is not contingent on what I do, but instead it depends on what Jesus did on the cross. I have traveled far and have seen much. I believe I must continue what men like Ted Standing Elk, Joe Iron, and others stood for in difficult times. Like you, I have seen many Lakota men stand for Jesus and yet they failed because of the pressure to conform to the Christianity they were taught. I grew up with the two men mentioned, and they both lived passionate lives for Jesus. I remember hearing the Gospel Hour preached in Lakota and the songs from Joe Iron were amazing.

We are at a great threshold in history. The world is faced with globalization and the Bible prophesies many things. All things are set in place for the second coming, and we need a revival of faith in Jesus. Most of our people are medicating the pain of their lives, and we need to offer them hope. I now know what my message to the Oyate is "Jesus is alive and offers a more abundant life in a world of turmoil." Jesus has brought me to a point in my life where I have clarity of life. I know there are forces out there that do not want you to hear the truth, but Jesus is the Savior.

Cayuga Center of the Universe

Pine Ridge has been in the news for over a century, but what makes this Reservation news worthy? Being an Oglala Lakota I was getting a soda one day in Big Bat's Gas/Convenient Store when I ran into a Cayugu from Six Nations. He was the director of an organization, and I sensed he is a very intelligent man. He was attending a meeting at the tribal offices. The meeting had just finished, and he was stopping at Big Bat's before he drove back to Rapid City. He looked like he was pretty upset when he saw me and decided to have a few words. He told me, "Leon, I know what is wrong with you Oglala! You people think you are the center of the Universe!" I remember smiling as I realized he was meeting with the Education Committee of the Oglala Sioux Tribe. Of course, I believe our people have ethnocentricities like most people around the world. When you come here, even if you are from another tribe, it is difficult for all others. When someone tells me they are from another tribe, I tell them not to feel bad because they, too, can lead an almost normal life. After all, everyone cannot be Oglala. We have withstood every tactic the United States Government could throw at us in an attempt to destroy us. I realize we have issues that are overwhelming and seem very difficult because we see slow change in our system.

While Wounded Knee in 1890 was a huge and tragic event in our history, it was a victory of sorts for America. The Occupation of Wounded Knee was a great victory for the American Indian. In 1973, the American Indian did not have freedom of religion, children were being taken and given to non-Indian families, and policies of the United States were created to eradicate the American Indian. 1973 brought human rights violations to the front pages throughout America. When you look at it, the unemployment, dropout rates, death rates, and poverty have essentially stayed the same over the last forty years. I remember the takeover of the tribal offices, when the Grassroots Oyate or People took over to stop the corruption. It was an attempt to stop all of the ills of the tribe in one moment. I was a witness to remarkable people who decided it was time for change. There were issues of the treasurer and president fighting for control. Lots of accusations were flying all over the place. It was wild and people occupied the government facilities. I never did find out what happened to the records, but I do remember the Federal people came in and took many boxes of information. Stands like these have been a part of the life of Pine Ridge, and in the seventies there were many unsolved murders across the Reservation.

I have never met a nicer group of people through my travels than the Lakota people. Yet, they have seen so much violence and have so many problems across Pine Ridge. I personally believe the Oglala

251

of Pine Ridge Reservation have a great opportunity to do what God intended for them to do. Take the world by storm. The problem is the Oglala are in a struggle in their own lives. Oglala can change the world if they understand their potential. I hope to develop this idea more in my book, but for now I believe this short essay can be sufficient food for thought.

MY FAITH

I am a Christian and I
always will be

Seek Nothing
....from 8-25-10

I want to be inspired, and I believe with encouragement we can all be healthy. When I was growing up I had a teacher tell us to write down our life's goals. I thought I wanted to be a journalist when I was young, but Jesus had a different life's work for me. I believe God wanted me to serve him on the Pine Ridge. I know many people are wondering how I could possibly understand God's will for my life.

First of all, it is important to be connected with the power source. When I was a young boy I realized I did not know the Creator. At the time I thought I was searching and wanting to know the architect of my universe. I have come to understand the Creator was reaching out for me. I was eight years old and I felt the religion I was involved in did not bring me the knowledge I desired. I was a little Catholic boy who went to church, lit candles, prayed for loved ones, and went to the catechism offered by the local nunnery. My world was empty, and I knew there was hollowness in my soul. It appears many people have sensed this in their own lives, but have not been able to overcome the world's distractions.

I am not sure my being "human" can help anyone understand that you can change the void in your life. Even when you have filled the void with what actually fits in the emptiness you will struggle. It is clear we can become conquerors over the condition we call "human". As we forge into the battle we actually need to seek to empty ourselves. John the Baptist said, "He must become greater; I must become less." He was talking about Jesus who was the savior. John came before Jesus with the message of repentance. This is a key for the lives of our people because we have fallen into the world's way of getting things done. Culture is how we get things done in our day to day activities. The American way of life is based on the "Dream" - not Dusty Rhodes, but the American dream of living a life of comfort and leisure. It leaves behind a life of sacrifice and hard work as everyone seeking the "Dream" is fully involved in getting what they think they deserve, more.

255

When I talk about Him increasing and me decreasing as John stated, it should be clear that this does not go against the Lakota way of a life of humility. It does go against the American Dream. You can see people fully involved in their culture of choice as they seek to be selfish or selfless. We as humans are by nature selfish, and it is hard to overcome this way of life. You do not need to teach selfishness as it comes naturally. I believe our ancestors trained themselves to become more selfless and to not seek after more for themselves. In America it is not looked upon as a good thing if you seek to help others. When we talk about repentance, we need to understand it is against the natural, selfish, self-centered ways of being human. When we can turn from our ways to God's ways, it will be a better life for us individually and socially as well.

I seek to understand the world around me, and I have thought of our ancestors as they understood the world. Because I am a follower of the teachings of Jesus, there are some ideas that may not seem to mesh with the Lakota way. I have come across many people in my life who have been labeled. I have yet to come across the Lakota theologian who has taken thought to the next level. Practical ways are how we live our lives and get through our days. But thought can lead you down many paths, so it is important to use reason when you travel the road of seeking to more fully understand the world beyond.

In our lives we there are aspects of life that are satisfying, but in the end it is only the Creator who has left us with His essence. Ex nihilo is a Latin phrase meaning "out of nothing." Nothing begins to exercise the mind. I have often thought about nothing. It is truly mind boggling because even darkness is something. So what is nothing? I believe it is void of anything or everything, and it is beyond comprehension for a finite being. We are dealing with space and time; we have a beginning and an end. All people will leave this earth, but it is vital we understand our being. I have been inspired to develop my writing from a human who by nature is not the solution to my being. No one person can fulfill your purpose; after all we are on this earth to fulfill some kind of purpose. I would hope to live two lives, but in the end I know it was but one life I will have lived. A life with purpose where I can find peace in the both the storms and goodness of life would be great.

256

By now you must be thinking this rambler is writing in riddles, so I will try to be clear as I have often been told. The world in a Lakota understanding is our mother. In the understanding based in the way of Jesus, I believe the world was created out of nothing, or ex nihilo. The Creator left the essence of himself. And the way to success is not more but less. We need to give of ourselves. We need to seek to decrease and allow the Creator to increase in our lives. The Lakota way of thought and the Bible way do not contradict - they actually come together in a greater understanding. I believe our ancestors sought out the essence of the Creator, who I understand is Jesus. The only way you could possibly understand a being greater than nothing is if he himself walked among us. The truth I understood as a pre-teenager is Jesus is God.

I believe I need to be willing to give up everything in order to find my way in this world. The cost of following Jesus is you must be willing to give up everything in your life. In my mind I believe our Lakota ancestors strived for this way of life. We have been kept down for way too long, and we must seek to do the Creator's will. I believe I am in the will, but it is very difficult. I want to be clear as some people know who I am, but they cease to know me. The Creator God knows every detail and things I do not even know about myself. It is not a religion but a relationship with the one who made the heavens and the earth. Pray and ask Him to show Truth. Life on the Reservations is difficult. We have a lot of pain. I hope to find healing of my soul in the end.

Tats and Tales
....from 11-17-09

My laptop gave out and I am resuming my Ramblings on my desktop computer. I was thinking about my column this week and thought about writing about tattoos. I was fourteen or fifteen when I got my hands on some India ink, which, by the way, could very well be called Chinese ink. It was black and widely used for writing and printing. I cannot even begin to tell you where I got the ink, but I used it to give myself a tattoo or three. I do not know if my mom noticed but I remember I lived in New Crazy Horse in Pine Ridge Village. I have seen many "tats" in my adult life, but I wondered when the craze really started in America. My mom even had some writings on her hands so maybe if she noticed mine she just did not mind.

It was the early nineties when I started paying attention to our American culture. Rap music was just beginning to take off and Bruce Willis was young. The last Die Hard was like watching the last Rocky movie. I did not want to watch the movie, but I did because I had seen every movie one of the Die Hard and Rocky movies to that point. Of course Die Hard came out in 1988, and it was a great movie with some lines everyone remembers. Then in 1990 Die Hard 2 came out, and it should have stopped there. But, they got every dollar they could. My theory is Bruce Willis came on stage for an award show and had an earring in his left ear. It was shocking and that started the craze of earrings. Before we knew it, the American culture changed.

Lakota people have had men piercing their ears. I was never into the cultural aspect of this way of life. So I do not have a pierced ear and really never wanted to take part in the ritual. I remember people talking about taking potatoes and using them to protect the neck. So I believe the American culture was helped by Bruce Willis and he started the ear piercing. Then when all of the youth culture pierced everything they could, they moved on to tattoos. I might be completely wrong, but it is my opinion of the way things have come about in American culture. Some people probably had piercings and tattoos before the nineties, but many people have enhanced their markings.

I saw a young lady in the store the other day and she had wings of a butterfly on her back. I talked to a vet or two and one said when the Marines would ask if someone had a tattoo, they would tell them they were too manly for the Marines. Some people put their significant other's name on their body. I laugh when someone wants to change their tattoo because it has a name they no longer want. I tease my wife about getting Leon put on her. She shakes her head no. I think tattoos are a way of saying something to the world that is significant to its owner.

I have seen some interesting "tats," but last week I saw a guy who had a lot of them on his arms. I am sure there are more all over his body.

I might be afraid of the pain and the healing you have to go through in order to express yourself. It is said Jesus was pierced. I appreciate the pain he went through for me. It could be said tattooing was counter-cultural, but today in America it has become a common place in our schools, movies and even our athletics.

One day when I was washing up for dinner I started to try to clean my tattoo because I forgot it was there. How could I forget what I did when I was a young teenager? I put the most powerful image I ever saw on my right hand, a cross. It signifies my belief system and helps me to remember Jesus died for all of the bad things I have ever done. It means more to me than anything on this earth because it has set me free and gave me eternal life. When I understood what Jesus did for me in taking my death I was blown away by his sacrifice. So the next time you see a tattoo remember, maybe it has a story.

A New Day

A new day is an opportunity to begin life over. In my mind I have a Lakota man raising his hand toward the heavens and realizing he is very small in the vastness of our Creator. Powerful images can help us comprehend we are small in regard to creation, and we need to make our lives meaningful. Embrace it, and who knows where the journey will take you. I am struggling because of the oppression our people feel on the Pine Ridge. The theme in our service yesterday was to take off our chains and step out of the bondage. There is much bondage such as poverty and alcohol. We have many people who sit and wait for their next drink. This kind of life is not living at all; I believe it is dying. So we must make choices every day. Today I choose to live and feel it in my being. New blood would rush through my body and mind.

I was talking to my wife this morning and I explained to her we have a burden. The cross we carry is heavy, but the great joy is to realize Jesus wants to help us carry it. We are to pick up our cross and follow him, but so many people believe it is too heavy for them to carry. But when you realize and proclaim he is the Savior, the Savior comes and lifts our being and we can now walk upright. Our God is a forgiving God, and he wants to know each of us.

The darkness is gone, and I want what God wants for me. I will not let the oppression of the darkness overcome me. I hope you know what I am saying because when you understand what I am saying it will help you to move into God's place for you. My struggles wrestling with the evil powers of darkness have their root in an unforgiving heart. I believe unforgiveness is like a cancer that will eventually eat up its victim. I pray like the Lakota man who reaches up to the skies and humbles himself, understanding who he is in regard to the Universe. Someone said they thought they were the star of this movie, when in actuality they are just a supporting actor. I pray God helps me to be the best supporting actor.

Stop "The Man"

There are many people out there who are confused about life and this is troubling to me as a Lakota man. I see in my own struggles the pain of our people. My life has been relatively easy compared to most. But it is because at a point in my life, I chose to change some things. I became a part of a faith community. The Gospel Fellowship has been my lifeline. I chose to be in fellowship with other likeminded followers of the teachings of Jesus. I do not stand on my accomplishments or good deeds; my faith and hope are built on the promises in the Bible.

I know it may seem like I am saying it is easy to follow the teachings of Jesus, to love God, and to love our neighbors. I am not, because I know through my own pain and struggles it is not an easy road. We have many social programs in Indian Country and we even have some very bright people. But, I am convinced the one thing that can save us is a relationship with God. Our lives as American Indians are important because we represent a whole hemisphere of people. We were almost wiped out and many of the tribes and communities did not make it through the last five hundred years. My opinion is that we need to embrace Jesus. Not the religion of Christianity, but the teachings of Jesus because they will change our lives.

When I learned the history of our people I became bitter. It was only Jesus who has helped me to overcome the malice and bitterness in my heart. I hope to stand against the injustice that continues even in the 21st century. We can overcome the historical trauma, but it will take all of us to stand against the greed and selfishness. Our lives are testament to the grandfathers and grandmothers who were very strong and had fortitude. We can come together in strength and unity.

When I was growing up, I would often hear people talk about "The Man" and how he was trying to keep us down. Being an "Indian" was mostly how Hollywood depicted us, backward, dirty, drunk, and a list of other negatives. I remember being called a dirty Indian by a Mexican! I always thought of the Mexicans as Indigenous people who were grouped together and stripped of their "Indianness". Some may be thinking at this point Indianness is not a word. Of course the culture of Mexico was tribal and indigenous to Mesoamerica. They were American Indians with a distinct culture. After the United States took about fifty percent of the land, some stayed within the borders of the United States. It would seem the way America sees the American Indian would be through a Hollywood lens. I read once the Lakota would break the ice in winter to bathe. We were looked at as savages so they could have a clear conscience when they took more land. Treaties were broken in the name of God, which is the worst thing you could possibly do.

When the people of Mesoamerica were in their fullness it was clear they worshiped the sun. It was their deity, and they would often sacrifice humans on their temples. One day the leaders were confused because some clouds covered the power of the sun. They realized if clouds could take the deity's power, it could not possibly be the god they thought it was. Of course, the common people could not be told, because the leaders feared they would riot. The leaders made a choice to not tell the people even though they understood the sun was just an object. I tell this story because I believe it is important to understand revelation. The creator created and gave humans the ability to choose right from wrong. The essence of humanity is that we are all flawed, and the ability to choose right is a gift of the Creator.

Wankan is sacred or holy in the realm of Lakota thought. When Lakota seek prayer, they usually go through a Holy Man or Woman. Most people do not classify themselves as Wankan for this is left to a few who deal with the spirits or seek to communicate with the Creator. If you look at the contemporary society of Lakota you will see the majority of people do not engage in ceremony. If they have a need they will seek out a spiritual leader. It is the Lakota way to have a spiritual leader. These ways have been passed down through the ages.

In my studies of Jesus, he walked the earth blamelessly and had compassion for the common people. He came to serve the common people and not to be served. In my mind I saw the old people who did not accumulate for themselves. They walked with nothing because they sought to serve. Here is the key in understanding the realm of following Jesus. We can now go to the Creator through his Spirit. Not just the Wankan, but the common people are allowed to speak directly with the one who made us. Until people understand this we will continue to have problems in Lakota Country. A transformed spirit comes from within. We have sought to change the behaviors of people, but without the change of heart, we will continue to go in circles. The people need to take hold of the unblemished lamb, the one that is perfect. So we need to not rely on the human, but on the Creator of the human to bring hope of change within.

We have many issues. I am tired and frustrated like many of our people. We know there is an alcohol problem and yet nothing is done. There are people who fight for a dry reservation and allow others to make a fortune because they do not want us to quit drinking. I met with two young men, and we were talking about this issue. Joose came up because people are starting to have bad reaction to this malt liquor. It is marketed by the corporation to make more money. The target group is minorities. Our people are drinking malt liquor by the cases and the "Man" is allowing us to kill ourselves. We need to understand what is at stake. Our way of life as humans is being attacked for money.

I am reminded of my rocket scientist friend. By the way, I believe everyone should have at least one of these people as a friend. Every border town around us is getting rich from something we have made illegal. I have read many views on the issue, and I believe our tribal government needs to start making better business decisions. Take it to the people to decide at election time this year. The people who do not drink will not all of a sudden start drinking. The "Man" is laughing all the way to the bank. They treat our relatives like they are less than human. It is time to start growing up and making grown up decisions. We need to find ways of keeping our money on the Reservation.

I talked with a lady from a tourist spot in the Black Hills, and she said she feeds four hundred people a night. The busy summer season allows her family to make enough money to almost make it through the whole year. There are thousands, if not millions, who come to the Black Hills to hear about our Indianness. We need to draw people to our homelands and keep them coming. Stop having workshops in Rapid City; build a convention center here and bring the other tribes here. Let us work together for our future and stop talking about it. Just me rambling, so we can stop the "Man" and start living.

Free Will vs. Determinism

I thought I was a strong proponent for free will in my life. I agreed with people when they told me I should allow people to choose their life. Funny idea about free will, it all comes down to you having the ability make a good choice or bad one, but ultimately the individual chooses. I wrestled with this idea for some time because of circumstance. What is in our context that would make us choose one way over another? I feel odd at times, but did I actually choose the four shots of espresso or did the barista make a mistake and make two extra. Did I choose to have them? You could argue it was my choice to say yes, and it would be just as easy for me to say no. But of course being a good "Indian" I was taught that we are not to deny a gift; we are to accept the gift with gratitude. We often see non-Indians who say "no" to gifts from Lakota people. I have often said to non-Indians if an Indian offers you food you are to take it; if you do not, it would be disrespectful. It would offend the Lakota person involved, but it would not be the first time an Indian was offended. Well, back to the four shots of espresso, I believe I could be right in both cases of determinism and free will. Because of my upbringing and cultural heritage, I was left with a decision. There was a cause to the affect in my life to choose the extra two shots. Of course, I am human and could have gone beyond cultural norms and upbringing and decided it was too late to drink four shots rather than the two I ordered.

So what does this rambling mean? It means you could make the case for Lakota people that they did not choose to live in poverty, but it was the determinism that made this fate. But freewill will eventually bring a leader to our Lakota people. I am sure people are confused because of the situation we find ourselves a part of in our Reservation society. We can overcome but there may very well be a point where something changes the game. It could be Jesus who comes into a life and helps that person to become a free will thinker. I never thought that I would have begun a life of following Christ. Some believe they will lose everything if they choose to lay down their lives. But I believe if you lay down your life you gain it by the freedom Jesus offers. In the end I believe that by following Jesus and becoming his servant, I will gain all that I desire. Humbling oneself will bring complete freedom. What is the truth about everything said? We need to continue to fight for the truth and ignore the illusion. Are you ready to open yourself up to the TRUTH or do you want to hold tight to your life and miss what the Creator has offered as a gift? As Lakota we are to receive gifts freely as a sign of respect. If I do not accept the gift of God, I am disrespectful to God.

I do not rely on my own strength
....*from 12-01-09*

New beginnings and new goals need to be a platform for our lives in Native America. Our people need to see where they will be in the 21st century. In my own life I have never really thought about the year 2000 or 2010 for that matter. I guess I have lived my life knowing God is in control. He has watched over me and has kept me on my path. My journey ends with being with the Creator, not because I am good, but because I realize I am a sinner and I have asked him to forgive me. Now I no longer have a sin debt on my life. Now I am no longer bound by this debt because Jesus died for me and my sin offering. It is the mercy of the Father which makes me free. So begins this week's ramblings and a new chapter in life. I love being a follower of the "Way" because I can rest in his plan for my life.

I was thinking about writing many things this week. First, I want to share the greatest game I ever saw played outside of the state high school realm. Casey, Brewer, Salway, Three Stars, Giago, Jess R., and Josh Martin were playing a game down in Denver. Their team name was the Spear Chuckers. They were playing against the Crow. I guess in my mind the Crow looked like giants. They had a player that was almost seven foot tall. When the Crow were able to bring the ball across the half court line, they were met with the play of Josh and Jess both from Pine Ridge High School. These guys are only around six foot tall, but they were formidable opponents. They made the taller Crow players work very hard in the low block area. Of course the guards were spectacular because they pressured the ball during the whole game.

This week I will celebrate my 25th wedding anniversary and I am excited. It is difficult to have long time marriages. I know there are some who have been married for over 60 years; this is a great feat in our community. I know marriage is difficult because we are in a give and take relationship. Two people with different views and opinions living together will have difficult moments, but it is always good when you can work out your differences. I hope to be more like my Lord in the next twenty-five years. It is like the preacher who said, "I am not like Jesus, but I thank God am not like I used to be."

We should understand our lives are always changing, and we must stop believing the lies. We each have our burdens to carry. I want to help people and not hurt them. Human beings are meant for relationships; this causes great pain and struggle because it is other humans who hurt us. My plan is to begin the later chapters of my life with an eagerness to help our people heal. I have heard people say we need to heal not kneel. That may sound like a good sound bite, but in all seriousness we should all be on our knees praying and asking God to make us what He wants us to be.

I have seen pain and suffering just as you have. When this pain comes, we need to call on the Creator to help us with our problems. Last week I helped bury a young woman, and I felt the pain of our people all over as I thought of my precious daughter. I shared with the people the fact that we are a beautiful people; we should not believe the lies that we are bad people. Genocide was unsuccessful in Lakota Country. No matter what happens in the next few years, we need to fight off depression and know we have survived.

I do not rely on my own strength, but I rest on the belief system that Jesus has paid it all. I told my friend the other day that Christianity did a job on our Native people. I know people see me as a Christian and sometimes I believe they think I am out of my mind. In its purest form, Christianity is selfless and thinking of others. In its worst form, men who say they follow Christ do terrible things. When I reached out to the heavens, it was Jesus who took my hand. Now, I am his friend, and he is my God. I will never apologize for my faith; instead I will let you know I do not stand on my merit but on what Jesus did on the cross. I love my people and hope for understanding. Thank you for reading. Anytime you would like to speak with me, I hope you will introduce yourself to me.

The Rock Jesus

Jesus the Christ is one statement where people get it wrong. Christ is not the last name of Jesus, rather it is an office. Jesus was his name and he was from Nazareth. He was Jesus of Nazareth and this is how the people knew him. He changed the world with his teaching of picking up your burden and following him. Who would want to pick up a burden, with all of its weight to follow a teacher who would eventually be killed for his faith and way? Love, repentance, forgiveness, and freedom are what he taught, but more than anything he was teaching a fulfillment of the Law or the Ten Commandments. Maybe most would like them to be suggestions because the law was difficult to follow and the religious leaders made it even more difficult to follow. Jesus said the greatest commandment is to love God with your heart, soul, and mind and the second is to love your neighbor as yourself. Can you love people beyond yourself or even like yourself?

Jesus said, "On this rock I will build my church." There are some who would say it was Peter who would become the first Pope. Actually, it is the understanding of what Peter was saying. Jesus asked the question, "Who do people say I am?" John and other prophets were named, but the question was asked to Peter, "Who do you say I am?" Peter answered, "You are the Christ, the Son of the living God." It was on this statement Jesus would build the Church; it was understood that Jesus was the Savior sent from God the Father. This entails a great deal when you dig a little deeper. What it does is touch your being because it transforms. The unknown is very powerful, but you must not let it control your fears; it will bring freedom to your soul. Do you feel powerless? Can you put your trust in someone who says take up your cross or burden and follow me? You must realize he is calling you to freedom, and his desire for a life with you is strong. Jesus laid down his life so we could live. Wow, I am fully involved in my faith. It is pure and simple; he took away my sin which separates me from Him!

Know Thyself and Accept God's Grace
....from 7-14-10

A few words to the Oglala Sioux Tribal Council... I know your job is very difficult and demanding. I realize years later that it is a very difficult position to have, with little time to accomplish projects. I hope some of you will read this because I believe we are at the crossroads of development. This crossroads is here because of the Internet, which is called the information highway. I know you have to weed through much of the information, but if you do the work it will pay off. I heard from the smoke signals you may be considering selling Zeolite and mining for the product. My words of caution are that it needs to be looked into thoroughly first because it may have horrific effects on the ecology. I do not know much about the field of mining for minerals, but I know where they want to mine is in the badlands and very little grows out in the badlands. Where they want to mine is in direct line of Shannon, Bennett, and Cherry Creek Counties.

Many people have told me the United States was founded on a Jewish/Christian foundation of the Bible. In my study it is more than a faith foundation, and if you search the scriptures, or what Jesus said, you will find the United States it is actually the opposite. The Jesus way is about emptying oneself rather than taking more. I call the American Dream "The Culture of More" because it is best described a way of life that seeks to take as much as it can. It is an easy way of doing something because the natural tendency of humans is self-centeredness. If you develop a worldview with this understanding in mind you can see how people react to different scenarios.

Over the past few weeks I have been working on some ideas about being human. One interesting idea deals with me. When you seek to understand what makes up the world, a good place to start is with yourself. "Know Thyself," is a great philosophical understanding of the world and what makes it work. We need to examine who we are and what makes us human. When you deal with existentialism you must understand your being and how you are affected by the world around you. So in my own humanness I understand what makes me human.

Many people do not like that I am a Follower of Christ, but in my mind, I must admit I cannot find fault in the way Jesus lived. He fed people, he sat with the sinners, the ones who the religious leaders would have nothing to do with. You see, I am one that Jesus sits with, and he accepts me. I was in need of a Savior. I realize there are some who want to continue on their own path and they are satisfied. But, I believe there are people who need a helping hand. Jesus stands at the door and offers his hand to help us through our difficulties.

Furthermore, I have come to realize I have many flaws in my mind and body as well as my thinking. Try to understand the way of Jesus when he says to pray for those who would do you harm. In my human tendency, I would seek retribution and revenge. I want them to hurt if they hurt me. It is the natural way, but what Jesus teaches me through his spirit is to turn the other cheek. Of course, I fail Jesus more often than I would like to admit, but in the end he forgives me because of the grace he continuously offers me as his free gift. I rely on my relationship with Jesus to help me overcome my self-centered way of being human. That brings me back to the idea of what makes us human. To be imperfect is to be human and yet we need to strive to become more.

Life needs to be about forgiving each other and learning to love each other as God loves us. If we believe we are imperfect it will help us to humble ourselves. If you ever come across someone who believes he does not make mistakes, you will find an egomaniac that is full of pride. Pride is the first thing that keeps us separated from the Creator. It leads us to believe we can do a better job in our personal lives than the one who is unmoved Creator. The unmoved is something that does not need a cause to move; it is totally independent. To believe you can make better choices outside of the Creator is the worst thing you can do; it is pride.

I try to rely on the Wanka Taku Sku Sku or the Sacred Mover because I am imperfect. I believe the Creator is perfect and does not rely on me. My classmate told me he reads my articles and said he is praying for me. It is powerful when you know people are praying for you to give the right information. The Creator offers forgiveness for all wrongs, and I am totally at the mercy of his grace. My understanding of myself is I am an imperfect person living in a brutal world where people seek to be selfish. Try to understand - the American Dream is not the way of the cross. It could very well be an antithesis of the way Jesus lived.

Know the Creator, Know Thyself
....from 10-13-09

The reason I write is to express myself. I also try to understand our lives as Lakota. It did not dawn on me until this week that I had some readers in Rosebud. One kind gentleman asked my name the other day and I told him, Leon Matthews. He then asked me what relation I am to the guy who writes for the Lakota Country Times. I told him I am that guy. He encouraged me to keep writing, so here I sit rambling on about being Lakota and living on the Pine Ridge. I met some wonderful women from Rosebud as well. We kidded with each other and made Pine Ridge and Rosebud jokes. It was a pleasant meeting, and I appreciated their kind words. As we parted I said I would say hello in my article. So I would like to greet all of the Sicangu, and say thank you for reading.

There is a Psalm that begins with these words, "O LORD, you have searched me and you know me." My life has seen some difficult days, and I know I am in a battle for my life. When I started my journey of healing, I started with an inventory of my inner self. I felt the pain of our people, and I could not handle the pain. I realize we have too many people walking around with pain, and they do not want to feel it anymore. I mentioned some of the guys in White Clay called out my name and asked me to write their story. I used to think it was some type of unresolved grief issue they were dealing with. At one time I thought we were dealing with grief, but I now realize the problems we face as a people are compounded by the problems we face due to the Reservation life. I believe what the Psalmist states about the Lord searching us and knowing us.

People need to know who they are with regard to the Creator. In my theology I understand there is one Creation and one Creator. The one who moved has breathed life into our beings and knows us fully. My dedication is to draw closer to the Creator. I make the choice to come closer to the Creator I see myself more clearly. Humanity is imperfect and knowing who the Sacred Mover is will give you identity. I question what people think when they are all alone. My faith is strong, and I will seek to help people to know the Savior. This week has brought me to the understanding, he is my savior and now I must continue to make him my Lord.

My hope is to continue in community or tiospaye, because we need help in this journey. When all is said and done, we will know what the next life brings. I choose to walk with the desire to be more like Jesus because he lived for people. We need to fight for the truth and ignore the illusion. I often fight with feelings of not being good enough or feelings of failure. I believe in a God of love and his love covers my

270

failures and shortcomings. He has given me great friends, and I believe they are my family. My identity is with the Creator, and my prayers are for the Oyate. My heart hurts for the hurting. We have many people in pain. Let us come together and see how we can bring our people to healing.

High School Memories....Oglala Light

In the 1980s the school in Pine Ridge Village was called Oglala Community High School. Many people remember movie nights in the auditorium. They were usually full with students from the dorms and the village. We had the Sugar Shack during the school day where you could order a burger or get a soda. School was bustling with the buses rolling in on the west side of the school. Harvey Nelson was making American History come alive with his Fighting Sioux Education. John Moore was scaring underclassman with his no nonsense way of teaching Government. Bill Hotz taught art and did the annual year book with lots of photos. Depending on who was working on the yearbook, it would have more pictures of each respective sport's athletes, either wrestlers or basketball players. Mrs. Williams was teaching Biology, and after four decades she is still a wonderful lady. She drives from Hot Springs every day to teach Lakota teenagers biology. Jess Mendoza made a name for himself as he eventually won a state championship with the art and science of basketball. Charlie Z was by his side and eventually Char would get a girls' basketball championship. They called our school Oglala when reporting sports, and no one seemed to know who we were at the time.

They changed the name to Pine Ridge High School and the Thorpes have continued to garner respect from other schools because of their sports programs. I cannot forget the Detroit Area teacher, Bob Mayne, who was instrumental in encouraging me to be a journalist. He was a great English teacher and I was able to work with him on the school newspaper. Mayne was a long haired hippy type with an old leather coat. He smoked like a train. I remember seeing an ashtray full of finished cigarettes butts. I was the assistant editor during my time

271

at OCHS for the Oglala Light. It was a great paper, and I was able to have freedom in my editorials. I wrote some articles, too. I would walk around with a camera and take random pictures. I was able to get a lot of smiles in the hallways. I remember my aunt Mary Ellen worked in the Principal's office and I would stop by and visit for a moment when I got the chance.

I was vocal about my faith for about a week. I believe people assumed I was a good kid or a church attendee so they thought I was good. Of course I had many issues, but I enjoyed being called preacher boy. Times were young on the Pine Ridge. I first flew on a plane my senior year of high school. It was a time of change. The eighties brought change in the way we would eventually travel and communicate.

Life has changed since the eighties, but I believe the eighties have been imprinted in my mind. I felt much rejection by people because I felt different. I do not believe I have ever hidden my faith and was ready to talk about it with people if they wanted to know. I was able to finish high school on the Reservation even though my family moved back to Denver. I stayed with the missionary couple and their family. The Hedlunds were great and were instrumental in helping me be where I am today. I took the ministry after Rev. Earl Hedlund. He was a great student of the Bible, and I suspect he read many books in his study. He was the main person who kept me balanced. That was not always easy, but I felt the love and grace from him when I did not make the best decisions. God has given me many people who have helped me along the way. Like my friend Rick Demerest says, "It is a good thing you are married to Belle, because you would run over any other woman." I needed a strong woman to balance me because of my strong tendencies to be human and make mistakes.

Well, people like to ask me to behave so I should. I am trying to blog to help ease their fears. I am writing about school after playing basketball with 20-something year olds last night. I am a little sore, but I feel stronger today. I think I will behave and make some bread. Last thought, my uncle Roy was a great soup maker, and he brought balance in my life. I wish he was still here!

Choices...Master of our Fate and Captain of our Souls
....from 6-30-10

Summer is finally here and I hear some people talk about the West's drought being over. I remember growing up and often seeing rivers of water run down the streets when it rained. Then the drought came, and it was rare to see lots of rain. I remember as a child making paper boats and floating them down the street. I recall a quote from the movie Invictus, "I am the master of my fate; I am the captain of my soul." When I was a child I dreamed about on a ship. I wondered what it would be like on the vast ocean with the great sky above. Being on the water brings a feeling of freedom. I realize that putting your faith in God and trusting Him to be the master of your fate and the captain of your soul is a stretch for many. I would like to touch on this aspect of life because there is truly freedom in our choice.

Because I am a Follower of Christ, I have thought about my choice to believe in what Jesus did on the cross for my sin. He took everything I have ever done wrong and my penalty for my sins. My penalty should be death, but Christ's salvation gives me everlasting life. I do not know who started the rumor about perfect people. I have been around lots of people and have yet to find one perfect person. Sometimes when we consider the white missionaries we believe they do not sin. Of course, you have to live with them and watch them on a daily basis to see their sin. Here is one of my new sayings, "With every breath I can use, I say there are no perfect people in this world. We all struggle because we are human; it is what makes us human." With this understanding we can trust God for our grace and salvation. I choose to be a child of his and know he is my father in Heaven.

We all have free will, and we are responsible to make decisions in our lives. Sometimes we do not always make the best choices. We all can choose what and who we are going to serve. The Lakota were forced to say they were "Christians". The Churches became weapons for the Government to kill the culture. The Lakota went underground before the 70s. Many of the leaders kept the Wo Lakota. My knowledge comes from listening to the elders about how they were able to keep the ceremonies going. My grandfathers went about their business as they sought to continue using the Inipi out in the country. It was an impossible task to try to outlaw the ways of our people. Because of the policies of the United States Government, we as Lakota have not understood the true way of Jesus. I will never deny my faith and know that I can be assured the Spirit of God will continue to help me grow to be a better person.

I was in White Clay last week. We were handing out a few sandwiches and some water. I took my extended family and the kids were able to pass out some of the items we took for our relatives. One man told me he reads my column and encouraged me to keep writing. A few weeks ago I was going through some stress and burn out. I was hearing Wanka Sica, or the evil one, telling me I do not belong here. I seek the truth, and I believe I fully understand who I am. I am an Oglala Lakota Wicasa, and I belong to my family. My family comes from the Pine Ridge Reservation. To my relatives in White Clay, you belong to your people and you belong with your family. You must fight the pain and seek healing from God. It is my prayer we can become "…the master of our fate; the captain of our souls." Because when it all comes to the bare bones, it is our choice who we will serve.

As I host many visitors and groups from around the country, it is clear to me that these people have become a blessing to the Lakota people. And yes, these groups are from American churches. It is a powerful when you understand you have family throughout the country. One church group who has come and served in the Pine Ridge is Lakeland Church from Illinois. They have researched the issues and have come to truly serve our people. It is a wonderful thing to see people who want to come and help. Someone asked me one time why I allow people to come for a week and stay with us. It is because there are two billion followers of Christ throughout the world, and we are a family. One large tiospaye of people on the same journey, and our Itanca is Jesus. We choose to follow him, and we know he died for all of our sin. Not just some of it, but the sin yesterday, today and tomorrow.

A Search for Love

I have a friend who is as different from me as I could ever imagine. He is a good friend and a mentor. We have been friends through some difficult days. We were visiting today, and he talked with me about a lady friend of his. He said he has searched his whole life for her. I told him I thought even a moment with her would be better than having never met her in the first place. It made me think about my life and how we have many choices. Even though things seem to not work out, I believe they will in the end. Living a life without love would not be living at all. My friend has taught me about business and how to think when it comes to being in business. He has encouraged me when I have been in low places and has genuinely cared for me. I do not let people too close, but I feel that my friend knows my weakness and the blemishes. He has continued to have a great impact in my life because I get to be me. I wish him well with his life. I hope and keep believing he will work things out.

I shared this because it is a great little part of my life. God has brought many people into my life. I have seen some people who have everything and others who have nothing. Life is very short and we should make as many friends as we can because we are social beings. Life was meant to be lived with others. Some people lose focus because they forget the people who love them the most. I enjoy meeting people and visiting with them about their passions. I get to meet people in our coffee house, and then I get to bake bread and make meals that people seem to enjoy. I have seen many people come through Pine Ridge and have watched people grow to love our people. I hope to play a small role in developing relationships to bring hope and change to our Lakota people.

I have met many people who are struggling because they have lost their love. I think it is a viable question when someone asks you what you love most. Love is takes your breath away and leaves you weak in your body. I have another friend who says he would rather have respect than love. I would rather have my breath taken and my knees buckle because I am in love. "And now these three remain: faith, hope and love. But the greatest of these is love." - Paul of Tarsus. I wonder if

275

people ever think about Paul's statement. He has some great insight, but when you think of faith and hope you will understand they will pass. But love, well, love will be around for eternity. In the end, when you have nothing left to hope for or believe in, we will still have love. In all of your life, will you have the opportunity to have a moment of love?

There are many types of love, but there is one love that is very powerful and is overwhelming. In my quest to find love as a child I turned to the sky. I say sky because I realized at the age of eight I did not know God. I was walking down a street. I looked up to the sky and asked him to show me who he was. I would interject I believe the American Indian has been duped when it comes to the White Man's Gospel or God. The deity I serve is not white. My God is above our earthly flesh, the Creator. I believe he chose to walk as a tribal man with dark hair, dark eyes, and dark skin. The blue eyed, blonde hair, and light skin Jesus is not true. I believe he looked more like us than the Europeans. I realized the Uncreated Being loved me enough to draw me to him. It is such a powerful thing to understand the Creator loved me so much he died for every bad thing I have done. There are some people who do not believe in sin. In the Lakota belief system the young man had thought impure thoughts about the White Buffalo Calf Woman. He was turned into a pile of bones. This shows us we need to understand that we do sin. So when I say Jesus took the penalty of death from me, he died for all of my sin. I no longer have to worry about my fate and am in the hands of God.

I have been called a radical or basically someone who cannot be controlled. I have been cut off by mainstream Christianity because I do not fit into their idea of following Christ. I believe I am where the Uncreated Mover has placed me. I have faith and hope. And, I realize I do have love. I hope you can find a love that never fails.

Dropping Rain.....Left with more Questions than Answers
....*from 12-22-09*

Our lives teach us many lessons, and we need to reach down and make every moment count. I have seen our peoples' pain and I feel that we need more for our people. I just got back from the Sportsmanship Basketball Tournament. It was another great time in Martin, South Dakota. I saw a young man praying before his game and that always brings me joy. I was sitting on their bench waiting for our game. I was having a great time watching the young men go up and down the court. I heard this young man tell them to hold for the last shot, and he would "can" it. Sure enough, with the game tied. In overtime they passed the ball around; Jerry Dreamer got the ball with seconds to go and, bang he dropped a three to win the game. I had to give him credit because he was very confident. So when you get a chance to honor someone, you should take the time.

I got home just in time to catch the Championship Game of the Lakota Nation Invitational. Wow, it was a heart breaker to listen to the game. Some people believe it is good to lose early so it will make you hungry. I like listening to the KILI guys – Tom, Todd, Tally, Beau, and Ricky. It is not as easy as it sounds to go through all of the games. I remember when I did the games with my Uncle Tom Crash, and he could barely talk when we got to the championship games. Do you remember seeing people? It is so great to see them. I like to meet many people around the Rez and wish them well. Charley White Elk was one of these guys; he would laugh and make your day. He will surely be missed; I want to give my condolences to the family. I hope to not lose an opportunity to greet people, so if you are out there and see me, say hello.

I was going to get my mail the other day. As I was walking out of the Post Office, a man told me he loved Jesus too. He told me that when we were in school at Oglala Community High School together, he was getting ganged and I suckered him. I laughed because that was not me. I told him I never suckered him or anyone else. He was very nice to me and said that he prayed to Jesus and now Jesus was in his heart. I was glad I was able to stay on the Ridge most of the week. I have listened to the LNI games on the radio and see a few people. I believe we need to encourage our people more. I want to share and help people with the One I work for here on the Pine Ridge. Jesus has truly changed my life, and I know sometimes we forget, but I am committed to living for him.

Rez Ramblings

We are now facing 2010 and we are out of the single digits. Our goals need to be looked over and changed and focused. I would like to see Billy Mills Hall opened for our people. Basketball is a great way to relieve stress and take off a few pounds. Volleyball is also a fun sport, and I know people play and it is good to see the players come into the hall. It is time for us as people to begin to take a stand and begin new life changes. I am looking at 2010 to be a great year for our people. We have many issues coming with financial strain, and if we could just begin to work on the things we can change we will have a better life. I do not have all the answers, but I am willing to help where I can, and I choose to help the young men and women with the issues they face in the next decade. We need to get our heads out of the sand and start to make real changes. I bet if I talked with every council person they would agree that we need to work harder in our communities.

So this leaves us with more questions than answers. I would love to see round dances at Billy Mills Hall. I would love to see people, young and old, enjoying themselves in a place that was built for hope. Billy is one of us, and his name is on there for a reason; it is because he proved to the world that he could win the Gold. Our people are great. I hope that we can start to see little changes in the way we do things in our communities. Let us not live with regrets, but live with hope of a better tomorrow. Change does not come easily, but with a little effort I hope we can see great changes for our children. I believe we need to know our weaknesses and this will make us stronger. I believe it is the power of God that will change us as we ask for his help. I want so much for us as a people. I pray God will help us in the next decade. Oh yeah, and "The Rev" Leon Brewer was dropping rain in Martin. Great job guys!

All Kinds of Christians
....*from 7-22-09*

This week I met some people who were well dressed (if you go for the ties and dresses). I thought they were Mormon, but it turned out they were Jehovah Witnesses. I told them a few years ago some people came to my door and knocked. My younger daughter answered the door and said, hello. They told her they were Jehovah Witnesses and began to share about what they were doing at our door. My daughter stopped them and said she didn't even see the accident. Of course it was poor humor, but I laughed at their expressions. I enjoyed my time talking with what I will refer to as the JWs. They were persistent and mostly calm. I asked them if they knew what cults were. One of them answered, "Any religion where a man leads the belief system." I thought that was a good answer, but I gave them my definition. It is any belief system that is unorthodox. Unorthodox means failing to follow a conventional or traditional practice or belief system, and is most commonly used in reference to Christianity here in America.

Many times we find that people do not understand Christianity. There are fanatical Christians, radical Christians, nominal Christians, and carnal Christians. My preference is being known as a radical follower of Christ. So much evil has been done by the "Christians". I was talking to some graduate students this past week as well, and we were talking about depravity. Depravity has to do with moral corruption. I believe this is what we deal with as humans, because given over to their own device, man becomes selfish. This is why I like the idealism of the Lakota because selflessness is a virtue upheld. I remember watching an elder who, for the most part, could have been very rich. Instead, he gave everything he had to others.

Now I know I started some thoughts and did not finish them completely. Jesus, of course, is the man I follow because it is stated in the Bible he became a servant unto death. My faith believes he rose from the grave and ascended into heaven. The promise I search for is when he comes back like he left. He died for all of the depravity or moral corruption that is within me. I gave my life to him when I was young and have failed in my life many times, but he is faithful to forgive me. I battle with being a hypocrite, so I pray for strength. I was taught by Earl Hedlund and went to college to understand more of the Bible. The Jehovah Witnesses, or JWs, do not believe many things as I do, but the main difference is I believe Jesus is God. When I was talking with them, I told one of the women about the Bible I study, and then she tried to tell me about my reading. I asked her if she knew what text criticism meant in regard to the Bibles we read. She did not. I learned about text criticism in school because many people do not understand how the bible was translated.

As to the different types of Christians, well there is no perfect person and there have been many bad things done in the name of Christ. At best, they were poor representations of Jesus because he did not harm anyone. At the worst, they are not followers of the teachings of Jesus. Because Jesus taught us to have compassion and love toward one another, we are called to not be selfish. We need to look after our fellow man.

In the practical manner, it is important for us to seek to help all mankind and not just our closest relatives. We say we are all related, and yet we do so much damage to each other. This is why I try to teach the young men and women on our basketball court what it means to be Lakota. When we teach our children our values, we also need to practice them in our daily lives. Being humble is knowing we will sometimes fail, but we must press on to finish the race. I seek to live like Jesus. I know it is only through his Spirit I can transform from being selfish to unselfish. Our leaders such as Crazy Horse and Red Cloud lived for the people.

Inspirations from the Dream Café
....from 12-08-09

Our lives are changing every day. My fear is we are not doing enough to help each other. This week we begin a new society, and I am sending a calling out to the men of our Lakota Nation. The Quest for Authentic Manhood is a study based on a biblical view of manhood. Taking steps to change our reservations and homelands is vital to the future of our people. I told a group of people last week that I am not as concerned about our women as much as I am worried about our men. There have been too many tragedies among our people in the past one hundred and fifty years. I believe we can change the way we do things among our people. I have seen the riches of America and the materialism. These can bring about competition between families as its members try to live up to each other's standard of living. It is not my plan to make Lakota ways mimics the American Dream, but we need to begin to find ways our people can thrive in a globalized world.

Because I am human, I could actually lie to you. I can act humble when I myself fight with arrogance. I can cheat and I can even pray like I am close to the Father, God. All of these things are just a small list of my being human and coming to a realization; I need to know what it means to become an authentic man in a world that is changing every day. We are influenced by the mass media and the world is coming into our living rooms on a daily basis. We can watch the British Broadcasting Corporation on the internet and see what the world sees in seconds. Instead of looking up to us, our children are looking up to basketball stars, movie stars, and every other star you can think of as we see our world change.

We need to begin to dream; our dreams need to begin in the heart. When I traveled across the world to a little place in India, I came across a little café, the Dream Café. It was a great place. We met with some leaders who were very much like the American Indian Movement was for the American Indian. They dream of a better world where their children can grow up in a free Nation. I was moved by the young people as they served food and made drinks. When I came home I realized we need to see our people dream and hope. Our young people need visions and dreams to accomplish what our ancestors prayed for when they looked into the future. My desire is to help people with their dreams and this is a very difficult task because of the struggles we face as Lakota people, mainly hopelessness.

When I was a young man in high school I wanted to write for the Oglala Light. I never found out who named our high school paper, but it is truly a brilliant name. I lived where I live today. The Lakota Times was on my block. I remember the time it was fire bombed. I remember Tim Giago telling me to get my journalism degree and he would hire me. Of course it was a dream I started to work on, but things did not work out for me in journalism. I went on to fulfill my other dream of becoming a minister. So now I write for the Lakota Country Times, and they allow me the freedom to write my thoughts. This is a great accomplishment. When I think of what I have been able to do in my life, these two goals remind me my life is successful. Writing for a paper that has history and quality, and presenting my faith on Sunday mornings are dreams I have prayed for in my life.

People are talking about our suicide rates in Pine Ridge and Rosebud. I often gauge leaders by their awareness of issues around the Reservation and by what they are reading and listening to across Lakota country. Here is a clear and concise message to our elected leaders. Call our people together for healing. We need our leaders to bring us together because it is the way things are supposed to be. Call off work, stop time, and draw us together for a moment where we can begin to change the future of our people. We are a beautiful people but we are hurting as well. As I write this open challenge we saw another young person take his own life. We do not need a band aid on an open wound; we need to work together, which means many groups and individuals will come to the aid of the Lakota to overcome the wounds they have endured for centuries. It is just like Hilary Clinton and others have said, it takes a whole community to raise a child.

I want to take this opportunity to thank President Two Bulls and Councilman Rick Grey Grass for having a meeting last week to brainstorm about the suicide issues on the Pine Ridge. This dialog needs to continue and I hope it will somehow stop the deaths. We need to dream and have visions. If there is any way I can help in Pine Ridge or Rosebud, let me know. I have a lot to share with youth and have been around the world. I have completed my goals and dream of a better world. Please ask me what I can do, and I will work very hard to help our Lakota people.

Ramblings from Kansas
....from 8-18-10

As I sit in Kansas pondering the next few weeks, and maybe even the next few years, I realize time is short. We need to live life to its fullest. School is starting and there are many parents across the country who are saying goodbye to their children on college campuses. It is hard to let your children go, and I have seen the lost look of the parents and the wide-eyed excited students. I think it is harder on mothers, but I believe fathers can struggle too. My first time, I was at Indiana State and we were dropping our daughter off in a town I had never been; it was extremely difficult. Here I am today, at a different school in a time. I want to encourage the parents because I believe success comes with sacrifice. The time away is worth every struggle and burden we go through. In the end your children will be able to achieve their life goals and this will make them stronger.

It is good to reset goals and develop strategy to achieve your goals when you get a chance. When I was a young person I battled with the idea of serving the Creator. I wanted to become a journalist and write for a living. It has been a dream of mine to be able to write my thoughts and ideas down on paper. If you told me in the early eighties I would be typing articles and views on a computer I would have walked away in disbelief. Of course the computers then seemed more work than their worth. I am thankful for my typing teacher in high school. Technology is growing and getting faster all the time. It makes me wonder what we as humans will be capable of in the coming years. So, I sit in the heartland of America thinking about the coming future. What kind of changes and or obstacles will arise in the coming days, weeks, months, and years? These are the thoughts running through my mind as I sit and write this week's ramblings in Kansas.

Our lives are in constant change even when we feel like there is little movement around us. I remember when I was a child. It seemed the summer would last for an eternity, but it was my perspective and now my worldview has changed. The summers seem to fly by without having a chance to catch a breath, and I realize the days are moving more quickly all the time. One area of our lives revolves around time, and yet the way we see time can be confusing and frustrating. We live in two worlds where we need to be able to operate in different cultures when it comes to time. In most places in America there are schedules, and some say we need to be five minutes early and/or on time. If you miss an appointment it can be hard to reschedule. In Indian country, and maybe some other obscure places in America, people are more flexible. Of course, this can frustrate the scheduled cultures to complete frustration. My preference is Indian Country time or more appropriately, "Indian Time". We start when everyone has arrived where it would be deemed appropriate.

I have been home for fifteen years now, and if you ask if I believe if it was worth coming home after college, I would say, absolutely. I believe it has been both great and sad at times, but the one constant in my life is my faith. Even though I have seen storms and great times of success, I have always known my faith has been strong. Many people tell me they do not know how they could live with losing a child and all of the difficulties Pine Ridge Indian Reservation gives day to day. It has been my faith that has sustained me, and it is what I offer as a remedy to the ills of our Reservation society. It is said that between twenty and thirty percent of the population in America is emotionally unhealthy at any given time, but on the Pine Ridge Reservation I believe the number is closer to seventy or eighty percent who are emotionally unhealthy. We carry the burden of our lives on our backs, and it would be natural for our young people to start losing hope of a better day. Our youth look around and see very little change in their difficult lives. We need to offer hope to every young person on the Pine Ridge and Rosebud Reservation.

We can change this by starting to live up to the expectations of our ancestors. To care for each other is the way our people lived 150 years ago. We had tenets in our society that kept us tied together as a people and it worked. As a boy I only knew I was "Indian," but as I grew, I found a whole way of life – with contradiction, but a great way of life. I found I had great people in my heritage. It gave me chills to know of my ancestors. Lakota people are magnificent people. Too often we have been affected with negativities around our homeland. It is time to rise up and begin to rebuild our society as the great plain's people. We were able to thrive in the worst conditions the earth could dish out one hundred and fifty years ago. It took the destruction of the food source to drive us to our knees, but our spirit has not been taken.

The Lakota people need to come together. Put our heads together and see what we can do for our children and their children. It is time to put down our agendas and humble ourselves in order for us to solve the issues we have as a people. There is no amount of "help for us" that will sustain true change. We as a people need to have a meeting where we can start changing our way of life in the 21st century. I would ask the leaders to have a meeting and invite all people to come and participate for change. Let us see the leaders rise up and develop a new beginning!

The Ultimate Question
....from 3-23-10

Here is the ultimate question that people have asked for years. Can money buy everything? I had someone tell me last week, "Money can buy anything - love, friends, and most anything you can imagine." But I took this question and asked around town. Most people disagreed with this opinion; money cannot buy everything. Because I am a Christian, I believe in the absolute truth, meaning the God of the Universe. Philosophically speaking, I have talked to some people about an absolute truth. Before psychology developed, most philosophers made the assumption there was absolute truth, and this referred to the Creator. Western thought began to focus on the rebirth of humanity, and sociology emerged. Now we are faced with a post-modern world where it is common to believe in more than one truth. Relativism permeates our modern thought. It reminds me of the movement that stated, "If it feels good, do it."

Pleasure can be a good thing and a bad thing; it is how you use pleasure. I have been reading, writing, and cooking these past few months. I find it more pleasurable to cook than most other things I do throughout my day. I had one of the mission team members from a college ask me a question last week. He asked, "What kind of things do you do during the day?" I quickly told him, "Human things." And then he told me he asked because he did not see me much during the day. I guess I should not have become defensive, but it bothers me when people assume I don't do anything throughout the day. I am busy with ministry first, and then I do the things I enjoy. I have many unfinished projects like a chair that was masterfully constructed that I would like to finish with a cushion. I am usually at the Higher Ground making coffees and smoothies, along with some of the lunch specials. I dream of baking Italian breads and like to ponder life's interesting questions.

rez# Rez Ramblings

Back to the question of money; it cannot buy everything as my good friend Howard Olson told me. He said money cannot buy poverty. I thought this was a great point because everyone else told me it cannot buy love. Of course, you would have to first define true love and that would take some debate. I believe love to be laying down your life and serving others; thinking of others better than yourself and not looking at your own interests but the interests of others. Now that is a powerful definition of love. Ultimately it is laying down your life for another. Many people would love to be served, but fewer love to serve. I believe our Lakota leaders, or Itancans, were the greatest servants of the people. They loved their people.

Happiness is another subject to consider. Can money buy you happiness? I believe you can find some pleasures that can bring you to happiness, but eventually happiness from pleasures will end.

Suffering makes us stronger. When we suffer we will call out the name of God and want him to fix our problems. This act of humility is powerful. By calling out to the Creator you are essentially saying you do not have the power to change your circumstance. I have experienced many instances in my own life where I have realized I cannot change without the Creator of this world helping me. I realize I cannot change the conditions of our reservations; I can only change me. I am engaged in decade long conversations, and I know that we have not yet solved the issues we are face in Lakota Country. My prayer is that our leaders will seek to serve like our ancestors. This is not to say we do not have leaders doing this, but it will be apparent when our leaders turn to the Creator and seek His wisdom. It will not just benefit their families, but it will help the whole Lakota Nation. The Government divided us and now we must come together and seek change among our members.

I do not have all of the answers, but I hope that together we can make a better life for our children's children. Our people deserve more, and it is time we start taking up our burdens and allow the Creator to help us carry them in the twenty-first century. My brother told me something that was powerful last week. He said, "I don't judge them, because I was just as bad or worse". And then he went on to say, "I trust God, and he has placed me in this place. I have to live my life the best I can for Him." Our lives can change with hope; I find my hope in Wanikiya, because I needed a savior. I believe my life would have been over if I had not turned my life over to Jesus. It is where truth begins for me. I could never pay or work for my salvation because it is a free gift. Oh, one last thing that money can't buy.... salvation.

Movement Requires a Mover.....Taku Sku Sku

Here is my two cents worth of a movement. I talked with a guy yesterday, and he asked me if I wanted to know why he did not believe anything about Jesus. I told him I did not want to hear about his reason. He was shocked or looked shocked, but the reason I do not want to hear is because for an illumination you must first be encountered by the Spirit. My position is we have heard the message but until it penetrates the heart, no one will listen. A few years ago I had a conversation with an influential person. He said, "Leon, how are you going to reach the Rez?" I told him one person at a time. My personal belief is we need a movement from Taku Sku Sku, or the Sacred Mover, for us to see real change. As a Lakota, I believe it must come from the Spirit because this movement cannot be stopped by man. When you see people come before the Creator in humbleness it will blow your mind. Our Tribal leaders need to seek the guidance of the Spirit; until this happens we will continue in poverty and its affects.

This Thanksgiving, I stand to help
....from 11-24-09

A pastor friend of mine called me last week, and I told him I was writing my column. He asked if I was writing my Thanksgiving piece. Here I was writing about piercings and tattoos. That is crazy. I am not your typical minister. I am sure there are many pastors around the country doing sermons about how thankful we should be and what our Lord has done for us in the 21st century. That is well and good, but I am a little upset with my reality at the moment. I see death all around and people are trying to put the fire out. It is the prevention I am focused on because when something happens people react. I pray for the people who are actually out there doing the leg work to prevent tragedy.

People can do something to bring hope to our Lakota Nation. We could build our communities with a place for young couples to begin their lives together without their mother-in-laws or in-laws all together in their lives. We have struggled with the idea of multiple families living together and this has not worked. Our young people need places to learn to live together. For too long our young people have had to begin their marriages with in-laws. This is a very good way of thinking but it hurts the young couples on our Reservation. We need places where the young couples can start their home lives together without interference. Working out their conflict in a healthy manner will do wonders for the young couples.

I remember my mother-in-law very well. She did not talk to me and always talked through my wife if she wanted me to know or do something. It was a good relationship, and I have good memories of her. In the old ways, mothers-in-law did not speak to the sons-in-law; I believe it was a great way of life. Our grandfathers had many ways we do not practice now, but I believe we need to begin to bring them back into our lives in the 21st century. One of the Lakota ways was to have honoring dinners. Some of this is still going on in and around our communities. I like to hear about the Payabaya community honoring their soldiers and veterans. These honoring meals make me happy.

Hope will help our people to embrace life. It is a powerful force. My hope is life will get better in Lakota country, and people will begin to live with abundance. This week we will celebrate a Thanksgiving Day, and I pray our people will have enough food. We have a few friends coming over to our home and I am excited! We get to share a day where we can look at our lives and be hopeful. Our children are our greatest asset. We need to bring them hope. We live in days with many hurting people and we need to protect our future. We have all heard it before - it is time we begin to strengthen our young people.

This week marks history because there are some that are no

longer with us. We are left to suffer on the earth. We need each other to bring hope back to our people. I was talking with Gerald Cournoyer this past week, and he shared with me about symbology, a study of symbols. I was blown away by the study of different cultures. I went to his website and saw some great artwork; Mark Harmon (NCIS television star) was given a portrait. We have many people in our midst who bring hope into our communities. I see young people every week who have bright futures and will be vital members of our Reservation.

Our Lakota people are a beautiful people and have some great potential. In the next few weeks we will see the great high school basketball tournament with thousands coming to Rapid City. I am excited to see Orie Brown and Carl Swallow play their senior years of basketball. I talked with Coach Rama and wished him a great year. Of course I was saying our Pine Ridge Thorpes have the greatest basketball coach in South Dakota. If you knew how much it takes for a Lakota team to win a state championship you would understand why Dusty Lebeau is the best coach in South Dakota history. Our people have much to be hopeful about, and it is time we move in the right direction. Basketball, art, education - the list of our people's greatness is endless.

I am excited for the future, because I know our people have been through genocide and have survived. I like what Robert Grey Eagle said one day, "Leon our people are behaving pretty well considering the unemployment statistics. What would Rapid City be like with an eighty percent unemployment figure?" He was right. When you are on the bottom, the only place to go is up. They told me to come and build a church family fourteen years ago. We are building this family, and everyone is welcome to make Jesus a part of your life. He ultimately brings me hope.

While visiting India in 2004 I traveled through the jungles of northwest India to a little place called Nagaland. The Indian and Burma (new name Myanmar) governments split the Nagas, and now half are Indian and half Burmese. This was done because of Independence in 1948. Today, Nagaland is still fighting for independence from the Indian Government. Ninety percent of Nagaland is Christian. Many Nagas have lost their lives in this war between them and India. Most people have never heard of the People of Nagaland but they have continued to grow as followers of Christ. There are seminaries and Christian schools made for their population. When the Christian missionaries left, the people began to take up their own churches and faith. I remember walking through the jungle trails where I would speak to ten thousand people. Many walked for days to hear from the Americans. I pray for my brothers and sisters in Nagaland because they still battle with many of the same issues we do here in Lakota country. Their children want to become teachers, doctors, actors, and every other dream imaginable to a young person.

On October 1, 1949 Mao Zedong proclaimed The People's Republic of China, and it was clear the Christian missionaries had limited time in China. The Communists won the civil war in China. I have heard there were around 2-3 million Christians in China when the Communists took over the government. It was almost 60 years ago and where is the Chinese Christian Church? There are estimates that speak of 100 million Christians. They are sending out missionaries, and they are going through Islamic countries sharing the Good News of Christ. What was meant to stop the worldwide movement of Christianity has instead strengthened the work of Christianity.

So what does this mean to us as Lakota people? It means we know in 1978 the United States Congress passed the Freedom of Religion Act for Native Americans. In 1981 I saw the churches on Pine Ridge full of people praying and worshiping in these churches. The church is not a building! The church is people. When you pray through Jesus Christ you are part of a worldwide movement. I am saddened by the closing of churches. No one even knows about the Wesleyan churches closing, but the people in Oglala village knows what it means when outsiders make business decisions and close the doors. We know of about the nine churches that are closing through the Episcopal Church. So even though business was used to close these churches, business will not close down all churches. We need to take up our own ministries.

The church is not a building. A church is the people who put their faith in Jesus Christ and what he did while he was on earth. While church buildings are being closed on the Pine Ridge, you must persevere and realize they cannot stop the movement. The world is changing and we need to understand change is coming. You can be a part of a positive change or the negative. But mark this, we are in the end of this financial age, and we are on the brink of cataclysmic change in the world we know. The hope of our people needs to be in our faith. Lakota people like you and me have been here for some time. We can help the world, but we need to be in unity. My hope is built on a better world. We as Lakota need to be healed through forgiveness. We need to forgive our relatives and work for change. What do you have to forgive your relatives for in the new coming age? I believe the Lakota have the answer to the world problems. It will come from us. We are small in regard to the world, but the power will come from us. It is the power of Christ that will change the world. I believe in the Lakota people! The world seeks a cure but we are busy with other obstacles. We need to be ready to help the people of the world. Our people can stand with truth or disappear as the world changes. I stand to help the world in these difficult times ahead of us.

OUR HISTORY

Colonization

Christian a Case of Denial

The first missionaries came in 1666; they were Jesuits and Franciscans. They came into contact with the Dakota Sioux people and would later move toward the Lakota. One day, I had a salesperson call me and ask me if I wanted to place an advertisement for Red Cloud School. Being the person I am, I started talking about the Thorpe-Crusader rivalry we have had for a long time. The sales person had no idea of what I was talking about. Then I started talking about the Catholic Church and its role in the destruction of Lakota people. They were "Christians" who came to Lakota Country to seek to make us human. They beat our children for speaking their own language and some have accused them of sexual abuse. Yes, these were "Christians" who brought pain and suffering to the Lakota Nation. We have seen the extreme of "Christian" acts of terror against Indigenous children in Canada. It was said some "Christians" would put healthy children in with sick dying children hoping the healthy would get sick and die too. Why did they do this? It was to destroy a people for land and greed.

It is reported the first "Christians" came across the Mississippi River with federal dollars to help them civilize the savages. When I was in college I had an ethics class. I wrote a paper called, "Would the Real Savage Please Stand Up". I kick myself now because I loaned the paper to a friend, and he never returned it to me. But I have much knowledge of what was done to the Indigenous people. Many of these acts were done by "Christians." The "Christians" played a huge role in the almost complete destruction of American Indians, so I rarely call myself a Christian. But, I refer to myself as a Follower of the Teachings of Christ. There was an ethnic cleansing and an extermination process that rivals the African situation. A "Christian" friend of mine wrote, "We will know them by their fruit." So what has America done? I hope this blows some minds. The fruit of the American Christian was destruction and chaos which has brought pain to Indian people.

I fully understand the white European "Christians" have brought the message of Jesus to the world. I fully understand the impact of the

295

Gospel of Jesus Christ. I have walked in the country of South Korea, and I saw the churches on every corner. I have walked the jungles of Nagaland where 90% percent of the State considers themselves followers of Christ. I hear stories of other places around the world where the Bible has had a profound effect on every aspect of the culture. Christianity is reaching out to a world of suffering.

A young man came to Pine Ridge a few years ago and did some crazy things. He left a child on the side of the road to walk home. The roads here are dangerous with people driving above 65 miles per hour without shoulders. This young man fought with his boss and rebelled for what he felt was right. This is the fruit that was left in Pine Ridge. So should we judge him by his fruit? Here is the bottom line, let's look at America. There are close to fifty million babies being killed through abortion. They enslaved a people from a continent. They killed the majority of America's Indigenous people. So when someone writes, "We will know them by their fruit," you need to understand that the rotten fruit of American "Christians" far outweighs the good fruit.

I am saddened that we are dealing with issues of race and ethnos, but the bottom line is people need to get their heads out of the sand. Some people will assume I do not like white people. That is a "White" lie. I believe people cannot handle the truth. I was accused of a lot of things yesterday. A friend told me that you cannot reason with an unreasonable person. Interestingly, that friend happens to be white. I do not want to be called a Christian because of the baggage the word brings with it to people's lives. Self-righteousness and ethnocentric idealism brings superiority, whereas the message of the cross is self-denial. I live in a world where people assume all "White" people are "Christian," and yet you have people online who have proven the case of denial. I believe "Christians" can be the biggest deterrent to people understanding the truth about the message of Jesus. I will call myself a follower of Jesus' teachings because I believe they have the power to transform from within. The power of the Spirit can be felt around the world.

Here in Pine Ridge and South Dakota, we celebrate Native American Day on what others celebrate as Columbus Day. The cultural truth is this, Lakota and other tribes understand Columbus brought pain, affliction, and the worst day in the American continent's history. It was the day the destruction of a God-like people began. They were "In Dios", or in the image of God, because they were a beautiful people. I believe the message of the cross came to America for salvation. Instead of salvation, it was destruction the Europeans brought. No, not all white people are bad, just as not all Indians are good.

Colonization followed by the Church led to the destruction of the Indian

Colonization brings destruction to whole people groups. Outsiders seek to gain wealth, money and resources, from an area by taking and developing of the land. In the process, the existing people, communities, and systems are forever changed and often devastated. In the year 1492, it is estimated there were between 12-20 million Indigenous Indians living in what we call the United States. By the year 1900, it is estimated there were only 240,000 Native Indians left. These numbers can be grossly underestimated. We can easily believe there were more, but it was impossible to accurately track the population at that time. The effects of colonization are great and many. Some of the change is positive and while some of the change is negative. When I think about the colonization movements today, I think of Iraq. The United States and its allies are offering freedom and democracy as the new colonial tools in an effort to gain resources and money. We as Americans are addicted to oil and will do everything in our power to keep our prices down. In the end we all know the Iraq war was about oil; in the process to control price and access to oil, Iraq is being colonized. Last week I was visiting with a guy. I said, if America sincerely cared about helping oppressed peoples throughout the world, they would be in Darfur where a million people have lost their lives because of civil unrest and war. People are dying around the world, but we are only engaged in key strategic areas where we have vested interest.

Many people want to help with issues in Native America, but they do not know how to help without doing more harm than good. I want to start a new movement to bring changes to our everyday lives. I am going to need some people who are willing to go the extra mile as we create an organization that will change the culture of death into a culture of life. In the last forty years things should have changed. We have lost our way because people are in power for themselves. I was asked if I was happy with the election by a good friend, and I am not at all happy because we have the same people in power. And in two years we will still have the same issues and most likely the same problems. We have the start of an organization that I believe can be a great vehicle for change because it will restore the dignity of the Lakota Nation and beyond. We have seen our whole way of life destroyed, and it is talked about but nothing changes. We have been colonized to the point of helplessness. This change should have begun; but true change comes from the heart. Do you have enough heart to begin to change the culture of death?

I came home 31 years ago from the war on Lakota. Oh you believe the Indian wars ended in the 1800s? They were ended in 1975 when people stood up and were willing to die because of the policies of termination the United States used in a cultural war. The churches were full in the 70s because every Indian was mandated to become civilized, and the church was used in the destruction of the language and rituals of the people. Social justice should be on the list of priorities for the American church but they are consumed with the idealism of America and the wealth it seems to worship. After 500 years of hearing about Jesus less than 5% of Indians believe in God in the flesh. I am a follower of Jesus and will be until the day I die and meet him in heaven. It is all that I live for because I know he has brought hope into my life. The problem is the church has destroyed its credibility because they have believed a lie. I once heard the biggest deception ever was the devil got people to believe he did not exist. I believe the biggest lie was Manifest Destiny and the thought that God gave the North American continent for the church to rule and lord over the land. We actually have people living on Pine Ridge who believe that because they are white or Euro-American Christians they should make the decisions for the Indians because we are incapable of living out our faith and life as believers in Jesus. Here I am rambling and it is almost 1:30 am. Until later.........

Kill the Indian, Save the Man

Cultural genocide has been happening to the Indigenous people of the Americas since the first landings. Early European history in the Americas points to conquering the land and its people. As a student I learned of the exploits of the explorers from Europe. Most of the early years were driven by the desire to acquire resources. Columbus sailed for the purpose of finding trade routes to the East. They were correct in their assumption that the world was round. Unfortunately for us they ran into our continent. Yes, I know what you are thinking. The Norsemen were early explorers and there is evidence they were here long before Columbus sailed. I have to admit I believe these men were out of their minds to get into these rickety boats and brave the ocean currents. I have traveled to Columbus, Ohio and have seen the replica of one of the ships. I have seen the Pacific and Atlantic oceans, and you would never have gotten me in those boats without lots kicking and screaming.

The trip to Ohio reminds me of some people who have since been found out to be just like Columbus. He was out to destroy Indians just like some other people I have met. These people were from Columbus, Ohio. I like being called an Indian. The other day I was talking to a young man who was telling me he was playing basketball in Rapid City with some guys. I asked him if they were "Skins". I know some people are thinking to themselves that I should not use the word "Skins," but the young man said they were "Skins". I have involved myself with the mascot issue in the past, but I find myself thinking those are the little things. We have bigger issues to deal with. We need to work hard on our communities to see them thrive and become a place of hope once more.

I was going to a store in White Clay, Nebraska. When I got out of my van, some guys yelled out my name and said they wanted me to write their story. "You know why we are up here in White Clay?" one of them asked. My mind started going. It is difficult to think of what would drive people to this point. They told me I could take pictures and tell their story. I was blown away and humbled at this point because I did not know what to say. Yeah, yeah, Leon speechless, is a rare moment. I hurt for our relatives. They have so much pain, and we have not found

299

a solution for helping them. Rapid City talks about "those people". It is our people they are referring to when they speak of people struggling around the bridges. Young people are shooting at them with pellet guns and throwing urine on them. We have many relatives panhandling in the downtown district, and the police are now trying to watch our Indian people.

So what does all of this mean? Cultural genocide is still affecting our Lakota people. We have not properly grieved for the loss of a whole way of life. I saw in some other papers there were people protesting the Catholic Social Services for their curriculum, but I want to share with you about a certain type of people that are capitalistic. I do not believe I have a new idea. Wasicu is word that comes from our ancestors. It meant greedy. Mistakes were made in the past because the United States wanted to wipe out the Indigenous peoples of America. They used Christianity to "Kill the Indian and Save the Man". We are still here and alive, but we need to seek to thrive in our communities. I have many great European American friends and some of them are capitalistic. I try not to let their values affect mine.

I try to follow the teachings of Jesus Christ, and I fail to live up to many of the teachings. I assure you I will not turn my back on my faith because Jesus is my hope. He makes me a complete person because I believe he has the power to keep making me a better person. We have many followers of Jesus on the Rosebud and Pine Ridge, and we are a good people. Jesus did not intend to destroy our people. This happened because of the actions of the greedy people who sought to take the land and resource. Jesus came to restore that which was broken. Let us explore how we can fight off the effects of cultural genocide. My identity is built first in Jesus Christ because of the changes in my life. Secondly, my identity is rooted in my ancestors. They have given me life, and as an Oglala Lakota it is a privilege to be known through my grandmothers and grandfathers.

How many relatives do you have who have suffer with diabetes? My mother had diabetes type II, and I have it as well. I remember when it started; I went into Sioux Nation Shopping Center looking for a Welch's Strawberry soda. I could not quench my thirst and everything

I drank seemed to go right through me. I eventually ended up in an emergency room in Arkansas where a machine the nurse was using to check my sugars would not register a number. The doctors gave me some pills and told me to visit the hospital when I got home. I went to the hospital as soon as I returned home and have been treated by the Pine Ridge Clinic since then. Well, it has been eight years now, and I still struggle to keep my sugars under control. We have a sixty percent diabetes rate among American Indians. What that means is either we are diabetic or borderline diabetic.

We have many people who have lost limbs, and it needs to stop. Complications with diabetes are out of control and have not been getting better since the epidemic has started. Since I have been diagnosed with this condition I have seen many people struggle, but no one seems too worried. We just keep building bigger dialysis centers. This is outrageous, and I assure you we need to be concerned about the condition of our people.

Social Justice

I was thinking about something after watching a video made at the Trinity Theological Seminary. What is the role of the Evangelical Followers of Christ with regard to social justice? JR Kerr mentions there is a lot of negativity related to Christianity for today's generation of young people. The experts believe there are between 2%-5% of American Indians who would refer to themselves as Christian. There has been over 500 years of evangelism or at least contact with Euro-Christians and the result is a 2-5% conversion. There has been so much contact with a group of people and less than 5% of Indigenous people accept the Way of Jesus. I have my own ideas of the reasons, but it is difficult for many people because they do not want to feel the shame and pain of what was done in the name of Jesus.

While developing my worldview and trying to understand my own faith, I came across some thought-provoking historical stories. While listening to an elder I heard a story of an eastern tribe who

301

accepted the message of Jesus and his redemption. Their whole tribe became Christians and was living on the frontier. My good friend Russell Means, the activist turned actor, was sharing his thoughts one day in the Coffee House in Pine Ridge. He was talking about treaties that were made between the tribes and the King of England. Russell shared that the only place you could find freedom was on the frontier. Land ownership meant everything during pre-revolution times. When 1776 came and the Declaration of Independence was formed, they wanted more land. Since the King of England had a treaty with the Indians about not expanding the thirteen original colonies, the revolutionaries needed to revolt. All men are created equal sounds really great if you were white and owned land. Look, women did not have the same rights of their husbands, and for sure the African slaves and American Indians did not have rights in this new government. It is clear there were hidden agendas.

I have had issues about the Tea Party of the 21st century because of the protestors who came to Boston to dump tea. Here is an excerpt from, http://www.bostonteapartyship.com/history.asp

"On the cold evening of December 16, 1773, a large band of patriots, disguised as Mohawk Indians, burst from the South Meeting House with the spirit of freedom burning in their eyes."

There were issues of taxation without representation and the revolutionaries were getting more upset because they thought they were being treated unfairly. So, this is the context of the 18th century. What did all of this mean to the frontier? It meant even the undesirables had true freedom because they were not under the oppression of the King and his taxes.

So, back to the tribe who accepted Jesus as the Lord. They were living as Christians on the frontier in freedom. After the American Revolution the Euro-Americans were looking to satisfy their blood thirst for land. They came across the tribe of Christians and coveted the land. Of course, this is against the Ten Commandments that are still written on the Supreme Court's Wall. Thou shall not covet is the tenth commandment but no less important. So the Euro-Americans had to come up with a plan so they could take the Christian tribe's land. You have to understand the whole tribe became Christians, and the people who brought the message of Jesus to them were now going to take their land. The settlers decided it was best to send the tribe Small Pox infested blankets so it would wipe them out. And people get upset because Saddam Hussein gassed the Kurds. Look, I am just as upset as the next guy with bio-warfare, but this was happening early in the history the History of American Government.

I try to help people to understand the issues with Christians in American Indian history. I know the "Christians" played a role in the destruction of whole people group. Because of the misinterpretation of scripture and implementation of said scriptures, the Euro-American Christian has played a huge role in stealing a continent. Every treaty made with Americans Indians has been broken. It is said the only promise that was kept was they promised to take our land. I need to be clear because although "Christians" have damaged American Indians, not all Christians have played a role in this forced acculturation. I have talked on tape about the Reverend Earl Hedlund as my mentor and a father I needed growing up. He gave me lots of grace and love with plenty of encouragement. I must share a story from my junior year of high school.

I was in the yearbook class. I was a bit of a cut up in high school, but also a serious student at times. When I made it to the class the teacher was not there, and I started bothering another student. He got a little upset and then more upset and a fight ensued. Of course, I was knocking him around without getting hit, and the teacher walks in. He grabs me by the back of the shirt and says, "What's going on?" I turned around to look at him, and just when I looked back at the other student, he hits me in the mouth. We were sent to the Principal's office and, of course, it was the walk of pain and anxiety. We were waiting to go into Looking Horse's office. She was less than five feet tall but the thought of her discipline brought great fear. She was pretty mean and tough and could handle the young Indian men in her school. We walked into the office. While we were standing in front of her desk, a shadowy figure entered behind us. It was Arvol Looking Horse, the current Keeper of the Sacred White Buffalo Woman's Pipe. Of course, I started by telling

Mrs. Looking Horse that it was my entire fault, and the other guy did not do anything. She then asked how I got a fat lip. I couldn't say anything, and we were both suspended for a couple days.

I was sent home. First we dropped off the other student, and then we arrived back at the Church where I was living. Pastor Hedlund saw me drive up with the Truant Officer. I got out of the truck, and the Pastor asked me what I was doing. I told him what happened. He smiled and walked away. I thought I would get a lecture, but I did not. I remember the experience vividly. I know there were many stories filled with acceptance and love. I appreciate everything he ever did for me, but mostly for being a great role model and a mentor of the Word of God.

So, where does this leave us when it comes to social justice? I believe the Church of America has a job to do when it comes to restoring the American Indian. They need to right the wrong. I have shared with many people the issue of what the church should do for American Indians. We live in one of the richest countries in the world, and the church alone has the ability to restore the Indian people. The wealth of America has been used to usher in the super power status of the United States. My hope is we can change the feelings about Christianity with the American Indians, and we can restore the relationship of the American Indian with the Creator of the universe. We can do this by helping to support change in government through pro-Indian legislation. I do not believe Indian Gaming is the answer for our tribes, but people are continuing to grasp at the profits of money taken through greed. We need people of Industry to come and set up opportunities so that the American Indian can feed their families. I believe feeding and meeting the basic needs of the people is vital for hope. Okay, I have typed the heck out of my computer; some hit tennis balls and others the heavy bag. I had to get this out so I could have it down in words.

In my defense as a follower of Jesus, I should explain to you that I searched as an eight year-old who did not know God. I now understand God called me to himself. I am seeking to do my job, and I believe it is important to help people understand. Jesus, through his Spirit, can change us from within. This is different than and much more powerful than the behavioral change many profess from Christendom.

Christianity from Colonization, not the True Way of Christ

....from 11-03-10

In order for colonization to be successful, the colonized people will continue to lose their culture even after the colonizing force has left. I have been researching colonization and how it has affected the Lakota Nation. First and foremost on the list of areas colonized is religion.

Now, I know people will say Lakota do not have a religion, but when you have rituals and specific ways of living day to day and rituals that are practices yearly, you have a religion. The seven sacred rites of Lakota given by the White Buffalo Calf Woman have been around for centuries. All of the ceremonies are important. We can see how this "religion" has affected the world, spiritual gurus killing people, casinos charging people and places like Australia adopting the Inipi or cleansing lodge. In talking with Russell Means, he told me the "sweat lodge" has bad connotations. I agree. When I consider the "Christian" influence on the Pine Ridge, it is clear that the efforts to Christianize the Lakota have failed. I hope my tombstone to read, "Lived a life for Christ." The Apostle Paul once said, "For I resolved to know nothing while I was with you, except Jesus Christ and him crucified." These are powerful words that describe a man who understood his own religion.

Some may try to criticize my faith. But, I have studied my own belief system, and I am trained in the interpretation of scripture or the Bible. I am not a perfect person, nor do I try to make believe I have all the answers. I am not in charge of the universe, but I am just a traveler who will someday die and meet my Lord and my God. So what affect has the effort to Christianize the Lakota people had on the Oglala Nation? I believe the early missionaries explained Jesus to our people incorrectly. They stressed a set of rules, and those rules brought forced acculturation to the Euro-American way of life. They did not offer the true meaning of what it means to follow Jesus and understand the sacrifice he gave for us to live. I believe many of the people who did accept Jesus into their lives were killed for the pursuit of more in America. I am a radical follower of Jesus and nothing will change this fact. So yes, in a sense I am everything the United States set out to

305

accomplish. I also understand what was done wrong to the Lakota people in the name of Christianity. I will not turn from my faith. Instead I will continue to share the freedom I have in a Savior I have accepted into my life.

Many people have sought to understand faith in Jesus. Here in Pine Ridge we have seen devastation when it comes to becoming a Christian. So let us look at how many people follow Jesus on the Pine Ridge. There is a term, nominal Christian; it basically means people who are in name Christians but do not practice what is called for in the faith. We may have many people in this category. This is the end result of enculturation, which is the process of a person learning the requirements of the American culture because it surrounds us. The nominal Christian may attend church a couple times a year but has missed the point of being a follower of Jesus. Then there is the fundamentalist Christian who holds to a strict regimen of the Christian faith and can be rigid in the way he or she lives out their lives. We have a polarized Christianity, but it is the result of the Assimilation tactics of the American Government. There are extremes on both ends, but there is one more way to clarify the Christian question of colonization.

I like to refer to a radical following of the teachings of Jesus. A radical follower is someone who lives out their faith in an everyday setting. The radical follower's life encourages others by sharing their faith in Jesus and hopes others will follow the truth. So how many radical followers of Jesus do we have? Let us say we have forty thousand people on the Pine Ridge. It may seem high, but the hospital proves we have more than that number using the facility in Pine Ridge. Okay, so we could look at the question of 2% percent of the forty thousand; that number would be eight hundred. So, do you believe we could possibly have 800 radical followers of Jesus Christ on the Pine Ridge? Highly unlikely, and if you look at 1%, which would be four hundred, you would be hard pressed to locate 400 radical followers of Jesus on the Pine Ridge. So, would the number be less than four hundred? I believe there is less than 1% of the population who would be known as radical followers of the teachings of Jesus. Love God and love your neighbor as yourself is what Jesus exemplified in his life and communicated in his teachings.

So when we seek to understand what has been done in Lakota country as a result of colonization, we must understand the true way of Christ has not been followed. Supra-cultural is an understanding of time and space. When referring to faith in Jesus as a radical follower, we need to understand there are principles that transcend culture. Jesus is above culture. Some people would have you believe Jesus is a puritan, but he was a man who sought out the people who were hurting. Jesus loved people and was involved in the lives of people who needed him. The religious people of the Pine Ridge believe they are right and that is their choice. I prefer to talk to people who are seeking knowledge. Jesus is not a white man's system, rather Jesus is a way of life that calls people to a relationship with the Creator, Taku Sku Sku, the unmoved mover. I talked to a couple and told them the Wanka Tanka is from a Catholic understanding of monotheism and Tunkasila is a contemporary term. To seek the unmoved mover of Taku Sku Sku is what the Lakota have sought forever. If in fact I am a leader of the Lakota in the 21st Century, I want to be clear. Jesus brought freedom, not bondage, and the missionaries brought bondage, not freedom. As a radical follower of Jesus, I believe I am a man who trusts in what Jesus did on the cross. He was put on the cross for me, and I no longer need to pay for my sin; he paid for it all.

Corporate Churches
....from 7-21-10

I have been thinking about summer and how fast it goes by when you are busy. We are closing in on the Oglala Nation Pow Wow and Rodeo. After this event summer turns to a return of school and fall schedules. Many people travel back to the Reservation for family visits and various ceremonies from Naming to Sundances. The largest gathering is usually the Oglala Nation Fair. This past week the Christians gathered in Rapid City right by the Civic Center. I enjoyed one band called Reilly who defined their music as Violin Rock. Their songs were full of dueling fiddles and guitars. I enjoyed the Irish song and was amazed at the passion. I was recognized by a couple of people from the college I attended, Crown College.

While I was walking around the vendors and looking at the displays, I noticed there was a Barbecue Pork Stand. I decided I did not want to try it, but the lady told my friend if we tried it we would want to buy a sandwich. I thought it was a bit absurd so I told her I would give her all of the money I had on me for the cause her sales were supporting. I pulled out three or four dollars and laid it on the table. It was for a children's home of some kind. They were raising money for an orphanage in a third world country. I did not give the money with a bad attitude but because it was a good cause. Every child in the world deserves better; I have been in some places where it broke my heart to see hurting children.

The Hills Alive Christian Music festival draws many people from surrounding states, but I realized there was a missing ingredient. I believe there are less than 2% of people living for Jesus on the Pine Ridge, so it would seem the standard for the event to not have many American Indians in attendance. That still did not bother me because I understand most people do not want to hear Christian Music. Christianity has its own culture and has become separate from the world. I will include myself because I am a part of a religion that boasts 2.5 billion followers. We have our own television channels, radio stations, music, books, travel agencies, and the list goes on. While Hills Alive was going on I realized the event planners did not seem to take the American Indian seriously.

We have an 80% unemployment rate; poverty like no other county in the country. Our children are in need of proper care, and yet the Hills Alive leadership chooses a group of people far from Pine Ridge to support. We have become an invisible people group to the largest Christian gathering in Western South Dakota. There is an underlying tone in South Dakota; it is called racism and prejudice. I usually see hope in the Christian world, but I believe the American Church is moving toward "corporation" at a faster rate than I suspected. They have the mindset of economic quarters to make their decisions. They seem to worry about the best business decision and act accordingly. Everything is pointed at developing the corporation rather than seeking first to love God and our neighbor.

I try to live my life without the same values of Christian corporations. When I host people from different parts of the country in Pine Ridge, I try to help them understand the extended family principles. It is difficult because they fight to have a schedule and control their week. We build a broad schedule and allow them to operate within a flexible framework. My hope is we can help people to understand it is not about the bottom dollar, but it is about family. We need people to understand from a family perspective rather than a corporate worldview. My belief is in God and not man. Man will fail us all, but the God of the Bible will never fail.

A group asked me what my favorite quote from the Bible is. The Apostle Paul says, "For I resolved to know nothing while I was with you but Christ and him crucified." In the darkest hours of Paul's work he understood it is all about Jesus and the work of the cross. Many people seem to be hurt by what they would call the White Man's Religion, but it is not. Jesus was a dark skinned man who lived close to nature and was out in the hot sun most of the time. He speaks to my life because he talks about having compassion for people. He hung on a cross for my sins and gave the ultimate sacrifice so I could have life. It is said some would consider dying for a good man, but Jesus died for me when I was a bad man. My humanity of being imperfect is what he died for, and I trust what he did. He gives me the free gift of being alive spiritually. The corporation will fail us all, but the Love of Christ will never fail because he gave us everything.

Music Healer of the Soul

In the darkest times in my life I have found music to comfort my soul. Our lives would be very dull without lyrics that move us. When I was a boy I remember singing to the radio and listening to love songs. I truly found peace in the 70s. It was a time of great lyrics and the civil rights movement was just ending. I remember how I would drift off and let the music touch my being. I would later find another love that moved me as much as music. I was very young and would dream of romance. Of course, I did not know what love was but it was a great time listening to the singers who seemed to know what love felt like. So what I am rambling about is the idea behind music and how it moves people in times of stagnation.

A few years ago I was speaking in St Paul, Minnesota at the Christian Ethnomusicology conference. You see, in Native America there is debate about the drums of the Lakota and other tribes. I was there to speak about the debate going on in Native American Christianity. It was called Dancing our Prayers or Burning our Regalia. I actually heard a Lakota Elder Christian talk about him burning his regalia when he became a Christian. Now I will say clearly I am not for this or the ones who are totally embracing dancing for the Christian faith. Since I grew up with the seventy's love songs, it is hard for me to throw myself fully into the Lakota Song. I was at least aware of the controversy and was asked to speak to some ethnomusicologists. My field is in the study of culture and the development of cross cultural ministry.

So what does that have to do with this article? Culture is not static, meaning it is always moving and changing. It is dynamic. Our people have changed their culture. It would be fascinating to see the contrast between the culture of two hundred years ago and the way our people live today.

Transportation is one aspect of the culture to examine. The horse was not originally from the Americas but was brought by the Spaniards. The introduction of horse into Lakota culture changed our lives dramatically. I believe our ancestors embraced this new addition into our way of life. Still today we have many people who have horses. We even have some great cowboys and rodeo participants. My point is we have adapted. I am not speaking particularly about transportation; I am speaking of culture as a whole. We have incorporated many American cultural items in our daily lives.

I believe the music forms have been powerful in Pan-Indianism. Pan-Indianism is a word I use to describe the attempt of others to adopt parts of Indian culture. I think of the Lost Boys in Peter Pan who tried to mimic the real Indians. However, this effort often lacks true understanding and authenticity. Back to music....people are drawn to the Lakota drum. It is a powerful aspect of our culture. Chris Eagle Hawk makes me proud when he talks of the Lakota heartbeat. When he speaks of the wars from the Battle of Little Big Horn all the way to the Gulf and Afghanistan wars, he brings great pride in the way our people use the drum to honor our Lakota Warriors. I have a drum and my friend, the DJ, gave me a drum stick. I hope to sing the songs of our elders. Our people have much to offer the world; it could very well be the heartbeat of the people. I guess Pan-Indianism's attempt to mimic our ways is a form of complement, but it must be done with respect and knowledge. Behind many great movements and cultures there has been music. I contemplate the next great movement. I believe music will be a part of it, and I hope to see our people writing songs for the future. Culture will always change and the future generations will call us their ancestors. Music can be one of the forces that can change the Reservations.

In my study of history of the Americas, I have seen the forced Christianity. It was oppressive and had negative effects on the Lakota as well as other people around the Americas. They say 2-5% of Native Americans would say they are Born Again Christians. Those numbers do not reflect mainline groups such as Catholics and Anglican groups. What it says is there are 2-5% living a daily life of following the Christian faith. Lately I have been listening to Bob Marley. He sang about the Lord and Jah. As a philosopher I try to look at particular issues we face and realize we have been changed by the oppressive onslaught of the white American Christianity. I try to be clear that I am a follower of Jesus who was tribal and knew oppression. Hellenization, like Americanization, sought to colonize his people. Jesus lived a simple life. I met a few older medicine men, or they could be called holy men. They, like Jesus, lived simple lives. He fed people when he did not have much himself, and he knew his people. I let people know my faith in Jesus has truly affected every aspect of my culture. Jesus' first miracle was changing water into wine. This was against natural law because the time and material did not exist for this to truly occur. Fermentation requires time and juice in order produce wine. My belief is alcohol is not the killer of our people but it is the loss of a beautiful way of life. A life where people took care of each other, but the government of the

United States calculated the destruction of our people. Alcohol does great harm to our people but it all began with abuse of power and trust that put us onto the Reservations. So what now? We need to reverse this act of aggression and begin a new way of life. I believe in "one love" and "one heart" like Bob Marley. We need to overcome the tactics and destructions of the Reservation System. It is a Death System; do not let anyone tell you differently.

Ghetto or Reservation

What is the difference between the ghetto and the Reservation? In this post I would like to explore the difference between these two places in America. Here is one definition taken from Wikipedia: A ghetto is now described as a "portion of a city in which members of a minority group live; especially because of social, legal, or economic pressure."

I grew up in what was commonly known as a ghetto. You sometimes hear the phrase, "That's Ghetto." It usually refers to something that is poor, old, beat up, and a list of other negative words. When I grew up in the inner-city, I did not ever think about growing up and moving away. There were people interested in social mobility, getting better jobs, education and moving on, but I never thought about a change. I lived my life and did the activities others did in our side of the city. It was urban and we were free to go to other parts of the city, but I have to admit I had contact sheets done on me a few times. That is when the officer stops you and writes your name down on a paper. If something happens around the same time they stopped you, they would look at your info and come and question you. So we could move or get a better job even though we lived in the ghetto.

This is true on the Reservation today, but it was not always true in the history of the Reservation system. There was a time when you had to get special permission from the Agent of your tribe to leave the Reservation. We were placed here because the United States wanted to eradicate us. Socially it was better for them to put our ancestors in obscure places where we would be no more. As a matter of fact, there are people in the eastern part of the United States who believe we do not exist. The number two reason for people coming to South Dakota is to see the Indians or Lakota and how we live. That is just under the number one reason, visiting the Shrine of Democracy, Mount Rushmore.

The term ghetto originally described the area where poor Jewish people were placed in the old country. The Jewish people were oppressed for centuries, but they have had the mental fortitude to continue their plight for their homeland. The first ghettos in modern history were the American Indian Reservation system. The United States Government systematically sought to destroy the Indigenous people of North America. We as Indian people were forced to live within the boundaries of the Reservation and our land and resources were stolen. This story should be told because it has been covered up with false history. Our people, because of their trust in the Wasicu, were duped and led to believe that they would have free reign over a territory for hunting and living at peace with the Earth. This was far from the truth as the westward expansion exploded when gold was discovered in the Black Hills. Recently, I heard about a gold mine in New Mexico. The guy giving tours said it was the richest gold mine ever, but they have not extracted the rest of the gold out of the earth. I laughed because it is outlandish to believe the Wasicu would not go and get all of the gold.

After living in an urban ghetto and on the Reservation, I realize we need to start developing ways of making this a better place. We struggle because we have not taken our ancestors' ways of trade. I heard a story of our people going all the way to Mexico City. That is a distant land for our people to go since we have not always had the horse. We have had commerce for centuries, but the question needs to be asked, why have we lost our way?

1. We have been imprisoned by the United States Government for the purpose of eradication.

2. We have learned to accept the Government of the U.S. and their tactics.

3. We have become dependent on the Government for our way of life.

313

4. We have not taken education seriously.

5. We have a high rate of sickness.

6. Our dependency has crippled us because we fight over scraps.

7. While Wall Street deals with billions of dollars, our people fight over thousands.

8. Our families have become dysfunctional.

9. The list can go on and on . . .

Bottom line about ghetto or Reservation.....we have been a target of the United States and we need to start reclaiming what is rightfully ours in the 21st century. We can begin by taking our heads out of the sand and looking around. We need to see the problems and start to become part of the solutions. I am excited because we have the ability to overcome the Reservation, aka ghetto, if we begin to work together and rise up out of the economic stronghold that ties us.

The Matrix, The Cave, The Lakota Nation
....from 4-06-10

When I first watched the movie The Matrix years ago, it impressed me as more than an action movie. As I watched it many more times, I was able to see the world as some would fictionalize it. I find it bothersome when people talk about colonization. It is true we have been colonized, but I do not want to surrender to the wishes of the government. If we were going to tell a story about our colonization, I believe it would be similar to The Matrix. Most of the people would be trying to get through their days. The days would be weeks and then months and years, as people would be oblivious to the machine using our bodies as batteries. We wouldn't understand that there is a real world with dangers we could not fathom. We would all like to have the One come and bring us to reality and salvation. I guess I would hope our story would be a little different. We see the trilogy turn into a bizarre underworld with the One giving up his life. Then a new day to start the process over again until it comes to perfection, or rather a way of life chosen by a machine programmed to develop the right human condition.

If you have not read The Cave from The Republic written by Plato, you need to search it online and seek to understand the views we as humans can form in our minds. I like the allegory because it helps to understand false suppositions. When you start with a false premise, you will find yourself on an unstable foundation. Truth is a powerful tool to seek. It is like the story of a man who was driving down the highway and stopped in a little town. He saw an old man sitting on a bench and asked the man about the town. The old man then asked the passerby where he was from and what his town was like. The visitor said it was an awful town full of gossips and other negatives. The old man said, "This town is full of the same types of people." The passerby got back in his car and left. Then soon after another visitor came through town and stopped. Like the first visitor, he asked the old man about the town. The old man asked the second man about his home town. The second visitor said it was full of great people who were loving and helpful. The old man then said his town was the same. I wish I knew the story teller to give him or her credit for this great story. It helps us have a better perspective. When we start with bad attitudes and suppositions we will have already formed an opinion about the situation. Be positive as it will make your life happier.

When you start with a presupposition, you have a preset mind set on the way things are. And, when you have a preset view, you will often see those ideas come to pass. Now, I understand boarding schools and the forced assimilation and destruction of the government, but I refuse to have it impact my life in negative ways. Because of my chosen profession, I have had many opportunities to live and work in many different places. I have traveled to far distant lands where the people suffer just like our people. These sufferings come from some of the same issues due to colonization we face as American Indians. There are issues because of severe poverty and third world conditions. We live in a country full of success stories and opportunities to change our conditions. Unfortunately, our people continue to struggle with living in a world of confusion and, by choice, living a life of oblivion.

315

We have many people across Indian Country receiving doctorates and other degrees, and I believe life will change. Change is difficult because it involves taking a chance that the outcome will be better than the present life you are living. When I went to college, I was full of life and hope. When I went out into the workforce, I saw many opportunities to make money and support my family. I would have three and sometimes four jobs going when I was in school full-time. I learned how to make pizza and do the bookkeeping for a convenience store. I cleaned whole K-Marts in twelve hours by myself. I worked for a grocery store for seven years. I was an assistant manager there and enjoyed making lifetime friends. I was also able to learn how to make burgers. All of these jobs gave me knowledge and understanding I now use in my work.

My point is we can have a better life on our Reservation and turn what they meant for evil into something that is good. When our young people come home from college, we need to embrace them and thank them for trying to educate themselves in an attempt to find a better way of life. Our lives can change because, unlike the people in third world countries trying to get to American for a piece of the American Dream, we are already in America, a land of opportunity. We can succeed because they cannot defeat us. We need to continue to make a better way of life seeking the Truth and understanding what is at stake. I believe everything is at stake and we need to build our Nation, the Lakota Nation.

Justice and Freedom
....*from 7-01-09*

The Last of the Mohicans film released in 1992 is one of my favorite films, because it brought out many views of the European people. I recently heard Michael Medved, a radio talking head, trying to rewrite history. He was talking about white Americans and saying they did not exist until 1776. I was shaking my head as I listened to him give his opinion. He went on to say the Americans have always been on the side of justice. I was shaking my head and wondering about what the

African Americans were thinking, since they only received their freedom in the 1860s. It took another century for them to get their civil rights. It is impossible to deny the history. The United States was founded and formed based on greed. It was a battle between the Spanish, British, and French countries. There are both good and bad among all people groups. You have people who will stop at nothing to achieve materialism. They will seek to gain with their heart, soul, and mind. And you have people who care about others and want the best for all people.

Back to the movie, we see three trappers running through the New York forest. This was actually filmed in North Carolina. I was told by my friend Russ Lee, who, by the way, is not related to General Lee. (I call Russ the Alabama Slama even though he can't dunk the basketball.) The lead character, Hawkeye, played by Daniel Day-Lewis has portrayed many other great Indian characters in Man Called Horse, Little Big Man, and Dances with Wolves. All of these movies were primarily about the European adapting to the Indian way of life. They are defiantly against the John Wayne style movies our parents grew up with in the 1960s and 70s.

June 25th is the anniversary of my eldest daughter Kayla's journey to be with Jesus. We try to do special things on this day as a family. This year we went to hike Harney Peak. It is the highest point east of the Rockies. During the hike I was thinking about running through the trees like they did in Last of the Mohicans. I was thinking to myself Mr. Russell Means had to have had a stunt double. They were constantly running in the hills. I thought if I tried to run I would blow out my knees. My advice for you is to take the journey to the top of the highest point in the Black Hills because it is breathtaking. The view at the top is worth every grueling moment up the mountain.

There are many people out there who are confused about life, and this is troubling to me as a Lakota man. I see in my own struggles and the pain of our people. My life has been relatively easy compared to most. This is because there was a point in my life when I chose to change some things. I became a part of a faith community. The Gospel Fellowship has been my lifeline. I chose to be in fellowship with other likeminded followers of the teachings of Jesus. I do not stand on my

317

accomplishments or good deeds; my faith and hope are built on the promises in the Bible.

I know it may seem like I am saying it is easy to follow the teachings of Jesus, to love God, and to love our neighbors. I am not, because I know through my own pain and struggles it is not an easy road. We have many social programs in Indian Country, and we even have some very bright people. But, I am convinced the one thing that can save us is a relationship with God. Our lives as American Indians are important because we represent a whole hemisphere of people. We were almost wiped out and many of the tribes and communities did not make it through the last five hundred years. My opinion is that we need to embrace Jesus. Not the religion of Christianity, but the teachings of Jesus because they will change our lives.

When I learned the full history of our people I became bitter. It was only Jesus who has helped me to overcome the malice and bitterness in my heart. I hope to stand against the injustice that continues even in the 21st century. We can overcome the historical trauma, but it will take all of us to stand against the greed and selfishness. Our lives are testament to the grandfathers and grandmothers who were very strong and had great fortitude. We can come together in strength and unity.

Anti-Life, Anti-Christ

A man who lived his life like a meteorite and was a radical follower of Jesus died in a tragic accident. He was thrown from an SUV and hit by a tractor trailer. He once said, "If you know even just a little about what happened at Wounded Knee in 1890 and 1973 you will understand the Government is anti-life and anti-Christ." These words echoed in my ears as I drove to Rapid City one day. He spoke about the apathy of the church in America.

I was in a store looking around and wondering through products. I wanted to look at the books and the kitchen wares. I know it sounds weird, but I like books and cooking. I was looking at the earphones and electronics and I remembered I wanted to look at the voice recorders because of the digital age. I was looking through a few models and found one I thought might work for my notes. I am not a great shopper, and just like many men I find what I need and walk away. I was walking back to the front of the store and saw a guy I knew. I was teasing him about my being Mexican. He started into this, "What percentage?", and I was offended. I told him, "I ain't no dog that has a pedigree." I realize that was bad English, but I was fired up. I made my point and spoke my truth.

Well, this started a tirade of discussion on his belief that Republican means Christian. He asked me who I was going to vote for. I told him who I already voted for and who I will vote for in the next national election. He told me I was into controversy, but I am just opinionated. I told him if he wants to stand with a country that has killed 50 million babies through abortion, enslaved millions of people from the African Continent, and killed off the majority of the Indigenous People of North America he could stand proud. By this time he was stammering and yet he kept going. He said, "Why don't we just move?" He used the absurdity argument, but I told him I did not want to drink his Tea or drink his Kool-Aid. I think the Tea Party supporters are more into not paying taxes because they do not want to see more programs and bailouts. Well at this point the guy was still stammering for words. He was worried about offending me, but he had already done that by asking about a pedigree.

I then struck at the heart because Biblical prophecy says, "All Nations will come against Israel." If he would like to stand by his American government in their fight against Israel, he is welcome by me. I do not believe he was ready to be taking on a rebel and radical. I am sure my perspective is not the complete truth, but I do believe people have misunderstood who they are in Christ. Here are a few ideas: the Church is apathetic when it comes to Injustice; it is worried about quarters and has become a business based on income; it believes a political party represents its views; it has bought into the American Dream; it does not care about poverty issues; it is apathetic when it comes to injustice because they do not care about the treaties that have been broken. I know many say that was in the past and Indians just need to get over it. I know the mentality because I see it when it comes to talking with people about faith and politics.

Walk into some churches and you will hear, "Giving is down. We need to raise the quarterly income." These days most churches are run like non-profit corporations.

Being Christian is not the same as being Republican or Democrat. My personal preference is to be a social conservative because I believe it speaks to me. There is not a party like that.

The American Dream is based on greed and how much you can get. The Church should be willing to serve. Jesus emptied Himself.

Yes, the poverty issue is here. It also existed when Jesus walked the earth. We need to pay attention to who is searching for salvation. Both the poor and rich have their issues that keep them from the truth.

Overcoming the Culture of Death
....*from 12-11-09*

The culture of death is the greatest death machine in the history of the world. If you were going to create a system of destruction against a people group, you would begin by taking over their lands.

And if these people were in your way, you could send them blankets with smallpox to kill their villages - or you could just burn down those villages if you did not have time. If you just wanted to keep them out of the way, you could create a holding area called concentration camps or reservations. Adolf Hitler wanted to create such a system. Some believe he looked to the United States and emulated the reservation system where the American Indian was fighting off eradication.

I like to use the term "American Indian", because Russell Means once said, "The United States did not make treaties with Native Americans but with American Indians." I believe that being mindful of this is a vital part of the fight to keep the treaties alive. If you look at the "ethical" treatment of American Indians you will find it was not ethical.

The "Culture of Death" is something we all need to understand and seek to change in our daily lives. It is important daily, because culture is how we get things done in our daily lives. There are some who talk about the way of life that our ancestors lived. This is beautiful and needed; however, our lives today need to incorporate our ancestors' ways on a daily basis. The way we get our food and transport it is part of our culture, and our food source has changed. We have become a nation of survivors, and it is vital we change; we need to become victors of a new way of life.

Jobs and careers are the most important change we need to compete in a global commerce. Here is an illustration of this fact: I was sitting with my wife Belle in a coffee house in Rapid City. We both had our laptops out, and we were communicating with friends all across the United States. Our phones were sitting next to our laptops, and I realized we were in the midst of worldwide commerce. How powerful this is. You can work from anyplace via wireless laptops and wireless phone coverage? The possibilities are endless!

Since writing this column I have found many people with many issues. One thing I have come across in tribal politics and government is the talk of corruption. I have heard this, and it is disheartening to say the least. I am afraid that we have people governing in a manner that would not make our ancestors happy. We have seen such a turnover in our tribal council and this is actually not surprising. We have some people in tribal government who want to just take care of their own families. Because we are all related, our tribal leaders should seek to help the entire tribe as if each of us were a family member. This is the way of our ancestors.

My hope is that with the high turnaround in the council, we can see change. My message to the new council is this: Work for the better of the PEOPLE and the people will follow you. Do not engage in the politics of death. Be a part of life, a new way of life where our people are being cared for.

I question the understanding of the government officials and whether they see the difference between social economics and capitalistic philosophies. Greed has brought the world economy to its knees. History teaches us the wrongs and the rights. It is time for the Lakota Nation to learn from the past and put in place a new way of life.

There are many people who want to help us and we need to encourage this help. But, we also need to be careful, as "good" intentions have killed many American Indians. The poverty culture is a hazard, and we need to move out of this mentality to see our people thrive. We have many people who can help us, and I believe it is the successful people of our tribe who have the answers. Look around and see the people who have overcome obstacles and seek to network with these individuals.

In 2009, we need to begin dialog with each other. I propose we begin thinking about a time and a place. The answers lie within, and we can overcome the culture of death.

Grieve, be Healed, and Move Forward
....from 11-13-08

Hope, dreams, and visions are what have kept me in difficult times. Hope is what can keep you strong even when your strength is gone. My hope is built on God; I do not put my trust in myself, because I know I am weak in many areas of my life.

When I am weak, I gain strength because I can turn my worries over to my Creator. In my darkest hours, it was the Creator of the universe who took me and held me when I could not move forward. One of my favorite Chiefs is Sitting Bull because he was a Holy Man and a leader of the people. I believe he had hope in the Creator and this is what compelled him to be a great leader. When we as a people lose hope, we will perish. Our hope needs to be built on a strong foundation in order to survive. My hope is in my faith, and my faith brings me dreams of a better life and vision of a great future.

We should not blame others for the situations we are in today. We have all heard of Imperialism and the destruction it has left on Indigenous peoples around the world. We can continue to give this ideology power, or we can begin to heal ourselves and envision a better life for our people. Evil has existed since time has existed. Men have preyed upon each other. It has not been beneficial to continue to blame the past for misfortune. I have studied history and have seen the evil of mankind. I do not want to continue to bring up the past and place blame upon others for the situation I am in today.

It is time to begin a new life for the Lakota Nation. Yes, I am speaking about all Lakota and not just the Oglala, because we are just a part of a whole. My hope is in a Lakota Nation that will take the global stage as a leader in this current world condition. Healing is a part of our life.

I am not a direct product of the boarding schools. I do realize the boarding schools were a destructive force used by United States of America in an attempt to destroy us as a people. Nonetheless, they have not. The U.S. Government did not succeed because we are still here, and we are full of life. We have seen people come out of this system and thrive in the American system. I am too young to have been involved in this system, and since I am middle age, I guess there are many people who do not understand what happened in boarding school. My hope is we can begin to bring our resources together and bring change to the Reservation system. You see, I am not willing to blame anymore.

I want change, and the change needs to come from our own people. We have people who have gone through the system and they are survivors. Now we must strive to bring the rest of the people to healing. Healing needs to happen in order for our Lakota people to move forward and flourish in the twenty-first century. Grief is killing our people. These are the stages of grief:*

- **Denial** (This isn't happening to me!)

- **Anger** (Why is this happening to me?)

- **Bargaining** (I promise I'll be a better person if...)

*(http://www.cancersurvivors.org/Coping/en d%20term/stages.htm)

- **Depression** (I don't care anymore.)

- **Acceptance** (I'm ready for whatever comes.)

I believe we are stuck (for lack of a better word) in the middle of the grieving cycle. When you lose something, you need to go through the grieving process. If it is not completed, you will be caught in an endless cycle. My hope is that we will complete the grieving and move forward to healing. In order for our people to begin to dream and have vision, we will need to work through our loss of life. Many of our people are stuck in the "Why is this happening to me?" phase. We can overcome our grief. My prayer is that we will be able to see our people overcome the problems of the Lakota Nation. People need to come to an understanding about our loss of life. We need to overcome it! Let us pray and envision a new way of life, healing.

The American Holocaust
....from 4-20-10

Cultural conflict has been around since the beginnings of travel. Settler colonies, trading posts, and plantations are what we refer to when we talk about colonization. There were thirteen original colonies during the revolutionary war. After the war was won by the Americans it would take some time to grow the new nation. If you were to look at the British Commonwealth you would understand how far reaching the British were throughout the world. When you begin to understand why countries are colonizing around the globe, you see that it is about the acquisition of resources. The Greeks with Alexander the Great spoke about Hellenization, spreading their culture as far as India. They set up places everywhere they went, spreading culture and language. Jesus saw his people taken over by the Romans where they taxed people.

When you look at the Jewish Nation of Israel you can see strikingly similarities between the North American Indigenous peoples and first century Jews. It was predicted after the fall of Jerusalem in 70 AD the Nation of Israel would become a nation once again. There was displacement of the Jewish people, where their people were made to leave their homeland. Sounds like the Trail of Tears when the Cherokee were sent to Oklahoma. Britain ruled over the Promised Land of the Jewish people. In 1948 Israel became a nation once more. There are Jewish settlements, and people are being pushed out, but I see the decolonization movement of Israel as a great example of how to get the British out of their country. Israelis have decolonized because their land was given back. Israel has become a powerful country in an unstable region. Of course there was the Holocaust where an estimated six million Jews were killed by extermination, along with many other groups of people. The world understands there was an American Holocaust, but many Americans do not know about the extermination tactics of the American government.

While I could go on thinking about the similarities between the Jewish People and American Indians, it would not be fair if I did not mention that Jesus was from the tribe of Judah. Tribal societies were part of the first century, and Jesus saw his people's sovereignty stripped away by a foreigners setting up colonies and making them pay taxes. When Mr. Charles Trimble asked the question in his column last week, it brought many more questions to mind. History should teach us to not make the same mistakes over and over again. But when you look at history you can see the same mistakes being made throughout the ages. It is clear we have much work to do to help our people understand we need to get out of the dependency mentality.

When I was around ten years old, I was walking by Kidney Springs. This blond haired boy walked up to me and extended his hand out to me with a food stamp book. I looked and him and said, "You don't want them?" He said, "No." He then pointed to the top of the hill. He said his grandmother lived up there, and they did not need the food stamps. It was a great moment for me being ten years old with one hundred dollars' worth of food stamps. Well, I actually gave most of them to my mother, but I kept a little to have some fun with pop and other goodies. I remember the day I took the food stamps; it left an impression in my mind. My reason for telling this story is because many of us grew up on food stamps, and some of the same people are on EBT now.

Many people are seeking to decolonize their minds because of the adverse effects of American Colonization. We as American Indians have become a hybrid people; we have become American with a different kind of Indian. Our ceremonies have been passed down through the years, but we now celebrate the American holidays of Christmas and Easter. Our lives have changed as we hold citizenship in the United States of America. Our clothing, food, transportation, and other daily activities resemble the American culture. But, we still have our language, our songs, and our dances, which make us a people group within a country. We are a dependent sovereign nation within a nation. One of the areas that people miss is the clothing we wear on a daily basis. Most American Indians on the Reservation and in the city dress similar to other Americans. In the end the world was revolutionized by the textile industry. So as a professor once told me about defining my faith, I believe I need to define my identity as an Oglala Lakota Wicasa or Man as well. We as people hold the keys to our future, and it will be our responsibility to make the proper changes.

I do not have much to say about the end result for the decolonization because my faith came through the colonization of America. The Jesus movement started almost 2000 years ago by a man who had nothing. His way was to think of others first and pray for his enemies. He fed people and healed them. He eventually gave up his life for the people. When I think of the ideal society, it will always include my faith in Jesus. So it is hard for me to think in these terms. I still believe we need to work on developing our Lakota Nation. We come from a strong people, and we should not have to have our hand out. We can and should hold the Unites States to their words in the treaties. We need to interpret the treaties and seek the right compensation for the stolen land. I do not know if we can actually be free from America's freedom and democracy cultural movement. We need to be distinctive in our dealings with the Federal Government. Our approach must move away from the dependency and move to become mature in our God given responsibilities.

One last thought.... we have been profoundly affected by the American Dream of wealth and greed. We need to truly be about the people in the decolonization movement. We need our own forms, including government. Our lives need to be a strong reflection of our ancestors because they had the mental fortitude to be a thriving people in difficult stretches on the plains.

Made in the USA
Lexington, KY
28 November 2012